Level 4

**Risks and
Consequences**

•

Dollars and Sense

•

From Mystery to Medicine

•

Survival

•

Communication

•

A Changing America

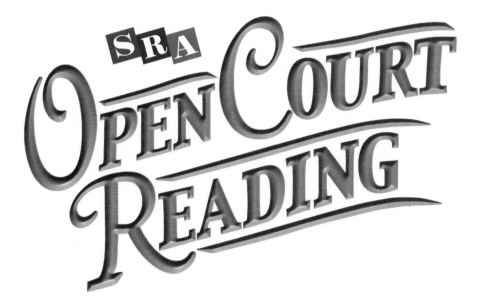

Level 4

— PROGRAM AUTHORS —

Carl Bereiter

Marilyn Jager Adams

Marlene Scardamalia

Anne McKeough

Michael Pressley

Marsha Roit

Jan Hirshberg

Joe Campione

Iva Carruthers

Gerald H. Treadway, Jr.

A Division of The **McGraw·Hill** Companies

Columbus, Ohio

Acknowledgments

Grateful acknowledgement is given to the following publishers and copyright owners for permissions granted to reprint selections from their publications. All possible care has been taken to trace ownership and secure permission for each selection included. In case of any errors or omissions, the Publisher will be pleased to make suitable acknowledgements in future editions.

RISKS AND CONSEQUENCES

"Mrs. Frisby and the Crow" reprinted with the permission of Atheneum Books for Young Readers, an imprint of Simon & Schuster Children's Publishing Division from MRS. FRISBY AND THE RATS OF NIMH by Robert C. O'Brien. Copyright © 1971 Robert C. O'Brien.

From TOTO by Marietta D. Moskin, text copyright © 1971 by Marietta Moskin. Used by permission of the of Coward-McCann, Inc., an imprint of Penguin Putnam Books for Young Readers, a division of Penguin Putnam Inc. From TOTO by Marietta D. Moskin, illustrated by Rocco Negri, illustrations copyright © 1971 by Rocco Negri. Used by permission of Coward-McCann, Inc., an imprint of Penguin Putnam Books for Young Readers, a division of Penguin Putnam Inc.

SARAH, PLAIN AND TALL COPYRIGHT © 1985 BY PATRICIA MACLACHLAN. Used by permission of HarperCollins Publishers.

"Escape" From CHARLOTTE'S WEB, COPYRIGHT 1952 BY E.B. WHITE RENEWED 1980 BY E.B. WHITE, ILLUSTRATIONS COPYRIGHT 1952 BY GARTH WILLIAMS RENEWED © 1980 BY GARTH WILLIAMS. Used by permission of HarperCollins Publishers.

"Hippo's Hope" from A LIGHT IN THE ATTIC by Shel Silverstein. COPYRIGHT © 1981 BY EVIL EYE MUSIC. Used by permission of HarperCollins Publishers.

From MAE JEMISON: SPACE SCIENTIST, text copyright © 1995 by Gail Sakurai. Reprinted by permission of Children's Press, a division of Grolier Publishing.

From TWO TICKETS TO FREEDOM. Text © 1971 Florence B. Freedman, illustrations © 1971 Ezra Jack Keats. Reprinted with permission of Peter Bedrick Books, an imprint of the McGraw-Hill Companies. All rights reserved.

"Freedom" from COLLECTED POEMS by Langston Hughes. Copyright © 1994 by the Estate of Langston Hughes. Reprinted by permission of Alfred A Knopf, a Division of Random House Inc.

"Daedalus and Icarus" reprinted with the permission of Margaret K. McElderry Books, an imprint of Simon & Schuster Children's Publishing Division from GREEK MYTHS Retold by Geraldine McCaughrean. Text copyright © 1992 Geraldine McCaughrean.

DOLLARS AND SENSE

"Starting a Business" from THE KIDS' BUSINESS BOOK by Arlene Erlbach. Copyright 1998 by Arlene Erlbach. Published by Lerner Publications: A Division of Lerner Publishing Group. Used by permission of the publisher. All rights reserved.

"Henry Wells and William Fargo" from FAMOUS BUILDERS OF CALIFORNIA, copyright © 1987 by Edward F. Dolan, Jr. Reprinted with permission of Curtis Brown, Ltd.. All rights reserved.

"Lemonade Stand" reprinted with the permission of Margaret K. McElderry Books, an imprint of Simon & Schuster Children's Publishing Division from WORLDS I KNOW AND OTHER POEMS by Myra Cohn Livingston. Text copyright © 1985 Myra Cohn Livingston.

"Elias Sifuentes, Restaurateur" Reprinted with the permission of Neil Johnson, c/o Mary Jack Wald Associates, Inc. from ALL IN A DAY'S WORK: Twelve Americans Talk About Their Jobs by Neil Johnson published by Joy Street Books/Little, Brown and Company, 3 Center Plaza, Boston, MA 02108. Copyright © 1989 by Neil Johnson.

From Business Is Looking Up by Barbara Aiello and Jeffrey Shulman. Copyright © 1988 by The Kids on the Block, Inc. Reprinted by permission of The Millbrook Press, Inc.

SALT by Harve Zemach, pictures by Margot Zemach. Copyright © 1965 by Margot Zemach. Reprinted by permission of Farrar, Straus & Giroux, LLC, on behalf of the Estate of Margot Zemach.

FROM MYSTERY TO MEDICINE

Maxine Kumin, "The Microscope." Copyright © 1968 by Maxine Kumin. Reprinted by permission of the author.

Adapted from Sure Hands, Strong Heart: The Life of Daniel Hale Williams by Lillie Patterson.

www.sra4kids.com

SRA/McGraw-Hill

A Division of The McGraw-Hill Companies

Send all inquiries to:
SRA/McGraw-Hill
8787 Orion Place
Columbus, Ohio 43240-4027

Printed in the United States of America.

ISBN 0-07-569248-1

3 4 5 6 7 8 9 RRW 05 04 03 02

Copyright © 1981 by Abingdon Press. Used by permission.

"Surgeons Must Be Very Careful" reprinted by permission of the publishers and the Trustees of Amherst College from THE POEMS OF EMILY DICKINSON, Thomas H. Johnson, ed., Cambridge, Mass.: The Belknap Press of Harvard University Press, Copyright © 1951, 1955, 1979, 1983 by the President and Fellows of Harvard University.

"The Germ" from VERSES FROM 1929 by Ogden Nash. Copyright © 1935 by Ogden Nash, renewed. Reprinted by permission of Curtis Brown, Ltd.

Carol Saller: THE BRIDGE DANCERS, by Carol Saller, text copyright 1991 by the author. THE BRIDGE DANCERS, illustrations copyright © 1991 by Gerald Talifero. Used by permission of the illustrator.

"Emily's Hands-On Science Experiment" from Current Science © 1998 by Weekly Reader Corp. All rights reserved!

"The New Doctor" from YOU CAN HEAR A MAGPIE SMILE, Copyright © 1980 by Paula Paul.

"The Story of Susan La Flesche Picotte" from Marion Marsh Brown's HOMEWARD THE ARROW'S FLIGHT © 1980. Revised edition 1995. © Field Mouse Productions, Grand Island, Nebraska.

Reprinted with the permission of Atheneum Books for Young Readers, an imprint of Simon & Schuster Children's Publishing Division from SHADOW OF A BULL by Maia Wojciechowska. Copyright © 1964 Maia Wojciechowska.

SURVIVAL

Chapter 10 from ISLAND OF THE BLUE DOLPHINS. Copyright © 1960, renewed 1988 by Scott O'Dell. Reprinted by permission of Houghton Mifflin Company. All rights reserved.

From The Arctic Explorer: The Story of Matthew Henson by Jeri Ferris, copyright 1989 by Jeri Ferris. Published by Carolrhoda Books, Inc. a Division of the Lerner Publishing Group. Used by permission of the publisher. All rights reserved.

MCBROOM AND THE BIG WIND by Sid Fleishman. TEXT COPYRIGHT © 1967 BY SID FLEISCHMAN. Used by permission HarperCollins Publishers. Illustrations copyright © 1982 by Walter H. Lorraine. By permission of the artist.

From ONE AT A TIME by David McCord. Copyright © 1952 by David McCord; copyright © renewed 1980 by David McCord. By permission of Little, Brown and Company (Inc.).

THE BIG WAVE by Pearl Buck COPYRIGHT © 1947 BY THE CURTIS PUBLISHING COMPANY; COPYRIGHT © 1948, 1976 BY PEARL S. BUCK. Used by permission of HarperCollins Publishers.

"Solitude", from NOW WE ARE SIX by A.A. Milne, illustrated by E.H. Shepard, copyright 1927 by E.P. Dutton, renewed © 1955 by A.A. Milne. Used by permission of Dutton Children's Books, an imprint of Penguin Putnam Books for Young Readers, a division of Penguin Putnam Inc.

From ANNE FRANK: THE DIARY OF A YOUNG GIRL by Anne Frank. Copyright 1952 by Otto H. Frank. Used by permission of Doubleday, a division of Random House, Inc.

"Many Thousand Gone" reprinted with the permission of Atheneum Books for Young Readers, an imprint of Simon & Schuster Children's Publishing Division from I'M GOING TO SING: BLACK AMERICAN SPIRITUALS. Selected and illustrated by Ashley Bryan. Copyright © 1982 Ashley Bryan.

"Walk Together Children" reprinted with the permission of Atheneum Books for Young Readers, an imprint of Simon & Schuster Children's Publishing Division from WALK TOGETHER CHILDREN: BLACK AMERICAN SPIRITUALS. Selected and illustrated by Ashley Bryan. Copyright © 1974 Ashley Bryan.

COMMUNICATION

"Messages by the Mile" from BEES DANCE AND WHALES SING: THE MYSTERIES OF ANIMAL COMMUNICATION, by Margery Facklam. Text copyright © 1992 by Margery Facklam. Reprinted by permission of Sierra Club Books for Children.

"Whalesong" from DRAGONSFIRE by Judith Nicholls, copyright © 1992. Reprinted with permission of Faber & Faber Limited. All rights reserved.

From WE'LL BE RIGHT BACK AFTER THESE MESSAGES © Shelagh Wallace reprinted with permission of Annick Press.

From BREAKING INTO PRINT: *Before and After the Invention of the Printing Press* by Stephen Krensky, illustrated by Bonnie Christensen. Text copyright © 1996 by Stephen Krensky. Used by permission of Rosenstone/Wender. BREAKING INTO PRINT, illustrations copyright © 1996 by Bonnie Christensen. Published in the United States by Little, Brown and Co. All rights reserved. Used with permission.

KOKO'S KITTEN by Dr. Francine Patterson, photographs by Ronald H. Cohn. Copyright © 1985 by The Gorilla Foundation. Photographs copyright © Ronald Cohn/The Gorilla Foundation/National Geographic Society.

From LOUIS BRAILLE: THE BOY WHO INVENTED BOOKS FOR THE BLIND by Margaret Davidson. Copyright © 1971 by Margaret Davidson. Reprinted by permission of Scholastic Inc.

Text of "Connections" Copyright © 1996 by Diane Siebert. Reprinted by permission of S©ott Treimel New York. Aaron Meshon-illustrator.

Excerpt from THE LITTLE PRINCE, copyright © 1943 by Harcourt Brace Jovanovich, Inc., copyright renewed 1971 by Consuelo de Saint-Exupery, English translation copyright © 2000 by Richard Howard, reprinted with permission of Harcourt, Inc.

A CHANGING AMERICA

"The Voyage of the Mayflower" from COBBLESTONE's November 1989 issue: Pilgrims to a New World, © 1989, Cobblestone Publishing Company, 30 Grove Street, Suite C, Peterborough, NH 03458. All rights reserved. Reprinted by permission of the publisher.

"Pocahontas" From THE VIRGINIA COLONY, text copyright © 1986 by Dennis B. Fradin. Reprinted by permission of Children's Press, a division of Grolier Publishing.

From Carole Charles' "Martha Helps the Rebel" © 1975 by The Child's World, Chanhassen, MN. Reprinted with permission of copyright holder.

— PROGRAM AUTHORS —

Carl Bereiter, Ph.D.
University of Toronto

Marilyn Jager Adams, Ph.D.
BBN Technologies

Michael Pressley, Ph.D.
University of Notre Dame

Marsha Roit, Ph.D.
National Reading Consultant

Anne McKeough, Ph.D.
University of Calgary

Jan Hirshberg, Ed.D.
Reading Specialist

Marlene Scardamalia, Ph.D.
University of Toronto

Joe Campione, Ph.D.
University of California at Berkeley

Iva Carruthers, Ph.D.
Northeastern Illinois University

Gerald H. Treadway, Jr., Ed.D.
San Diego State University

Table of Contents

Dollars and Sense

Table of Contents
From Mystery to Medicine 206

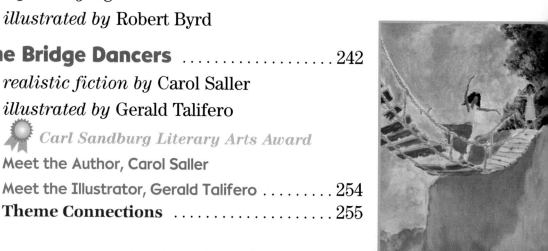

Table of Contents
Survival

Table of Contents

Communication 414

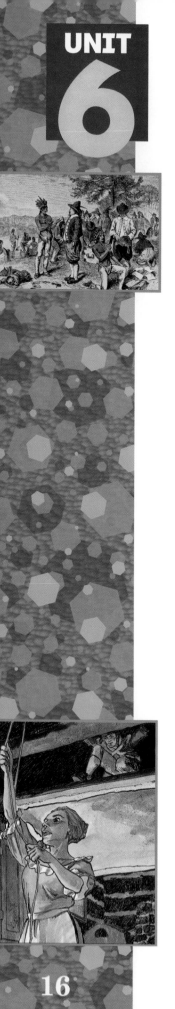

Table of Contents

A Changing America 482

Risks and Consequences

Have you ever taken a risk? What happened? We take risks every day—every time we decide to do something or not to do it. How do you decide which risks are worth taking?

Focus Questions Are there times when we must take a risk to help others? Can our own risks sometimes endanger others?

Mrs. Frisby and the Crow

from ***Mrs. Frisby and the Rats of NIMH***
by Robert C. O'Brien
illustrated by Barbara Lanza

Mrs. Frisby is a mouse that lives with her children in a country garden. When her son Timothy becomes ill, she undertakes a treacherous journey to bring him some medicine.

Mrs. Frisby looked again at the sun and saw that she faced an unpleasant choice. She could go home by the same roundabout way she had come, in which case she would surely end up walking alone in the woods in the dark—a frightening prospect, for at night the forest was alive with danger. Then the owl came out to hunt, and foxes, weasels and strange wild cats stalked among the tree trunks.

The other choice would be dangerous, too, but with luck it would get her home before dark. That would be to take a straighter route, across the farmyard between the barn and the chicken house, going not too close to the house but cutting the distance home by half. The cat would be there somewhere, but by daylight——and by staying in the open, away from the shrubs——she could probably spot him before he saw her.

The cat: He was called Dragon. Farmer Fitzgibbon's wife had given him the name as a joke when he was a small kitten pretending to be fierce. But when he grew up, the name turned out to be an apt one. He was enormous, with a huge, broad head and a large mouth full of curving fangs, needle sharp. He had seven claws on each foot and a thick, furry tail, which lashed angrily from side to side. In color he was orange and white, with glaring yellow eyes; and when he leaped to kill, he gave a high, strangled scream that froze his victims where they stood.

But Mrs. Frisby preferred not to think about that. Instead, as she came out of the woods from Mr. Ages' house and reached the farmyard fence she thought about Timothy. She thought of how his eyes shone with merriment when he made up small jokes, which he did frequently, and how invariably kind he was to his small, scatterbrained sister Cynthia. The other children sometimes laughed at her when she made mistakes, or grew impatient with her because she was forever losing things; but Timothy never did. Instead, he would help her find them. And when Cynthia herself had been sick in bed with a cold, he had sat by her side for hours and entertained her with stories. He made these up out of his head, and he seemed to have a bottomless supply of them.

Taking a firm grip on her packets of medicine, Mrs. Frisby went under the fence and set out toward the farmyard. The first stretch was a long pasture; the barn itself, square and red and big, rose in the distance to her right; to her left, farther off, were the chicken houses.

When at length she came abreast of the barn, she saw the cattle wire fence that marked the other end of the pasture; and as she approached it, she was startled by a sudden outburst of noise. She thought at first it was a hen, strayed from the chicken yard—caught by a fox? She looked down the fence and saw that it was no hen at all, but a young crow, flapping in the grass, acting most odd. As she watched, he fluttered to the top wire of the fence, where he perched nervously for a moment. Then he spread his wings, flapped hard, and took off—but after flying four feet he stopped with a snap and crashed to the ground again, shedding a flurry of black feathers and squawking loudly.

He was tied to the fence. A piece of something silvery—it looked like wire—was tangled around one of his legs; the other end of it was caught in the fence. Mrs. Frisby walked closer, and then she could see it was not wire after all, but a length of silver-colored string, probably left over from a Christmas package.

The crow was sitting on the fence, pecking ineffectively at the string with his bill, cawing softly to himself, a miserable sound. After a moment he spread his wings, and she could see he was going to try to fly again.

"Wait," said Mrs. Frisby.

The crow looked down and saw her in the grass.

"Why should I wait? Can't you see I'm caught? I've got to get loose."

"But if you make so much noise again the cat is sure to hear. If he hasn't heard already."

"You'd make noise, too, if you were tied to a fence with a piece of string, and with night coming on."

"I would not," said Mrs. Frisby, "if I had any sense and knew there was a cat nearby. Who tied you?" She was trying to calm the crow, who was obviously terrified.

He looked embarrassed and stared at his feet. "I picked up the string. It got tangled with my foot. I sat on the fence to try to get it off, and it caught on the fence."

"*Why* did you pick up the string?"

The crow, who was very young indeed—in fact, only a year old—said wearily, "Because it was shiny."

"You knew better."

"I had been told."

Birdbrain, thought Mrs. Frisby, and then recalled what her husband used to say: The size of the brain is no measure of its capacity. And well she might recall it, for the crow's head was double the size of her own.

"Sit quietly," she said. "Look toward the house and see if you see the cat."

"I don't see him. But I can't see behind the bushes. Oh, if I could just fly higher . . . "

"Don't," said Mrs. Frisby. She looked at the sun; it was setting behind the trees. She thought of Timothy, and of the medicine she was carrying. Yet she knew she could not leave the foolish crow there to be killed——and killed he surely would be before sunrise——just for want of a few minutes' work. She might still make it by dusk if she hurried.

"Come down here," she said. "I'll get the string off."

"How?" said the crow dubiously.

"Don't argue. I have only a few minutes." She said this in a voice so authoritative that the crow fluttered down immediately.

"But if the cat comes . . ." he said.

"If the cat comes, he'll knock you off the fence with one jump and catch you with the next. Be still." She was already at work with her sharp teeth, gnawing at the string. It was twined and twisted and twined again around his right ankle, and she saw she would have to cut through it three times to get it off.

As she finished the second strand, the crow, who was staring toward the house, suddenly cried out:

"I see the cat!"

"*Quiet!*" whispered Mrs. Frisby. "Does he see us?"

"I don't know. Yes. He's looking at me. I don't think he can see you."

"Stand perfectly still. Don't get in a panic." She did not look up, but started on the third strand.

"He's moving this way."

"Fast or slow?"

"Medium. I think he's trying to figure out what I'm doing."

She cut through the last strand, gave a tug, and the string fell off.

"There, you're free. Fly off, and be quick."

"But what about you?"

"Maybe he hasn't seen me."

"But he will. He's coming closer."

Mrs. Frisby looked around. There was not a bit of cover anywhere near, not a rock nor a hole nor a log; nothing at all closer than the chicken yard— and that was in the direction the cat was coming from, and a long way off.

"Look," said the crow. "Climb on my back. Quick. And hang on."

Mrs. Frisby did what she was told, first grasping the precious packages of medicine tightly between her teeth.

"Are you on?"

"Yes."

She gripped the feathers on his back, felt the beat of his powerful black wings, felt a dizzying upward surge, and shut her eyes tight.

"Just in time," said the crow, and she heard the angry scream of the cat as he leaped at where they had just been. "It's lucky you're so light. I can scarcely tell you're there." Lucky indeed, thought

Mrs. Frisby; if it had not been for your foolishness, I'd never have gotten into such a scrape. However, she thought it wise not to say so, under the circumstances.

"Where do you live?" asked the crow.

"In the garden patch. Near the big stone."

"I'll drop you off there." He banked alarmingly, and for a moment Mrs. Frisby thought he meant it literally. But a few seconds later—so fast does the crow fly—they were gliding to earth a yard from her front door.

"Thank you very much," said Mrs. Frisby, hopping to the ground.

"It's I who should be thanking you," said the crow. "You saved my life."

"And you mine."

"Ah, but that's not quite even. Yours wouldn't have been risked if it had not been for me—me and my piece of string." And since this was just what she had been thinking, Mrs. Frisby did not argue.

"We all help one another against the cat," she said.

"True. Just the same, I am in debt to you. If the time ever comes when I can help you, I hope you will ask me. My name is Jeremy. Mention it to any crow you see in these woods, and he will find me."

"Thank you," said Mrs. Frisby. "I will remember."

Jeremy flew away to the woods, and she entered her house, taking the three doses of medicine with her.

Mrs. Frisby and the Crow

Meet the Author

Robert C. O'Brien could sing before he could talk. His favorite "toy" was the family's wind-up Victrola (music player), and he spent hours listening to music. He learned to play piano when he was very young, and he stayed with it all his life.

His other favorite thing to do was create splendid imaginary worlds, with himself in dazzling, heroic roles. In his forties he decided to share those worlds with others so he started writing books.

"When I get a story idea," he said, *"I write it down before I forget it. It isn't always for children, but those are the stories I most like to write."*

Meet the Illustrator

Barbara Lanza says that fantasy books are her favorite genre. *"I love doing fantasy. I've always loved little secret worlds, whether they are in the backyard or in outer space."*

Her parents and her high school art teacher encouraged Ms. Lanza to pursue a career in art. She says of her work, *"You really need to understand yourself and be very committed to bringing your feelings into your work. When you are an illustrator, you're illuminating something for someone else. By having a clear focus yourself, you can better describe things for others."*

Theme Connections

Within the Selection

Record your answers to the questions below in the Response Journal section of your Writer's Notebook. In small groups, report the ideas you wrote. Discuss your ideas with the rest of your group. Then choose a person to report your group's answers to the class.

- Why did Mrs. Frisby choose to go home through the farmyard instead of the woods?
- Why did Mrs. Frisby risk her life to remove the string from the crow's leg?
- What risk did the crow take to save Mrs. Frisby's life?

Across Selections

Compare the consequences of the risks taken by Mrs. Frisby with the consequences of the risks taken by Rosa Parks in "Rosa Parks: My Story." How are they alike?

Beyond the Selection

- Mrs. Frisby took a risk to help the crow. Have you ever taken a risk to help someone else? Do you know anyone who has? Share this experience with the rest of your group, and discuss the consequences of the risk.
- Think about how "Mrs. Frisby and the Crow" adds to what you know about risks and consequences.
- Add items to the Concept/Question Board about risks and consequences.

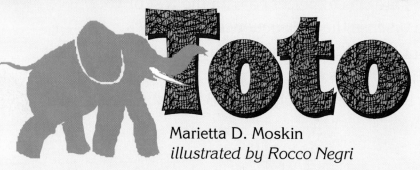

Toto

Marietta D. Moskin
illustrated by Rocco Negri

Deep in Africa, on the outer slopes of a gently rolling ring of hills, lived a timid young boy named Suku. His round thatched hut stood in a busy village where his tribe had always lived. Just a short distance away, on the other side of the blue and purple hills, was a quiet valley set aside for animals to live without fear of being hunted by men. Suku had often climbed to the top of the tallest hill and had watched the herds of animals moving through the grasslands far below. But that was as far as he ever went. His own world was outside the protected game reserve——with his family, in the safe, familiar village.

On a saucer-shaped plain sheltered by the ring of blue and purple hills lived a curious little elephant. His name was Toto——the little one——because he was the youngest and smallest elephant in the herd. With his large family he roamed across the silvery plains of his valley, feeding on the juicy grasses and bathing in the broad green river that twisted through the land. It was a good life for elephants and for the many other animals with whom they shared their peaceful valley.

Day by day the little elephant in the valley and the boy in the village grew stronger and bigger and learned the things they had to know.

Toto learned which berries and roots were good to eat and which ones would make him sick. He learned to recognize danger by smells in the air and sounds in the distance. He stood patiently while his mother doused him with water from her trunk, and he paid attention when she showed him how to powder himself with red dust to keep the insects away.

When his mother warned him never to stray outside their peaceful valley because there were dangers beyond the hills, Toto listened. Most of the time he was happy to play with his cousins among the thorn trees and with his friends, the antelope and the baby baboons. But sometimes Toto looked toward the blue and purple hills in the distance and wondered what lay behind their rounded crests.

Suku too learned a great many things a boy growing up in an African village had to learn. He carried water for his mother from the river and he collected dung to burn in the fire on which she cooked their midday meal. In the evening he helped his father and the other men to pen the tribe's cattle and goats within the village compound. But in the morning, when the boys and young men of the village went out to herd their cattle on the rich grazing lands in the valley, Suku did not go with them. He watched when the herd boys walked jauntily out of the village, brandishing their wooden staffs and shouting to their charges. At seven he was old enough to go, but Suku was frightened when he thought of the herd boys walking through the bush with nothing but a stick or crude iron spear to protect them from lions.

"Our ancestors were famous lion hunters," his mother scolded. "The men of our tribe have always walked fearlessly through the bush."

"Give Suku time," his father counseled. "Courage sometimes comes with need."

So Suku went on doing women's chores around the village and avoiding the boys who teased him.

And inside the ring of gently rolling purple hills, Toto, the little elephant, roamed with the herd across the grasslands. But whenever he saw the young weaverbirds flying from their hanging straw nests, he watched enviously as they sailed off into the sky far, far beyond the circle of hills.

One night Toto followed the elephant herd to the edge of their valley where the river flowed onto the plain through a gap in the hills. There, in a clearing between the trees, the young males of the herd fought mock battles with each other in the moonlight.

Sheltered by his mother's bulk, Toto watched for a while. Then, looking up at the velvety sky, he saw that the moon had traveled across the valley and was about to dip down below the highest hill.

I wonder where she goes, Toto thought. Perhaps I'll just follow the river a little ways and see. Not very far——just to where the river curves.

Slowly Toto moved away from the group of elephants. Nobody noticed. Not even his mother. But once he was in the shadows of trees, the moon was no longer there to guide him.

"Elephants have no enemies—Mother said so,"
he told himself bravely. Only the lion might stalk an
unprotected elephant child—but the lions had had
their kill earlier that night. Toto had seen them at
their meal.

Toto walked on through the darkness. Sometimes
he could see the moon reflected on the river, and he
hurried to catch up with it. But he didn't look back, and
so he didn't realize that the hills lay behind him now. He
didn't notice either that he could no longer hear the loud
trumpeting of the other elephants at play. He didn't know
that he was already in that mysterious world beyond
the hills he had longed to discover.

Suddenly Toto felt a sharp pain in his right front leg. Something hard and sharp had fastened around his foot. Toto pulled and pulled, but he couldn't free his foot. Each time he pulled, the pain got sharper.

Nothing his mother had told him about danger had prepared Toto for this. In fear and pain he trumpeted loudly. But he had walked too far to be heard. There was no answering call from his mother or from any of the other elephants. For the first time in his life, Toto was alone.

In the round thatched hut in the village, Suku slept on a woven mat next to his parents. Suku was a sound sleeper, but something—some noise—awoke him before dawn. It sounded like an elephant trumpeting, Suku thought sleepily. But elephants rarely strayed this far out of the game reserve in the valley. He must have been dreaming, Suku told himself. He couldn't have heard an elephant this close.

But Suku could not go back to sleep. When the first sunshine crept through the chinks under the door, he got up and slipped into his clothes. He had promised his mother he would cut some papyrus reeds at the river today so that she could mend their torn sleeping mats. Now that he was awake he would do it before the day grew hot.

Quietly, so as not to waken the rest of his family, Suku tiptoed out of the hut. Outside, no one stirred. Even the cattle were still asleep.

Clutching his sharp reed knife, Suku followed the winding path down the hill to the riverbank, searching for a good stand of feathery papyrus.

Suddenly the silence at the river was broken by a loud rustling sound. The sound came again—not just a rustling this time, but a snapping of twigs and a swishing of the tall grasses. Carefully, and a little fearfully, Suku moved around the next curve in the path. And then he stopped again.

Before him, in the trampled grass, lay a very young elephant. Around one of the elephant's legs the cruelly stiffened rope of a poacher's trap had been pulled so tight that the snare had bitten deeply into the flesh. The elephant had put up a fierce struggle, but now he was exhausted. He lay quietly on his side, squealing softly from time to time.

Anger exploded inside Suku—anger at the cruel poachers who had set their cunning trap so close to the game reserve. He approached the trapped elephant carefully. His father had taught him to be aware of wounded animals who could be far more dangerous in fear and pain. But the little elephant seemed to sense that Suku wanted to help him, and he held very still. Grasping his knife, Suku slashed at the thick, twisted rope. It took time to free the elephant's leg, but finally the last strand of the rope gave way. The boy jumped out of the way quickly, and the small elephant slowly got to his feet. Then he just stood there on the path, staring at Suku.

"Shoo, shoo, little elephant—quickly, run back into the valley," Suku urged. The poachers who had set the trap could be back at any time. But Toto, who had spent the night by himself, would not leave that strange two-legged creature with the oddly dangerous smell but the warm, comforting sounds. When Suku turned to walk back to the village, Toto started after him.

"Please, little one, please, hurry home," Suku pleaded. But the little elephant didn't budge.

"What are we going to do?" Suku asked in despair. "Will I have to lead you back to your family, you foolish little one?"

Suku didn't want to go into the bush. But he looked at the elephant baby and knew that there was no choice.

Suku began to walk, and the small elephant followed. He walked slowly and painfully, limping on the leg that had been cut so badly by the poacher's snare.

It was easy for Suku to find the way Toto had left the reserve. Trampled grass and elephant droppings formed a perfect track. After a while the boy and the elephant came to the clearing where the herd had watched the fight between the young bulls the night before. The clearing was empty, but a trail of droppings showed that the herd had moved on across the open bush.

Suku was so busy following the trail that he hadn't thought much about what he was doing. Suddenly he realized he was walking all by himself across the open grasslands. Just like the herd boys. And he didn't even have an iron spear for protection——nothing but a small reed cutting knife!

He walked on, trying not to think about the dangers. By now the sun was high in the sky, and at home they were surely wondering what had happened to him.

They walked and walked. Suku, who hadn't had any breakfast that morning, began to feel hungry and thirsty. Toto hadn't had breakfast either, but there was no time to stop and eat.

Suddenly Toto stopped. He raised his head and listened, trembling a little. Young as he was, Toto recognized the smells and sounds of danger.

Suku looked around to see what had frightened Toto. And then he saw the danger too. A few paces away, half-hidden in the silvery-tan grass, stood an enormous brown-maned lion.

The lion looked from the elephant to the boy, almost as if he were measuring which one would make the

easier victim. He looked haughty and strong and very big. Suku's fist tightened around the handle of his knife. He wasn't sure at all whether the knife would do him any good, but he was prepared to defend himself if the lion attacked. Behind him he could sense the little elephant stiffen. Even though the lion looked awfully big to him too, Toto had raised his trunk and spread his ears the way the big elephants did when they were ready to attack.

"Oh, please, make him go away, make him go away," Suku prayed silently. His hand around the knife handle felt clammy and stiff. It seemed to him that he and the elephant and the lion had stood there facing one another, forever.

It was Toto who broke the silence. He took a step toward the lion, and he trumpeted a warning.

The next moment—almost like an echo—another elephant call sounded across the bush. Then another and another. Turning his head, Suku saw a large herd of elephants advancing from behind a nearby stand of thorn trees. Toto's family had come to rescue their littlest one!

Then Suku heard another, more familiar sound. It was the rattling and roaring sound of a car traveling fast across rough ground. A second later the game warden's battered white Landrover appeared over the next small hill. Suku recognized the warden at the wheel, and next to the warden Suku saw his father standing up in the car with a gun in his hand.

"Stand still, Suku—just don't move," his father shouted. He aimed his gun at the lion, waiting to see what the lion would do.

The lion looked at his two young victims. Then he looked at the menacing group of elephants on his right and at the men in the car to his left. Mustering what dignity he could, he stalked slowly and deliberately away. Within moments he had disappeared into the tall dry grass.

Another loud, single call sounded from the elephant herd. Toto was being summoned. His mother was coming to take him back to the herd.

Slowly Toto raised his trunk to the boy who had brought him home. Then, still limping badly, he turned and followed his mother.

The warden had waited for the elephants to withdraw. Now he drove the Landrover over to where Suku stood.

"Get in, Suku—let's go," the warden said.

"You came just in time," Suku said.

"We found the cut snare and the elephant tracks— and someone in the village

had seen you going down to the river early this morning," his father explained.

"The poachers would have killed him for his hide," Suku said.

"You did right, Suku," the warden said. "I get so angry too when I catch these poachers. You would make a good game ranger some day, Suku. You love animals, and you are brave."

The warden's words made Suku feel good. He knew that he hadn't felt brave, but he had walked in the footsteps of his ancestors: he had gone into the bush, and he had faced a lion!

Now he would never feel shy of the village boys again. He knew he had earned his place in the tribe.

Under the leafy canopy of the forest, Toto nuzzled up close to his mother's flank. He had eaten his fill of crisp greens at the riverbank, and his mother had bathed his cut foot and smeared it with healing red mud. Now the herd was resting quietly in the shade near the river.

It was good to be back home, Toto thought contentedly. Let the moon and the sun and the birds travel beyond the hills if they wished. His place was here.

Toto

Meet the Author

Marietta D. Moskin said, *"I can't remember a time when I didn't want to write poems or stories."* As soon as she could write, Ms. Moskin began to create fantasy worlds. During World War II, Ms. Moskin and her family spent several years in concentration camps. Even then, she hoarded scraps of paper so she could write her stories and poems.

"In my books," she once said, *"I have tried to draw as often as possible on my own experiences and remembered feelings."* "Toto" grew out of a family trip to East Africa (Kenya, Tanzania, and Uganda).

Meet the Illustrator

Rocco Negri for a time thought he wanted to become a writer. He once said, *"As far as I can remember, I was always very quiet. I communicated more in writing."* But then he got interested in art and decided it was something he would enjoy enormously. Art allowed him to live in two worlds at the same time—the real world and the world of make-believe.

"One of my greatest satisfactions in life is illustrating children's books, because children are so pure in appreciation and perception. They have no inhibition or discrimination to cloud their minds or hearts."

Theme Connections

Within the Selection

Record your answers to the questions below in the Response Journal section of your Writer's Notebook. In small groups, report the ideas you wrote. Discuss your ideas with the rest of your group. Then choose a person to report your group's answers to the class.

- What risk did Toto take by leaving the herd to follow the moon?
- Why did Suku decide to walk into the bush after freeing Toto from the trap?
- What risk did Toto take to save himself and Suku from the lion?

Across Selections

- Toto risked his safety by leaving his herd to follow the moon. How is this risk similar to the risk taken by the crow in "Mrs. Frisby and the Crow"?
- What other stories have you read in which characters, like Suku, overcame their fears and took risks to help other characters?

Beyond the Selection

- Think about how "Toto" adds to what you know about risks and consequences.
- Add items to the Concept/Question Board about risks and consequences.

Sarah, Plain and Tall

from ***Sarah, Plain and Tall*** by Patricia MacLachlan
illustrated by Meg Kelleher Aubrey

"**D**id Mama sing every day?" asked Caleb. "Every-single-day?" He sat close to the fire, his chin in his hand. It was dusk, and the dogs lay beside him on the warm hearthstones.

"Every-single-day," I told him for the second time this week. For the twentieth time this month. The hundredth time this year? And the past few years?

"And did Papa sing, too?"

"Yes. Papa sang, too. Don't get so close, Caleb. You'll heat up."

He pushed his chair back. It made a hollow scraping sound on the hearthstones, and the dogs stirred. Lottie, small and black, wagged her tail and lifted her head. Nick slept on.

I turned the bread dough over and over on the marble slab on the kitchen table.

"Well, Papa doesn't sing anymore," said Caleb very softly. A log broke apart and crackled in the fireplace. He looked up at me. "What did I look like when I was born?"

"You didn't have any clothes on," I told him.

"I know that," he said.

"You looked like this." I held the bread dough up in a round pale ball.

"I had hair," said Caleb seriously.

"Not enough to talk about," I said.

"And she named me Caleb," he went on, filling in the old familiar story.

"*I* would have named you Troublesome," I said, making Caleb smile.

"And Mama handed me to you in the yellow blanket and said . . ." He waited for me to finish the story. "And said . . . ?"

I sighed. "And Mama said, 'Isn't he beautiful, Anna?'"

"And I was," Caleb finished.

Caleb thought the story was over, and I didn't tell him what I had really thought. He was homely and plain, and he had a terrible holler and a horrid smell. But these were not the worst of him. Mama died the next morning. That was the worst thing about Caleb.

"Isn't he beautiful, Anna?" Her last words to me. I had gone to bed thinking how wretched he looked. And I forgot to say good night.

I wiped my hands on my apron and went to the window. Outside, the prairie reached out and touched the places where the sky came down. Though winter was nearly over, there were patches of snow and ice everywhere. I looked at the long dirt road that crawled across the plains, remembering the morning that Mama had died, cruel and sunny. They had come for her in a wagon and taken her away to be buried. And then the cousins and aunts and uncles had come and tried to fill up the house. But they couldn't.

Slowly, one by one, they left. And then the days seemed long and dark like winter days, even though it wasn't winter. And Papa didn't sing.

Isn't he beautiful, Anna?

No, Mama.

It was hard to think of Caleb as beautiful. It took three whole days for me to love him, sitting in the chair by the fire, Papa washing up the supper dishes, Caleb's tiny hand brushing my cheek. And a smile. It was the smile, I know.

"Can you remember her songs?" asked Caleb. "Mama's songs?"

I turned from the window. "No. Only that she sang about flowers and birds. Sometimes about the moon at nighttime."

Caleb reached down and touched Lottie's head.

"Maybe," he said, his voice low, "if you remember the songs, then I might remember her, too."

My eyes widened and tears came. Then the door opened and wind blew in with Papa, and I went to stir the stew. Papa put his arms around me and put his nose in my hair.

"Nice soapy smell, that stew," he said.

I laughed. "That's my hair."

Caleb came over and threw his arms around Papa's neck and hung down as Papa swung him back and forth, and the dogs sat up.

"Cold in town," said Papa. "And Jack was feisty." Jack was Papa's horse that he'd raised from a colt. "Rascal," murmured Papa, smiling, because no matter what Jack did Papa loved him.

I spooned up the stew and lighted the oil lamp and we ate with the dogs crowding under the table, hoping for spills or handouts.

Papa might not have told us about Sarah that night if Caleb hadn't asked him the question. After the dishes were cleared and washed and Papa was filling the tin pail with ashes, Caleb spoke up. It wasn't a question, really.

"You don't sing anymore," he said. He said it harshly. Not because he meant to, but because he had been thinking of it for so long. "Why?" he asked more gently.

Slowly Papa straightened up. There was a long silence, and the dogs looked up, wondering at it.

"I've forgotten the old songs," said Papa quietly. He sat down. "But maybe there's a way to remember them." He looked up at us.

"How?" asked Caleb eagerly.

Papa leaned back in the chair. "I've placed an advertisement in the newspapers. For help."

"You mean a housekeeper?" I asked, surprised.

Caleb and I looked at each other and burst out laughing, remembering Hilly, our old housekeeper. She was round and slow and shuffling. She snored in a high whistle at night, like a teakettle, and let the fire go out.

"No," said Papa slowly. "Not a housekeeper." He paused. "A wife."

Caleb stared at Papa. "A wife? You mean a mother?"

Nick slid his face onto Papa's lap and Papa stroked his ears.

"That, too," said Papa. "Like Maggie."

Matthew, our neighbor to the south, had written to ask for a wife and mother for his children. And Maggie had come from Tennessee. Her hair was the color of turnips and she laughed.

Papa reached into his pocket and unfolded a letter written on white paper. "And I have received an answer." Papa read to us:

"Dear Mr. Jacob Witting,

"I am Sarah Wheaton from Maine as you will see from my letter. I am answering your advertisement. I have never been married, though I have been asked. I have lived with an older brother, William, who is about to be married. His wife-to-be is young and energetic.

"I have always loved to live by the sea, but at this time I feel a move is necessary. And the truth is, the sea is as far east as I can go. My choice, as you can see, is limited. This should not be taken as an insult. I am strong and I work hard and I am willing to travel. But I am not mild mannered. If you should still care to write, I would be interested in your children and about where you live. And you.

"Very truly yours,
"Sarah Elisabeth Wheaton
"P.S. Do you have opinions on cats? I have one."

No one spoke when Papa finished the letter. He kept looking at it in his hands, reading it over to himself. Finally I turned my head a bit to sneak a look at Caleb. He was smiling. I smiled, too.

"One thing," I said in the quiet of the room.

"What's that?" asked Papa, looking up.

I put my arm around Caleb.

"Ask her if she sings," I said.

Caleb and Papa and I wrote letters to Sarah, and before the ice and snow had melted from the fields, we all received answers. Mine came first.

Dear Anna,

Yes, I can braid hair and I can make stew and bake bread, though I prefer to build bookshelves and paint.

My favorite colors are the colors of the sea, blue and gray and green, depending on the weather. My brother William is a fisherman, and he tells me that when he is in the middle of a fogbound sea the water is a color for which there is no name. He catches flounder and sea bass and bluefish. Sometimes he sees whales. And birds, too, of course. I am enclosing a book of sea birds so you will see what William and I see every day.

Very truly yours,
Sarah Elisabeth Wheaton

Caleb read and read the letter so many times that the ink began to run and the folds tore. He read the book about sea birds over and over.

"Do you think she'll come?" asked Caleb. "And will she stay? What if she thinks we are loud and pesky?"

"You *are* loud and pesky," I told him. But I was worried, too. Sarah loved the sea, I could tell. Maybe she wouldn't leave there after all to come where there were fields and grass and sky and not much else.

"What if she comes and doesn't like our house?" Caleb asked. "I told her it was small. Maybe I shouldn't have told her it was small."

"Hush, Caleb. Hush."

Caleb's letter came soon after, with a picture of a cat drawn on the envelope.

Dear Caleb,

My cat's name is Seal because she is gray like the seals that swim offshore in Maine. She is glad that Lottie and Nick send their greetings. She likes dogs most of the time. She says their footprints are much larger than hers (which she is enclosing in return).

Your house sounds lovely, even though it is far out in the country with no close neighbors. My house is tall and the shingles are gray because of the salt from the sea. There are roses nearby.

Yes, I do like small rooms sometimes. Yes, I can keep a fire going at night. I do not know if I snore. Seal has never told me.

Very truly yours,
Sarah Elisabeth

"Did you really ask her about fires and snoring?" I asked, amazed.

"I wished to know," Caleb said.

He kept the letter with him, reading it in the barn and in the fields and by the cow pond. And always in bed at night.

One morning, early, Papa and Caleb and I were cleaning out the horse stalls and putting down new bedding. Papa stopped suddenly and leaned on his pitchfork.

"Sarah has said she will come for a month's time if we wish her to," he said, his voice loud in the dark barn. "To see how it is. Just to see."

Caleb stood by the stall door and folded his arms across his chest.

"I think," he began. Then, "I think," he said slowly, "that it would be good—to say yes," he finished in a rush.

Papa looked at me.

"I say yes," I told him, grinning.

"Yes," said Papa. "Then yes it is."

And the three of us, all smiling, went to work again.

The next day Papa went to town to mail his letter to Sarah. It was rainy for days, and the clouds followed. The house was cool and damp and quiet. Once I set four places at the table, then caught myself and put the extra plate away. Three lambs were born, one with a black face. And then Papa's letter came. It was very short.

Dear Jacob,

I will come by train. I will wear a yellow bonnet. I am plain and tall.

Sarah

"What's that?" asked Caleb excitedly, peering over Papa's shoulder. He pointed. "There, written at the bottom of the letter."

Papa read it to himself. Then he smiled, holding up the letter for us to see.

Tell them I sing was all it said.

Sarah came in the spring. She came through green grass fields that bloomed with Indian paintbrush, red and orange, and blue-eyed grass.

Papa got up early for the long day's trip to the train and back. He brushed his hair so slick and shiny that Caleb laughed. He wore a clean blue shirt, and a belt instead of suspenders.

He fed and watered the horses, talking to them as he hitched them up to the wagon. Old Bess, calm and kind; Jack, wild-eyed, reaching over to nip Bess on the neck.

"Clear day, Bess," said Papa, rubbing her nose.

"Settle down, Jack." He leaned his head on Jack.

And then Papa drove off along the dirt road to fetch Sarah. Papa's new wife. Maybe. Maybe our new mother.

Gophers ran back and forth across the road, stopping to stand up and watch the wagon. Far off in the field a woodchuck ate and listened. Ate and listened.

Caleb and I did our chores without talking. We shoveled out the stalls and laid down new hay. We fed the sheep. We swept and straightened and carried wood and water. And then our chores were done.

Caleb pulled on my shirt.

"Is my face clean?" he asked. "Can my face be *too* clean?" He looked alarmed.

"No, your face is clean but not too clean," I said.

Caleb slipped his hand into mine as we stood on the porch, watching the road. He was afraid.

"Will she be nice?" he asked. "Like Maggie?"

"Sarah will be nice," I told him.

"How far away is Maine?" he asked.

"You know how far. Far away, by the sea."

"Will Sarah bring some sea?" he asked.

"No, you cannot bring the sea."

The sheep ran in the field, and far off the cows moved slowly to the pond, like turtles.

"Will she like us?" asked Caleb very softly.

I watched a marsh hawk wheel down behind the barn.

He looked up at me.

"Of course she will like us." He answered his own question. "We are nice," he added, making me smile.

We waited and watched. I rocked on the porch and Caleb rolled a marble on the wood floor. Back and forth. Back and forth. The marble was blue.

We saw the dust from the wagon first, rising above the road, above the heads of Jack and Old Bess. Caleb climbed up onto the porch roof and shaded his eyes.

"A bonnet!" he cried. "I see a yellow bonnet!"

The dogs came out from under the porch, ears up, their eyes on the cloud of dust bringing Sarah. The wagon passed the fenced field, and the cows and sheep looked up, too. It rounded the windmill and the barn and the windbreak of Russian olive that Mama had planted long ago. Nick began to bark, then Lottie, and the wagon clattered into the yard and stopped by the steps.

"Hush," said Papa to the dogs.

And it was quiet.

Sarah stepped down from the wagon, a cloth bag in her hand. She reached up and took off her yellow bonnet, smoothing back her brown hair into a bun. She was plain and tall.

"Did you bring some sea?" cried Caleb beside me.

"Something from the sea," said Sarah, smiling. "And me." She turned and lifted a black case from the wagon. "And Seal, too."

Carefully she opened the case, and Seal, gray with white feet, stepped out. Lottie lay down, her head on her paws, staring. Nick leaned down to sniff. Then he lay down, too.

"The cat will be good in the barn," said Papa. "For mice."

Sarah smiled. "She will be good in the house, too."

Sarah took Caleb's hand, then mine. Her hands were large and rough. She gave Caleb a shell—a moon snail, she called it—that was curled and smelled of salt.

61

"The gulls fly high and drop the shells on the rocks below," she told Caleb. "When the shell is broken, they eat what is inside."

"That is very smart," said Caleb.

"For you, Anna," said Sarah, "a sea stone."

And she gave me the smoothest and whitest stone I had ever seen.

"The sea washes over and over and around the stone, rolling it until it is round and perfect."

"That is very smart, too," said Caleb. He looked up at Sarah. "We do not have the sea here."

Sarah turned and looked out over the plains.

"No," she said. "There is no sea here. But the land rolls a little like the sea."

My father did not see her look, but I did. And I knew that Caleb had seen it, too. Sarah was not smiling. Sarah was already lonely. In a month's time the preacher might come to marry Sarah and Papa. And a month was a long time. Time enough for her to change her mind and leave us.

Papa took Sarah's bags inside, where her room was ready with a quilt on the bed and blue flax dried in a vase on the night table.

Seal stretched and made a small cat sound. I watched her circle the dogs and sniff the air. Caleb came out and stood beside me.

"When will we sing?" he whispered.

I shook my head, turning the white stone over and over in my hand. I wished everything was as perfect as the stone. I wished that Papa and Caleb and I were perfect for Sarah. I wished we had a sea of our own.

Sarah, Plain and Tall

Meet the Author

Patricia MacLachlan grew up in Cheyenne, Wyoming, with parents who loved books and stories. *"We read them, discussed them, reread them, and acted out the parts."*

Ms. MacLachlan spent time writing about foster and adopted families for a family agency. When she decided to start writing books, she studied other writers first. She read 30 to 40 children's books each week.

Most of her books are about families, and her concern for families and for children has shaped her career. *"I write books about brothers and sisters, about what makes up a family, what works and what is nurturing."* Many of the characters she writes about are based on people in her own family.

Meet the Illustrator

Meg Kelleher Aubrey creates her work from photos she has taken. She loves to use her friends and family as models because, she says, *"Using familiar faces make[s] the project more personal and fun."* She received her degree in illustration from the Rhode Island School of Design and has won several awards for her art.

Theme Connections

Within the Selection

Record your answers to the questions below in the Response Journal section of your Writer's Notebook. In small groups, report the ideas you wrote. Discuss your ideas with the rest of your group. Then choose a person to report your group's answers to the class.

- What risk did Sarah take by coming to stay with Caleb, Anna, and Papa?
- Are the Wittings risking anything by having Sarah come to stay with them?

Across Selections

- Compare the risks taken by Toto in "Toto" with the risks taken by Sarah. How are they alike? How are they different?

Beyond the Selection

- Think about how "Sarah, Plain and Tall" adds to what you know about risks and consequences.
- Add items to the Concept/Question Board about risks and consequences.

Escape

from ***Charlotte's Web***
by E. B. White
illustrated by Garth Williams

The barn was very large. It was very old. It smelled of hay and it smelled of manure. It smelled of the perspiration of tired horses and the wonderful sweet breath of patient cows. It often had a sort of peaceful smell—as though nothing bad could happen ever again in the world. It smelled of grain and of harness dressing and of axle grease and of rubber boots and of new rope. And whenever the cat was given a fish-head to eat, the barn would smell of fish. But mostly it smelled of hay, for there was always hay in the great loft up overhead. And there was always hay being pitched down to the cows and the horses and the sheep.

The barn was pleasantly warm in winter when the animals spent most of their time indoors, and it was pleasantly cool in summer when the big doors stood wide open to the breeze. The barn had stalls on the main floor for the work horses, tie-ups on the main floor for the cows, a sheepfold down below for the sheep, a pigpen down below for Wilbur, and it was full of all sorts of things that you find in barns: ladders, grindstones, pitch forks, monkey wrenches, scythes, lawn mowers, snow shovels, ax handles, milk pails, water buckets, empty grain sacks, and rusty rat traps. It was the kind of barn that swallows like to build their nests in. It was the kind of barn that children like to play in. And the whole thing was owned by Fern's uncle, Mr. Homer L. Zuckerman.

Wilbur's new home was in the lower part of the barn, directly underneath the cows. Mr. Zuckerman knew that a manure pile is a good place to keep a young pig. Pigs need warmth, and it was warm and comfortable down there in the barn cellar on the south side.

Fern came almost every day to visit him. She found an old milking stool that had been discarded, and she placed the stool in the sheepfold next to Wilbur's pen. Here she sat quietly during the long afternoons, thinking and listening and watching Wilbur. The sheep soon got to know her and trust her. So did the geese, who lived with the sheep. All the animals trusted her, she was so quiet and friendly. Mr. Zuckerman did not allow her to take Wilbur out, and he did not allow her to get into the pigpen. But he told Fern that she could sit on the stool and watch Wilbur as long as she wanted to. It made her happy just to be near the pig, and it made Wilbur happy to know that she was sitting there, right outside his pen. But he never had any fun— no walks, no rides, no swims.

One afternoon in June, when Wilbur was almost two months old, he wandered out into his small yard outside the barn. Fern had not arrived for her usual visit. Wilbur stood in the sun feeling lonely and bored.

"There's never anything to do around here," he thought. He walked slowly to his food trough and sniffed to see if anything had been overlooked at lunch. He found a small strip of potato skin and ate it. His back itched, so he leaned against the fence and rubbed against the boards. When he tired of this, he walked indoors, climbed to the top of the manure pile, and sat down. He didn't feel like going to sleep, he didn't feel like digging, he was tired of standing still, tired of lying down. "I'm less than two months old and I'm tired of living," he said. He walked out to the yard again.

"When I'm out here," he said, "there's no place to go but in. When I'm indoors, there's no place to go but out in the yard."

"That's where you're wrong, my friend, my friend," said a voice.

Wilbur looked through the fence and saw the goose standing there.

"You don't have to stay in that dirty-little dirty-little dirty-little yard," said the goose, who talked rather fast. "One of those boards is loose. Push on it, push-push-push on it, and come on out!"

"What?" said Wilbur. "Say it slower!"

"At-at-at, at the risk of repeating myself," said the goose, "I suggest that you come on out. It's wonderful out here."

"Did you say a board was loose?"

"That I did, that I did," said the goose.

Wilbur walked up to the fence and saw that the goose was right—one board was loose. He put his head down, shut his eyes, and pushed. The board gave way. In a minute he had squeezed through the fence and was standing in the long grass outside his yard. The goose chuckled.

"How does it feel to be free?" she asked.

"I like it," said Wilbur. "That is, I *guess* I like it." Actually, Wilbur felt queer to be outside his fence, with nothing between him and the big world.

"Where do you think I'd better go?"

"Anywhere you like, anywhere you like," said the goose. "Go down through the orchard, root up the sod! Go down through the garden, dig up the radishes! Root up everything! Eat grass! Look for corn! Look for oats! Run all over! Skip and dance, jump and prance! Go down through the orchard and stroll in the woods! The world is a wonderful place when you're young."

"I can see that," replied Wilbur. He gave a jump in the air, twirled, ran a few steps, stopped, looked all around, sniffed the smells of afternoon, and then set off walking down through the orchard. Pausing in the shade of an apple tree, he put his strong snout into the ground and began pushing, digging, and rooting. He felt very happy. He had plowed up quite a piece of ground before anyone noticed him. Mrs. Zuckerman was the first to see him. She saw him from the kitchen window, and she immediately shouted for the men.

"Ho-*mer!*" she cried. "Pig's out! Lurvy! Pig's out! Homer! Lurvy! Pig's out. He's down there under that apple tree."

"Now the trouble starts," thought Wilbur. "Now I'll catch it."

The goose heard the racket and she, too, started hollering. "Run-run-run downhill, make for the woods, the woods!" she shouted to Wilbur. "They'll never-never-never catch you in the woods."

The cocker spaniel heard the commotion and he ran out from the barn to join the chase. Mr. Zuckerman heard, and he came out of the machine shed where he was mending a tool. Lurvy, the hired man, heard the noise and came up from the asparagus patch where he was pulling weeds. Everybody walked toward Wilbur and Wilbur didn't know what to do. The woods seemed a long way off, and anyway, he had never been down there in the woods and wasn't sure he would like it.

"Get around behind him, Lurvy," said Mr. Zuckerman, "and drive him toward the barn! And take it easy—don't rush him! I'll go and get a bucket of slops."

The news of Wilbur's escape spread rapidly among the animals on the place. Whenever any creature broke loose on Zuckerman's farm, the event was of great interest to the others. The goose shouted to the nearest cow that Wilbur was free, and soon all the cows knew. Then one of the cows told one of the sheep, and soon all the sheep knew.

The lambs learned about it from their mothers. The horses, in their stalls in the barn, pricked up their ears when they heard the goose hollering; and soon the horses had caught on to what was happening. "Wilbur's out," they said. Every animal stirred and lifted its head and became excited to know that one of his friends had got free and was no longer penned up or tied fast.

Wilbur didn't know what to do or which way to run. It seemed as though everybody was after him. "If this is what it's like to be free," he thought, "I believe I'd rather be penned up in my own yard."

The cocker spaniel was sneaking up on him from one side, Lurvy the hired man was sneaking up on him from the other side. Mrs. Zuckerman stood ready to head him off if he started for the garden, and now Mr. Zuckerman was coming down toward him carrying a pail. "This is really awful," thought Wilbur. "Why doesn't Fern come?" He began to cry.

The goose took command and began to give orders.

"Don't just stand there, Wilbur! Dodge about, dodge about!" cried the goose. "Skip around, run toward me, slip in and out, in and out, in and out! Make for the woods! Twist and turn!"

The cocker spaniel sprang for Wilbur's hind leg.
Wilbur jumped and ran. Lurvy reached out and
grabbed. Mrs. Zuckerman screamed at Lurvy. The
goose cheered for Wilbur. Wilbur dodged between
Lurvy's legs. Lurvy missed Wilbur and grabbed the
spaniel instead. "Nicely done, nicely done!" cried
the goose. "Try it again, try it again!"

"Run downhill!" suggested the cows.

"Run toward me!" yelled the gander.

"Run uphill!" cried the sheep.

"Turn and twist!" honked the goose.

"Jump and dance!" said the rooster.

"Look out for Lurvy!" called the cows.

"Look out for Zuckerman!" yelled the gander.

"Watch out for the dog!" cried the sheep.

"Listen to me, listen to me!" screamed the goose.

Poor Wilbur was dazed and frightened by this hullabaloo. He didn't like being the center of all this fuss. He tried to follow the instructions his friends were giving him, but he couldn't run downhill and uphill at the same time, and he couldn't turn and twist when he was jumping and dancing, and he was crying so hard he could barely see anything that was happening. After all, Wilbur was a very young pig—not much more than a baby, really. He wished Fern were there to take him in her arms and comfort him. When he looked up and saw Mr. Zuckerman standing quite close to him, holding a pail of warm slops, he felt relieved. He lifted his nose and sniffed. The smell was delicious—warm milk, potato skins, wheat middlings, Kellogg's Corn Flakes, and a popover left from the Zuckermans' breakfast.

"Come, pig!" said Mr. Zuckerman, tapping the pail. "Come pig!"

Wilbur took a step toward the pail.

"No-no-no!" said the goose. "It's the old pail trick, Wilbur. Don't fall for it, don't fall for it! He's trying to lure you back into captivity-ivity. He's appealing to your stomach."

Wilbur didn't care. The food smelled appetizing. He took another step toward the pail.

"Pig, pig!" said Mr. Zuckerman in a kind voice, and began walking slowly toward the barnyard, looking all about him innocently, as if he didn't know that a little white pig was following along behind him.

"You'll be sorry-sorry-sorry," called the goose.

Wilbur didn't care. He kept walking toward the pail of slops.

"You'll miss your freedom," honked the goose. "An hour of freedom is worth a barrel of slops."

Wilbur didn't care.

When Mr. Zuckerman reached the pigpen, he climbed over the fence and poured the slops into the trough. Then he pulled the loose board away from the fence, so that there was a wide hole for Wilbur to walk through.

"Reconsider, reconsider!" cried the goose.

Wilbur paid no attention. He stepped through the fence into his yard. He walked to the trough and took a long drink of slops, sucking in the milk hungrily and chewing the popover. It was good to be home again.

While Wilbur ate, Lurvy fetched a hammer and some 8-penny nails and nailed the board in place. Then he and Mr. Zuckerman leaned lazily on the fence and Mr. Zuckerman scratched Wilbur's back with a stick.

"He's quite a pig," said Lurvy.

"Yes, he'll make a good pig," said Mr. Zuckerman.

Wilbur heard the words of praise. He felt the warm milk inside his stomach. He felt the pleasant rubbing of the stick along his itchy back. He felt peaceful and happy and sleepy. This had been a tiring afternoon. It was still only about four o'clock but Wilbur was ready for bed.

"I'm really too young to go out into the world alone," he thought as he lay down.

Escape

Meet the Author

E. B. White E. B. White is best known for his classic children's books, *Stuart Little* and *Charlotte's Web*. He began to write his first book, *Stuart Little* after he had a vivid dream. Whenever one of his nieces or nephews wanted to be told a story, E. B. White would make up new adventures for his mouse-like hero whom he named Stuart Little. E. B. White began his writing career as a reporter, but his real passion was writing essays.

Meet the Illustrator

Garth Williams Garth Williams was born in New York City to parents who were both artists. "Everybody in my house was either painting or drawing," he said, "so I thought there was nothing else to do in life but make pictures." Later, Garth Williams wanted to become an architect, but he couldn't afford the cost of the college tuition. Instead, he won a painting scholarship to the Royal College of Art.

Williams tries to show humor, respect for others, and responsibility in his illustrations. He went on to illustrate many books, including *Stuart Little* and *Little House on the Prairie*.

Theme Connections

Within the Selection

Record your answers to the questions below in the Response Journal section of your Writer's Notebook. In small groups, report the ideas you wrote. Discuss your ideas with the rest of your group. Then choose a person to report your group's answers to the class.

- Why did Wilbur decide to escape from his yard?
- Why did Wilbur decide to follow Mr. Zuckerman back into the barnyard instead of listening to his friends' instructions to run away?
- What risk was there to Wilbur outside his pen?

Across Selections

Wilbur listened to the goose and escaped from his yard. Have you read any other stories in which the character listened to the advice of another character and was not happy with the consequences of that risk? How was that experience similar to Wilbur's experience? How was it different?

Beyond the Selection

- Wilbur escaped his yard, but he decided to follow Mr. Zuckerman back into it. Like Wilbur, have you ever taken a risk and realized you made the wrong decision?
- Think about how "Escape" adds to what you know about risks and consequences.
- Add items to the Concept/Question Board about risks and consequences.

Hippo's Hope

poem and drawings by Shel Silverstein

There once was a hippo who wanted to fly—
Fly-hi-dee, try-hi-dee, my-hi-dee-ho.
So he sewed him some wings that could flap through the sky—
Sky-hi-dee, fly-hi-dee, why-hi-dee-go.

He climbed to the top of a mountain of snow—
Snow-hi-dee, slow-hi-dee, oh-hi-dee-hoo.
With the clouds high above and the sea down below—
Where-hi-dee, there-hi-dee, scare-hi-dee-boo.

(Happy ending)
And he flipped and he flapped and he bellowed so loud—
Now-hi-dee, loud-hi-dee, proud-hi-dee-poop.
And he sailed like an eagle, off into the clouds—
High-hi-dee, fly-hi-dee, bye-hi-dee-boop.

(Unhappy ending)
And he leaped like a frog and he fell like a stone—
Stone-hi-dee, lone-hi-dee, own-hi-dee-flop.
And he crashed and he drowned and broke all his bones—
Bones-hi-dee, moans-hi-dee, groans-hi-dee-glop.

(Chicken ending)
He looked up at the sky and looked down at the sea—
Sea-hi-dee, free-hi-dee, whee-hi-dee-way.
And he turned and went home and had cookies and tea—
That's hi-dee, all hi-dee, I have to say.

Focus Questions What would the world be like if no one ever took a risk? Can you fulfill your dreams without taking some risks?

Mae Jemison
Space Scientist

by Gail Sakurai

THREE . . .

Two . . .

One . . .

Liftoff!

The space shuttle *Endeavour* thundered into the morning sky above Kennedy Space Center. Higher and higher it soared over the Atlantic Ocean. A few minutes later, *Endeavour* was in orbit around Earth.

Aboard the spacecraft, astronaut Mae Jemison could feel her heart pounding with excitement. A wide, happy grin split her face. She had just made history. She was the first African-American woman in space. The date was September 12, 1992.

But Mae wasn't thinking about dates in history books. Her thoughts were of the wonder and adventure of space travel. "I'm closer to the stars——somewhere I've always dreamed to be," Mae said during a live television broadcast from space.

Mae's dream didn't come true overnight. It happened only after many long years of hard work, training, and preparation. Her success

The space shuttle *Endeavour* lifts off.

While in space, the *Endeavour* astronauts pose for a portrait.

83

story began nearly thirty-six years earlier, in a small town in Alabama.

Mae Carol Jemison was born on October 17, 1956, in Decatur, Alabama. While she was still a toddler, Mae and her family moved to the big city of Chicago, Illinois. Mae considers Chicago her hometown because she grew up there.

Mae was the youngest child in her family. She had an older brother, Charles, and an older sister, Ada. Her parents, Charlie and Dorothy Jemison, were helpful and supportive of all of Mae's interests. "They put up with all kinds of stuff, like science projects, dance classes, and art lessons," Mae said. "They encouraged me to do it, and they would find the money, time, and energy to help me be involved."

Other adults were not as encouraging as Mae's parents. When Mae told her kindergarten teacher that she wanted to be a scientist, the teacher said, "Don't you mean a nurse?" In those days, very few African Americans or women were scientists. Many people, like Mae's teacher, couldn't imagine a little black girl growing up to become a scientist. But Mae refused to let other people's limited imaginations stop her from following her dreams.

Mae had always dreamed of becoming an astronaut. Her dream came true in 1987.

Mae loved to work on school science projects. She spent many hours at the public library, reading books about science and space. On summer nights, she liked to lie outside, look up at the stars, and dream of traveling in space. Mae was fascinated by the real-life space flights and moon landings that she watched on television. Mae Jemison knew that she wanted to be an astronaut. Although all the astronauts at the time were white and male, Mae wasn't discouraged.

Science and space were not young Mae's only interests. She also loved to dance. Mae started taking lessons in jazz and African dance at the age of nine. By the time she was in high school, Mae was an accomplished dancer, and she frequently performed on stage. She was also skilled at choreography, the art of creating a dance.

85

Mae at Stanford University

In 1973, Mae graduated from Chicago's Morgan Park High School, where she was an honor-roll student and excelled in science and math. That fall, Mae entered Stanford University in California. At Stanford, she specialized in African and Afro-American studies, and chemical engineering. Mae continued her dancing and choreography. She also became involved with student organizations, and she was elected president of the Black Student Union.

After receiving her Bachelor of Science degree from Stanford, Mae enrolled at Cornell University Medical College in New York. She had decided to become a doctor. Medical school was demanding, but Mae still found time to participate in student organizations. She served as president of both the Cornell Medical Student Executive Council and the Cornell chapter of the National Student Medical Association.

Mae traveled to several countries as part of her medical training. She studied medicine in Cuba. She helped provide basic medical care for people in rural Kenya and at a Cambodian refugee camp in Thailand.

Mae received her Doctor of Medicine degree from Cornell University in 1981. Like all new doctors, she served an internship, a period of practicing under experienced doctors. Mae completed her internship at the Los Angeles County/University of Southern California Medical Center. Then she started working as a doctor in Los Angeles.

Mae was working as a doctor in this Los Angeles office when NASA selected her for its astronaut program.

Although she had settled into a career as a doctor, Mae wasn't finished traveling yet. She remembered the trips she had taken during medical school, and she still wanted to help people in other parts of the world. Mae decided to join the Peace Corps, an organization of volunteers who work to improve conditions in developing nations.

Mae spent more than two years in West Africa. She was the Area Peace Corps Medical Officer for Sierra Leone and Liberia. She was in charge of health care for all Peace Corps volunteers and U.S. embassy employees in those two countries. It was an important responsibility for someone who was only twenty-six years old.

"I learned a lot from that experience," Mae said. "I was one of the youngest doctors over there, and I had to learn to deal with how people reacted to my age, while asserting myself as a physician."

When her tour of duty in the Peace Corps was over, Mae returned to Los Angeles and resumed her medical practice. She also started taking advanced engineering classes.

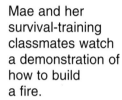
Mae sits in the cockpit of a shuttle trainer.

Mae and her survival-training classmates watch a demonstration of how to build a fire.

Mae had not forgotten her dream of traveling in space. Now that she had the necessary education and experience, Mae decided to try and become an astronaut. She applied to the National Aeronautics and Space Administration (NASA), which is responsible for U.S. space exploration. After undergoing background checks, physical exams, medical tests, and interviews, Dr. Mae Jemison was accepted into the astronaut program in June 1987. She was one of only fifteen people chosen from nearly two thousand qualified applicants!

Mae didn't let success go to her head. "I'm very aware of the fact that I'm not the first African-American woman who had the skills, the talent, the desire to be an astronaut," she said. "I happen to be the first one that NASA selected."

Mae moved to Houston, Texas, where she began a year of intensive training at NASA's Johnson Space Center. She studied space shuttle equipment and operations. To learn how to handle emergencies and deal with difficult situations, Mae practiced wilderness- and water-survival skills. Survival training also helps teach cooperation and teamwork. These are important abilities for astronauts who must live and work together for long periods in a cramped space shuttle.

Mae took lessons on how to move her body and operate tools in a weightless environment. On Earth, the force of gravity keeps us from floating off the ground. But in space, there is less gravity, so people and objects drift about. Since there is no "up" or "down" in space, astronauts don't need to lie down to sleep. They can sleep in any position. To keep them from drifting while asleep, they zip themselves into special sleeping bags attached to the shuttle's walls.

During training, Mae got a preview of weightlessness. She flew in a special training jet that simulates zero gravity. The jet climbs nearly straight up, then loops into a steep dive. This is similar to the loop-the-loops on many roller coasters. For thirty seconds at the top of the loop, trainees feel weightless. Their feet leave the floor and they can fly around inside the padded cabin.

At the end of her training year, Mae officially became a mission specialist astronaut. "We're the ones people often call the scientist astronauts," Mae explained. "Our responsibilities are to be familiar with the shuttle and how it operates, to do the experiments once you get into orbit, to help launch the payloads or satellites, and also do extravehicular activities, which are the space walks."

Mae in training (top) clinging to a life raft in water-survival training; (middle) practicing with the shuttle escape pole for emergency bailouts; (bottom) learning to use a parachute.

Bottom left: Mae and astronaut Jan Davis (left) hold onto each other in NASA's "zero-gravity" training aircraft.

This illustration shows how the space shuttle looks during flight. The cargo bay holds Spacelab, the science laboratory where *Endeavour*'s astronauts conducted most of their experiments.

In the 1970s, NASA designed the space shuttle as the first reusable spacecraft. A shuttle launches like a rocket, but it returns to Earth and lands on a runway like an airplane.

A space shuttle has many uses. It carries both equipment and people into space. Astronauts aboard a shuttle can capture, repair, and launch satellites. Shuttles are often used as orbiting laboratories, where space scientists conduct experiments in a zero-gravity environment. In the future, space shuttles might transport supplies and workers for building space stations.

The *Endeavour* crew on their way to the launch pad.

Although Mae was a full-fledged astronaut, she still had to wait four more years before she went into space. While she waited, Mae worked with the scientists who were developing experiments for her mission. She also trained with her fellow crew members. In her spare time, Mae liked to read, travel, ski, garden, dance, and exercise. She also enjoyed taking care of Sneeze, her white, gray, and silver African wildcat.

On September 12, 1992, the long wait was over. Space shuttle *Endeavour* perched on the launch pad like a great white bird waiting to take flight. Everything was ready for the liftoff.

Mae awoke early to shower and dress. She ate breakfast with the other astronauts. Then, Mae and the crew put on their orange space suits and boarded a van for the short drive to the launch pad. For two-and-a-half hours until liftoff, they lay on their backs, strapped into their seats, as the countdown progressed. At 10:23 A.M., precisely on time, *Endeavour* lifted off on its historic space journey.

Dr. Mae Jemison earned her place in the history books as the first African-American woman in space. Mae said, "My participation in the space shuttle mission helps to say that all peoples of the world have astronomers, physicists, and explorers."

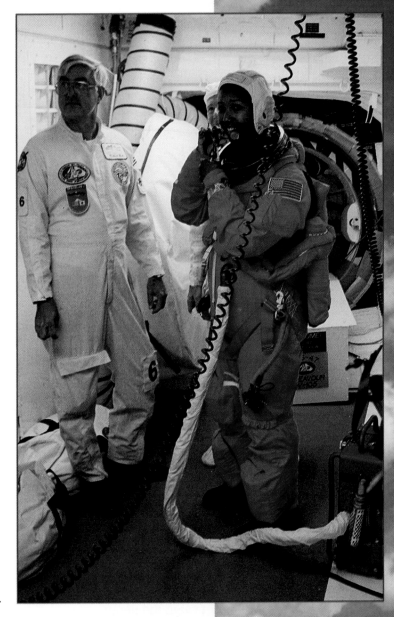

Mae prepares to board the shuttle.

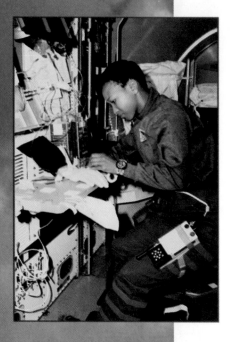
Mae injects liquid into a mannequin's hand. She is testing new medical equipment that is specially designed for a weightless environment.

Endeavour's mission was devoted to scientific research. Mae was responsible for several key experiments. She had helped design an experiment to study the loss of bone cells in space. Astronauts lose bone cells in weightlessness, and the longer they stay in space, the more they lose. If too many cells are lost, bones become weak and can break easily. Scientists hope to find a way to prevent this loss.

Mae explained, "The real issue is how to keep people healthy while they're in space."

Mae investigated a new way of controlling space motion sickness. Half of all astronauts experience space sickness during their first few days in space. They often feel dizzy and nauseated. Astronauts can take medicine to control space sickness, but the medicine can make them tired.

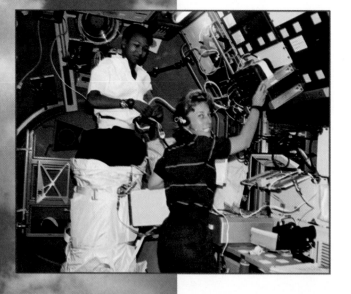
Mae and Jan Davis conduct a zero-gravity experiment. In space, a person's fluids shift toward the upper body. The device Mae is wearing simulates normal gravity and forces the fluids back to the lower body.

To carry out the space-sickness experiment, Mae had been trained in the use of "biofeedback" techniques. Biofeedback uses meditation and relaxation to control the body's functions. Mae wore special monitoring equipment to record her heart rate, breathing, temperature, and other body functions. If she started to feel ill, she would meditate. She concentrated intensely on bringing her body back to normal. The purpose of the experiment was to see if Mae could avoid space sickness without taking medication. The results of the experiment were not conclusive, but space researchers still hope to use biofeedback in the future.

Mae is all wired up for the biofeedback experiment.

Mae was also in charge of the frog experiment. Early in the flight, she fertilized eggs from female South African frogs. A few days later, tadpoles hatched. She then watched the tadpoles carefully. Her goal was to find out if the tadpoles would develop normally in the near-zero gravity of space. "What we've seen is that the eggs were fertilized and the tadpoles looked pretty good," said Mae. "It was exciting because that's a question that we didn't have any information on before."

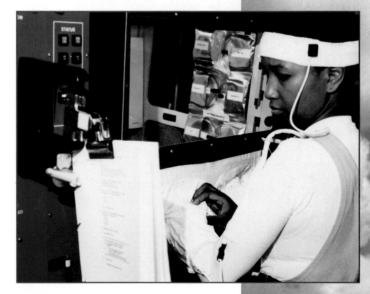

Mae works with the frog experiment.

Home again.
Endeavour lands on the runway at the Kennedy Space Center.

Mae with Morgan Park High School's principal, Earl Bryant, at a special homecoming ceremony in her honor.

On September 20, 1992, at 8:53 A.M., *Endeavour* landed at Kennedy Space Center. The crew had spent more than 190 hours (almost eight days) in space. They had traveled 3.3 million miles and had completed 127 orbits of Earth!

After her space mission, Mae returned home to Chicago. Her hometown welcomed her with six days of parades, speeches, and celebrations. Then she went to Hollywood to accept the American Black Achievement Awards' Trailblazer Award for being the first African-American woman in space. In 1993, Mae was inducted into the National Women's Hall of Fame in Seneca Falls, New York.

Mae Jemison had made her childhood dream come true. She was ready for new challenges. A few months after her space flight, Mae took a leave of absence from NASA to teach and to do research at Dartmouth College in New Hampshire. Then, on March 8, 1993, she permanently resigned from the astronaut corps.

Mae formed her own company called The Jemison Group, Inc. The Jemison Group's goal is to develop ways of using science and technology to improve the quality of life. Mae's company makes a special effort to improve conditions in poor and developing countries.

Mae encourages youngsters to follow their dreams. She is shown here with thirteen-year-old Jill Giovanelli, the winner of the International Peace Poster Contest.

The company's first project used satellite communications to provide better health care for people in West Africa. Mae also established an international summer science camp for young people.

Besides her work with The Jemison Group, Mae spends much of her time traveling around the country, giving speeches, and encouraging young people to follow their dreams. Mae Jemison believes in the motto:

"Don't be limited by others' limited imaginations."

Mae Jemison
Space Scientist

Meet the Author

Gail Sakurai was born in Detroit, Michigan. As soon as she learned to read, she knew she wanted to be a writer.

Ms. Sakurai gets story ideas from the world around her. Her book about Dr. Mae Jemison, the first female African-American astronaut, grew out of a lifelong interest in space exploration. She says, *"I get the ideas for my books from everywhere—from things I read, from my children, and even from television. I have more ideas than I'll ever have time to use."*

Ms. Sakurai's advice to aspiring young writers is simple. *"Read. Read everything you can get your hands on!"*

Theme Connections

Within the Selection

Record your answers to the questions below in the Response Journal section of your Writer's Notebook. In small groups, report the ideas you wrote. Discuss your ideas with the rest of your group. Then choose a person to report your group's answers to the class.

- What was Mae Jemison's childhood dream?
- How did Mae Jemison make her dream come true?

Across Selections

How are the risks taken by Rosa Parks in "Rosa Parks: My Story" similar to the risks taken by Mae Jemison in "Mae Jemison: Space Scientist"? How are they different?

Beyond the Selection

- Share with the members of your group the story of someone you know or have read about who, like Mae Jemison, took a risk to reach an important goal.
- Think about how "Mae Jemison: Space Scientist" adds to what you know about risks and consequences.
- Add items to the Concept/Question Board about risks and consequences.

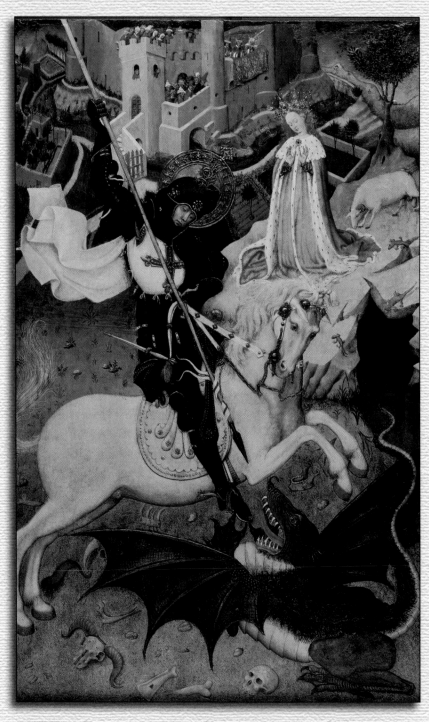

Saint George Killing the Dragon. 1430–35. **Bernardo Martorell.**
Tempera on panel. 115.3 cm × 98 cm. The Art Institute of Chicago.

Kajikazawa in Kai Province. From the series Thirty-Six Views of Mount Fuji. 1823–29. **Katsushika Hokusai.** Woodblock print. $10 \times 15\frac{1}{8}$ in. The Metropolitan Museum of Art, New York, NY.

Margaret Bourke-White Atop the Chrysler Building. 1931–1933. Silver gelatin print.

Two Tickets to Freedom

from *Two Tickets to Freedom: The True Story of Ellen and William Craft, Fugitive Slaves*
by Florence B. Freedman
illustrated by Doris Ettlinger

Among the many slaves in Georgia in 1848 were a young couple named William and Ellen Craft. Ellen was a maid and William a skilled cabinetmaker. Their lives were not as harsh as those of many other slaves, but the desire to be free never left them. However, escaping would be difficult!

William had been saving money for tickets to escape. He had a plan for himself and Ellen, who was light-skinned enough to pass for white. Ellen would dress up as an injured man, bandaging her face to further disguise the fact that she was a woman, and bandaging her right arm and hand to prevent anyone from asking her to write. She would then travel with William as her slave.

*Their journey would include a train ride
to Fredericksburg, Virginia, followed by a boat trip to
Washington, D.C., and finally a train ride to Philadelphia,
the first stop on the Underground Railroad.*

*By the time they left the train in Fredericksburg and
boarded a ship for Washington, D.C., William and Ellen felt
sure they were safe. They were unaware that the most
difficult part of their daring escape was just around the
corner. Would they ever make it to Philadelphia?*

In a few minutes, the ship landed at Washington, and there William and Ellen took a carriage to the train for Baltimore, the last slave port they were to see. They had left their cottage on Wednesday morning, the 21st of December. It was Christmas Eve, December 24, 1848, when they arrived in Baltimore.

William and Ellen were more tense than ever. They were so near their goal . . . yet they knew that officials in Baltimore were particularly watchful to prevent slaves from escaping across the border to Pennsylvania and freedom.

William settled his "master" in a first-class carriage on the train and went to the car in which blacks traveled. Before he entered, a Yankee officer stopped him, saying sternly, "Where are you going, boy?"

"Philadelphia, sir," William replied humbly.

"What are you going there for?" asked the officer.

"I am traveling with my master who is in another carriage, sir."

"I think you had better get him out, and be quick about it, because the train will soon be starting," the officer ordered. "It is against the rules to let any man take a slave past here unless he can satisfy them in the office that he has a right to take him along." The officer moved on, leaving William on the platform.

William's heart was beating furiously. To have come so far—and now this! How would Ellen be able to prove ownership? He consoled himself with the thought that God, who had been so good as to allow them to come this far, would not let them be turned aside now.

William hastened into the car to tell his master the bad news. "Mr. Johnson," seated comfortably in the railroad car, smiled at him. They were so near their destination.

"How are you feeling, sir?" asked William.

"Much better," answered his "master." "Thank God we are getting on so nicely."

"Not so nicely, sir, I am sorry to say," William said. "You must leave the train and convince the officials that I am your slave."

"Mr. Johnson" shuddered.

"Good heavens!" he whispered. "Is it possible that we will be sent back into slavery?"

They were silent for a few despairing moments. Then they left the train and made their way to the office.

Ellen summoned her last bit of courage.

"Do you wish to see me, sir?" "Mr. Johnson" asked the man who appeared to be the chief officer.

"Yes," he answered. "It is against our rules, sir, to allow any person to take a slave out of Baltimore into Philadelphia unless he can satisfy us that he has a right to take him along."

"Why is that?" asked "Mr. Johnson" innocently.

"Because, sir," the officer answered in a voice and manner that almost chilled the blood of the fugitives, "if we should allow any gentleman to take a slave past here into Philadelphia, and should the gentleman with whom the slave was traveling turn out to be not his rightful owner, and if the real owner should prove that his slave escaped on our railroad, we should have to pay for him."

This conversation attracted the attention of a large number of curious passengers. They seemed sympathetic to "Mr. Johnson," because he was so obviously ill.

Seeing the sympathy of the other passengers, the officer asked, more politely, "Do you know someone in Baltimore who might vouch for you and assure us that you have a right to take this slave into Pennsylvania?"

"No, I do not," asserted "Mr. Johnson" regretfully. He then added more forcefully, "I bought tickets in Charleston to pass us through to Philadelphia, and you have no right to detain us here!"

The officer was firm. "Right or wrong, I shan't let you go."

William and Ellen looked at each other, but did not dare to say a word for fear they would give themselves away. They knew that, if the officer suspected them, he had the right to put them in prison. When their true identity became known, they would surely be sent back into slavery, and they knew they would rather be dead. They silently prayed to be delivered from this new danger.

Just then, the conductor of the train on which they had come from Washington, came in.

"Did this gentleman and his slave come on your train?" asked the official.

"They did," answered the conductor, and left.

Suddenly the bell rang for the train to leave. The other passengers fixed their eyes upon the officer, "Mr. Johnson," and his slave, their expressions showing their interest and concern.

The officer seemed agitated. Running his fingers through his hair, he finally said, "I don't know what to do." Then looking around, he added, "I calculate it is all right. Run and tell the conductor that it will be all right to let this gentleman and his slave proceed," he told one of the clerks. "Since he is not well, it is a pity to stop him here. We will let him go."

"Mr. Johnson" thanked him and stepped out, crossing the platform as quickly as possible, with his slave close behind. William escorted his master into one of the best carriages of the train and reached his own just as the train pulled out.

It was eight o'clock on Christmas Eve, just eight days after William had first thought of their plan. In the four days before they left Macon, he and Ellen had both been working; they had seen each other only at night, when they talked over each detail of their plan. They had had hardly any sleep for the four days of planning and the four days of the journey. Now that the last hurdle was passed, William realized how terribly tired he was. Knowing that they would be in Philadelphia in the morning, and that there were no important stations between Baltimore and Philadelphia, William relaxed his guard, and fell asleep. It proved to be the wrong time for sleeping.

When the train reached Havre-de-Grace, all the first-class passengers were told to get off the train and onto a ferryboat, to be ferried across the Susquehanna River to take the train again on the opposite side. This was to spare the passengers the jolting of rolling the cars onto the boat. The baggage cars, however, were rolled on the boat to be taken off on the other side. The sleeping William was near the baggage car, so they did not wake him.

When Ellen left the railroad carriage to get on the ferryboat, it was cold and dark and rainy. She was alone, without William, for the first time on the journey. She was frightened and confused.

"Have you seen my boy?" "Mr. Johnson" asked the conductor.

The conductor, who may well have been an abolitionist, thought he would tease this Southern slaveowner.

"No, I haven't seen anything of him for some time; no doubt he has run away and has reached Philadelphia long before now. He is probably a free man by now, sir."

"Mr. Johnson" knew better. "Please try to find him," he asked the conductor.

"I am no slave hunter," the conductor indignantly replied. "As far as I am concerned, everybody must look after his own slaves." With that, he strode away.

Ellen was frightened. She feared that William had been kidnaped into slavery, or perhaps killed on the train. She was in a predicament for another reason. She had no money at all. Although Ellen had been carrying the money up to then, she had given it all to William the night before after hearing that there were pickpockets in Philadelphia who preyed on travelers. A pickpocket would not think of a slave as a likely victim.

Ellen did have the tickets, however. Frightened and confused though she was, she realized that there was no use in her staying there at Havre-de-Grace. She must board the ferry and complete her journey, hoping and praying that she and William would find each other again in freedom.

The ferry ride over, the passengers went back on the train. After the train was well on its way to Philadelphia, the guard came to the car where William was sleeping and gave him a violent shake, saying, "Boy, wake up!"

William started, not knowing for a moment where he was.

"Your master is scared half to death about you," the guard continued. It was William's turn to be scared. He was sure that Ellen had been found out.

"What is the matter?" William managed to ask.

"Your master thinks you have run away from him," the guard explained.

Knowing that Ellen would never think any such thing, William felt reassured and went to his "master" immediately.

After talking with "Mr. Johnson" for a few minutes, William returned to his place, where the guard was talking with the conductor.

"What did your master want, boy?" asked the guard.

"He just wanted to know what had become of me."

"No," said the guard. "That's not it. He thought you had taken leave for parts unknown. I never saw a man so badly scared about losing his slave in my life. Now," continued the guard, "let me give you a little friendly advice. When you get to Philadelphia, run away and leave that cripple, and have your liberty."

"No, sir," replied William. "I can't promise to do that."

"Why not?" asked the conductor, evidently much surprised. "Don't you want your liberty?"

"Yes, sir," he replied, "but I shall never run away from such a good master as I have at present."

One of the men said to the guard, "Let him alone. I guess he'll open his eyes when he gets to Philadelphia."

In spite of William's seeming lack of interest, the men gave him a good deal of information about how to run away from his master in Philadelphia, information which he appeared not to be taking to heart, but which he found useful for both of them later.

On the train, William also met a free black man, who recommended to him a boardinghouse in Philadelphia kept by an abolitionist, where he would be quite safe if he decided to run away from his master. William thanked him, but did not let him know who he and his "master" really were.

Later on in the night, William heard a fearful whistling of the steam engine; he looked out the window and saw many flickering lights. A passenger in the next car also stuck his head out the window and called to his companion, "Wake up! We are in Philadelphia." The sight of the city in the distance and the words he heard made William feel as if a burden had rolled off his back; he felt really happy for the first time in his life.

As soon as the train reached the platform, he went to get "Mr. Johnson," took their luggage, put it into a carriage, got in and drove off to the abolitionist's boardinghouse recommended to him by the free black man.

No sooner had they left the station than Ellen, who had concealed her fears and played her part with so much courage and wit throughout the journey, grasped William's hand and said, "Thank God we are safe!" She burst into tears, and wept like a child.

When they reached the boardinghouse, Ellen was so weak and faint that she could scarcely stand alone. As soon as they were shown their room, William and Ellen knelt down and thanked God for His goodness in enabling them to overcome so many dangers in escaping from slavery to freedom.

That was Sunday, December 25, Christmas Day of 1848.

Ellen was twenty-two years old, and William a few years older. They thought all their troubles were over. They were young, strong, and in love. And they were free.

Philadelphia was the first stop on the Underground Railroad for William and Ellen. Eventually, they made their way to England, where their children were born. After the Civil War, they returned to Georgia with their family and bought a large plantation. There they established the Woodville Cooperative Farm School for poor families, to which they devoted the rest of their lives.

Two Tickets to Freedom

Meet the Author

Florence B. Freedman was born in Brooklyn, New York. She went to school at Columbia University and later became a teacher of English and Hebrew.

Many of Ms. Freedman's books are based on stories she heard or read when she was growing up. *Two Tickets to Freedom* is a true story. To write it, Ms. Freedman researched old newspaper articles, journals, and William Craft's own narrative of what happened.

Meet the Illustrator

Doris Ettlinger grew up in Staten Island, New York. She took painting lessons from local artists, read "How to Draw" books, and copied the comics from the newspaper. She studied illustration at the Rhode Island School of Design, graduating in 1973, and has illustrated professionally ever since. Today Ms. Ettlinger lives on the banks of the Musconetcong River in New Jersey with her husband and two children. Several days a week she teaches art to children and adults. She tells her students that *"drawing every day improves my skills, just as a musician practices an instrument or an athlete works out."*

Theme Connections

Within the Selection

Record your answers to the questions below in the Response Journal section of your Writer's Notebook. In small groups, report the ideas you wrote. Discuss your ideas with the rest of your group. Then choose a person to report your group's answers to the class.

- Why did William and Ellen Craft take their risk-filled journey?
- What were the possible consequences of their escape?

Across Selections

- William and Ellen Craft risked their lives to escape slavery. Which other characters that you have read about in this unit have taken dangerous risks to better their lives and the lives of others?
- William and Ellen Craft escaped slavery and eventually moved to England. What other stories have you read in which a character took a risk that paid off?

Beyond the Selection

- Think about how "Two Tickets to Freedom" adds to what you know about risks and consequences.
- Add items to the Concept/Question Board about risks and consequences.

Freedom

Langston Hughes
illustrated by Tyrone Geter

Freedom will not come
Today, this year
          Nor ever
Through compromise and fear.

I have as much right
As the other fellow has
          To stand
On my two feet
And own the land.

I tire so of hearing people say,
Let things take their course.
Tomorrow is another day.
I do not need my freedom when I'm dead.
I cannot live on tomorrow's bread.
          Freedom
          Is a strong seed
          Planted
          In a great need.
          I live here, too.
          I want freedom
          Just as you.

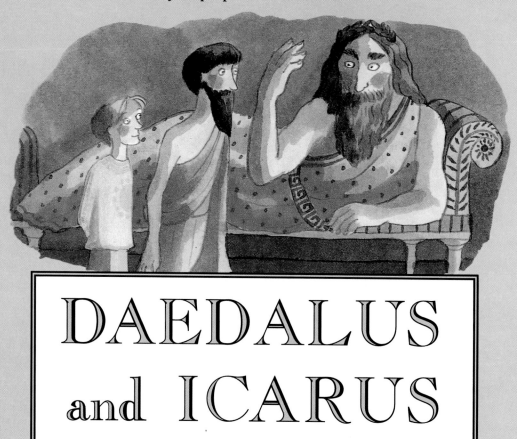

DAEDALUS and ICARUS

retold by Geraldine McCaughrean
illustrated by Emma Chichester Clark

Daedalus and Icarus lived in great comfort in King Minos's palace. But they lived the life of prisoners. Their rooms were in the tallest palace tower, with beautiful views across the island. They ate delectable food and wore expensive clothes. But at night the door to their fine apartment was locked, and a guard stood outside. It was a comfortable prison, but it was a prison, even so. Daedalus was deeply unhappy.

Every day he put seed out on the windowsill, for the birds. He liked to study their brilliant colors, the clever overlapping of their feathers, the way they soared on the sea wind. It comforted him to think that they at least were free to come and go. The birds had only to spread their wings and they could leave Crete behind them, whereas Daedalus and Icarus must stay forever in their luxurious cage.

116

Young Icarus could not understand his father's unhappiness. "But I like it here," he said. "The king gives us gold and this tall tower to live in."

Daedalus groaned. "But to work for such a wicked man, Icarus! And to be prisoners all our days!...We shan't stay. We shan't!"

"But we can't get away, can we?" said Icarus. "How can anybody escape from an island? Fly?" He snorted with laughter.

Daedalus did not answer. He scratched his head and stared out of the window at the birds pecking seed on the sill.

From that day onward, he got up early each morning and stood at the open window. When a bird came for the seed, Daedalus begged it to spare him one feather. Then each night, when everyone else had gone to bed, Daedalus worked by candlelight on his greatest invention of all.

Early mornings. Late nights. A whole year went by. Then one morning Icarus was awakened by his father shaking his shoulder. "Get up, Icarus, and don't make a sound. We are leaving Crete."

"But how? It's impossible!"

Daedalus pulled out a bundle from under his bed. "I've been making something, Icarus." Inside were four great folded fans of feathers. He stretched them out on the bed. They were wings! "I sewed the feathers together with strands of wool from my blanket. Now hold still."

Daedalus melted down a candle and daubed his son's shoulders with sticky wax. "Yes, I know it's hot, but it will soon cool." While the wax was still soft, he stuck the wings to Icarus's shoulder blades.

"Now you must help me put on my wings, Son. When the wax sets hard, you and I will fly away from here, as free as birds!"

"I'm scared!" whispered Icarus as he stood on the narrow window ledge, his knees knocking and his huge wings drooping down behind. The lawns and courtyards of the palace lay far below. The royal guards looked as small as ants. "This won't work!"

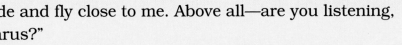

"Courage, Son!" said Daedalus. "Keep your arms out wide and fly close to me. Above all—are you listening, Icarus?"

"Y-y-yes, Father."

"Above all, don't fly too high! Don't fly too close to the sun!"

"Don't fly too close to the sun," Icarus repeated, with his eyes tight shut. Then he gave a cry as his father nudged him off the windowsill.

He plunged downward. With a crack, the feathers behind him filled with wind, and Icarus found himself flying. Flying!

"*I'm flying!*" he crowed.

The guards looked up in astonishment, and wagged their swords, and pointed and shouted, "Tell the king! Daedalus and Icarus are...are...flying away!"

119

By dipping first one wing, then the other, Icarus found that he could turn to the left and the right. The wind tugged at his hair. His legs trailed out behind him. He saw the fields and streams as he had never seen them before!

Then they were out over the sea. The sea gulls pecked at him angrily, so Icarus flew higher, where they could not reach him.

He copied their shrill cry and taunted them: "You can't catch me!"

"Now remember, don't fly too high!" called Daedalus, but his words were drowned by the screaming of the gulls.

I'm the first boy ever to fly! I'm making history! I shall be famous! thought Icarus, as he flew up and up, higher and higher.

At last Icarus was looking the sun itself in the face. "Think you're the highest thing in the sky, do you?" he jeered. "I can fly just as high as you! Higher, even!" He did not notice the drops of sweat on his forehead: He was so determined to outfly the sun.

Soon its vast heat beat on his face and on his back and on the great wings stuck on with wax. The wax softened. The wax trickled. The wax dripped. One feather came unstuck. Then a plume of feathers fluttered slowly down.

Icarus stopped flapping his wings. His father's words came back to him clearly now: "*Don't fly too close to the sun!*"

With a great sucking noise, the wax on his shoulders came unstuck. Icarus tried to catch hold of the wings, but they just folded up in his hands. He plunged down, his two fists full of feathers—down and down and down.

The clouds did not stop his fall.

The sea gulls did not catch him in their beaks.

His own father could only watch as Icarus hurtled head first into the glittering sea and sank deep down among the sharks and eels and squid. And all that was left of proud Icarus was a litter of waxy feathers floating on the sea.

DAEDALUS and ICARUS

Meet the Author

Geraldine McCaughrean After Geraldine McCaughrean struggled with several unsuccessful and unpublished novels, she found that her true talent was in writing for children. In her retelling of both *The Odyssey* and *Greek Myths* she uses humor to create interest and excitement in age-old stories. McCaughrean has also translated several Japanese classics including *The Cherry Tree* and *Over the Deep Blue Sea.*

Meet the Illustrator

Emma Chichester Clark was born in London, England. She draws the eyes of most of her characters in a very distinctive way—as circles with pupil dots. This gives the character a childlike, curiously expressive appearance. Many of Emma Chichester Clark's books, such as *Tea At Aunt Agatha's*, show characters wearing wide-brimmed hats. Expressive eyes and wide-brimmed hats are the trademarks of Emma Chichester Clark.

Theme Connections

Within the Selection

Record your answers to the questions below in the Response Journal section of your Writer's Notebook. In small groups, report the ideas you wrote. Discuss your ideas with the rest of your group. Then choose a person to report your group's answers to the class.

- Why did Icarus and Daedalus risk their lives to leave the palace?
- Icarus ignored his father's advice and flew too close to the sun. What was the consequence of this risk?

Across Selections

- How is the risk taken by Icarus similar to the risk taken by the crow in "Mrs. Frisby and the Crow"?
- William and Ellen Craft escaped slavery in "Two Tickets to Freedom," and Daedalus and Icarus escaped the palace in "Daedalus and Icarus." Compare the risks taken by these characters and their consequences.

Beyond the Selection

- Think about how "Daedalus and Icarus" adds to what you know about risks and consequences.
- Add items to the Concept/Question Board about risks and consequences.

Dollars and Sense

What do these people have in common? Josie has her own hot dog stand on a busy street corner. Angeline buys used designer jeans and sells them in her shop. Nancy has started a company that makes educational computer games. Don't say they're all women. That's true, but it's not the point. The point is that they all run their own businesses instead of working for someone else. Would you like to do that? It isn't easy. You'll learn why in this unit. But for many people it's the only way to go.

Starting a BUSINESS

by Arlene Erlbach

Going into business means making lots of decisions and having a business plan. Successful entrepreneurs take time to plan their business before they start. They ask themselves many questions. You can answer questions about your business in a business journal or notebook.

Good planners get ideas here...

Start by thinking about your business goals. Do you want a short term business that earns money for a specific item, like a new bike, musical instrument, or pet? Do you want an ongoing business that brings in steady money? Or maybe you'd like to only run your business during school vacations.

You'll also need to think about how much time you'll be able to spend on your business. Be realistic. If you already are expected to do lots of chores at home, you won't have as much time to devote to your business as a kid who has few family obligations. Ditto if you take lots of lessons or have the hardest teacher at school this year.

What Do I Like and What Am I Good At?

Most important, your business should be something you think is fun and something that's easy for you to do. To help you decide what kind of business to try, make a chart like the one below. Write down what you like to do and what you're good at. Then jot down businesses related to your likes and talents.

...and write them down here.

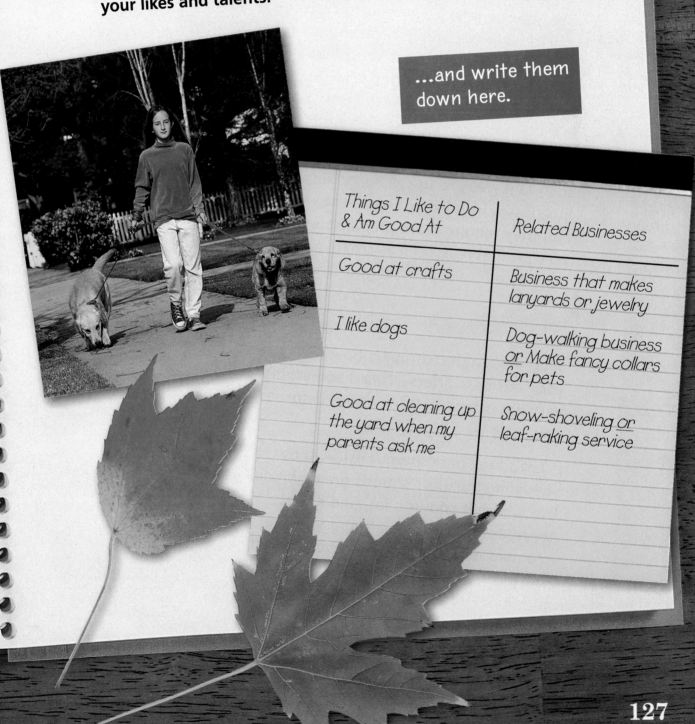

Things I Like to Do & Am Good At	Related Businesses
Good at crafts	Business that makes lanyards or jewelry
I like dogs	Dog-walking business or Make fancy collars for pets
Good at cleaning up the yard when my parents ask me	Snow-shoveling or leaf-raking service

Your manufacturing business could be making lanyards (also known as friendship bracelets).

Some businesses are service businesses. Others are manufacturing businesses. Service businesses provide care, maintenance, or repair to customers—such as dog walking, yard cleaning, or lawn mowing. Customers pay service businesses to do things they themselves don't have the time or desire to do. Most kids have service businesses, because they cost less to run than manufacturing businesses, and they are easier to start.

Manufacturing businesses make and sell products, such as jewelry, dog collars, or lanyards. Manufacturing businesses usually cost more than service businesses, and they require more preparation, but they can be very profitable as well as creative. Manufacturing businesses are especially good for artistic people.

What Is the Business Market?

Would enough customers need what your business offers? This is something very important to think about before you start.

Let's look back at your list. A snow shoveling business sounds great—if you live where it snows a lot, and if there are houses around you. But if you live in a neighborhood of condominiums or apartments, you might not get much business. The management for these buildings has probably made other arrangements for snow removal.

Is there another service you could offer in your community? In a neighborhood with lots of apartment buildings and condominiums, there may be a lot of older people. Maybe some of these people would like you to pick up their groceries, newspapers, or dry cleaning for them when the weather is cold and snowy. They may even need your services in good weather.

When you ask yourself these questions, you are analyzing the business market for an area. You are thinking about the people in that area, finding a need they have, and filling that need. Keeping your market in mind is a great start for brainstorming business ideas. Just follow these steps:

1. Think about items or services that might be needed in your neighborhood.

2. Think of a business that already exists in the area. Could you perform the same service, or provide a similar product, better or at a lower price?

3. Ask your family, neighbors, and friends what business they think is needed.

4. Make a list of the results, then ask yourself if the businesses are activities you would enjoy and be good at doing.

What do you like to do? Be honest!

Businesses Needed in My Neighborhood	Would I Like To Do It?
Dog clean up	No!
Delivery service	Yes—but I'll need to buy a wagon.
Birthday party helper	Yes—I love birthday parties. Won't need to buy a wagon.

Starting a
BUSINESS

Meet the Author

Arlene Erlbach has always loved to write. Mrs. Erlbach said, "When I was in grade school I'd make up stories about children while I lay in bed." In addition to being an author, Mrs. Erlbach is an elementary school teacher and is in charge of the school's Young Authors program. Mrs. Erlbach says she gets ideas for her writing "from my childhood, my son's experiences, the news, and the kids at the school where I teach."

Theme Connections

Within the Selection

Record your answers to the questions below in the Response Journal section of your Writer's Notebook. In small groups, report the ideas you wrote. Discuss your ideas with the rest of your group. Then choose a person to report your group's answers to the class.

- What are some things to consider when creating a business plan?
- What is the most important thing to consider when starting a business?
- What is the difference between a manufacturing business and a service business?

Across Selections

Mae Jemison started her own business, The Jemison Group, in "Mae Jemison: Space Scientist." Based on the information you read about in "Starting a Business," why do you think this was a good business for Mae Jemison to start?

Beyond the Selection

- What kind of business would you start? Using the information you read about in "Starting a Business," make a chart to help you decide which business to start. On the chart, write down things that you like to do and are good at.
- Think about how "Starting a Business" adds to what you know about business.
- Add items to the Concept/Question Board about business.

Focus Questions What makes a good business partner?
Why are some people better than others at spotting
business opportunities?

Henry Wells and William G. Fargo

by Edward F. Dolan, Jr.

There is an odd fact about two of the most important men in California history. Neither ever lived in the state. Yet they gave California a giant company of stagecoaches, freight wagons, banking offices, and mail deliveries. The two men were Henry Wells and William G. Fargo, the founders of Wells Fargo & Company.

Henry Wells

Born December 12, 1805, Henry Wells was raised at Thetford, a small Vermont town. As a young man, he moved to New York State and went to work for Harnden's Express. In keeping with the word *express*—which means "rapid conveyance"—the company was in the business of making deliveries as swiftly as possible. It delivered all kinds of things, from letters and packages to merchandise and money.

Harnden's was just one of many such companies. They were all a great help to businesses and families in the time before today's systems of rapid communication and transportation came into being.

The slender Wells began as one of Harnden's deliverymen. He proved so good at his job that he was promoted to positions of greater responsibility. He also proved to be an ambitious man who wanted to be in business for himself. And so, in 1842, he formed his own express company with two friends. Close on its heels came a second firm, which he called Wells & Company. A third firm took shape in 1850—the American Express Company, today a giant operation doing business throughout the world.

By now, Wells was forty-five years old and a wealthy man. And, by now, he and William G. Fargo had been close friends for eight years.

William G. Fargo

William George Fargo was thirteen years younger than Wells. The date of his birth was May 20, 1818. His birthplace was the city of Albany, New York. After working as a railroad conductor, he took a job as an express company deliveryman. He went to work for Wells in 1842 when Wells formed his first company.

Fargo was a fine employee. His deliveries were very swift because he was an excellent horseman. He became such a valued worker that Wells made him a partner when Wells & Company was formed. Fargo became a high-ranking executive with American Express when that company took shape.

By 1852, the two friends were important businessmen in the East. They began to look to the West. Because of the gold rush that had started in 1848, northern California had become one of the busiest regions in the nation. Its many mining towns were all in need of food and supplies. They were being served by a number of express companies, some large and some small. But the region was so busy that the two men were certain it could use another. They decided that they must establish a company in the new state. On May 18, 1852, Wells Fargo & Company was established.

134

The California Visit

The company's main office was located in New York City. There, Wells and Fargo laid plans for their new venture.

First, they decided that the company would build offices in the many mining towns now dotting the Sierra Mountains. Then it would purchase gold from the miners, ship it down to San Francisco, and send it to New York. The company would make a profit by buying the gold for slightly less than it was worth in the East and then selling it or using it to make investments when it reached New York. Next, the company would provide a stagecoach service for travelers going to and from the gold fields. Finally, it would ship all types of needed goods from the East to San Francisco.

Two of the firm's top employees traveled to San Francisco in the spring of 1852. There, they opened the first Wells Fargo office in California. Henry Wells followed them a few weeks later. He wanted to visit

the Sierra mining towns so that he could learn firsthand the problems that working among them might bring. His trek into the mountains netted him a number of fine ideas for the company. One of the first had to do with mail from home for the miners.

Wells learned that nearly all of the miners had come west alone, leaving their families safe at home. Their hope had been to "strike it rich" fast and return to give their loved ones a better life. Now they yearned for news of family and friends. But mail delivery was a problem because the miners were constantly on the move. They were always moving to new diggings when the earth failed to reveal its hidden wealth. They were often impossible for the U.S. Postal Service to find.

Wells decided that his company would take on an extra job. It would start a mail service. The service would carry letters for a slightly higher fee than the Postal Service charged. He was sure no one would mind the fee because of a plan that had come to mind. It was a plan to make the miners easy to find and thus insure that their mail reached them.

The plan called for a miner to leave his name at the local Wells Fargo office whenever he came into a new town. The name would be placed on a card that would be sent to the San Francisco office. Then, when mail arrived in San Francisco, the employees there would look up the miner's latest card and forward the letter to its proper destination. The system worked beautifully. It was used by countless families everywhere.

Wells soon reached another decision. He knew that the offices in the mining towns would need rugged safes to hold the gold dust purchased by the company. There was no other way to protect the gold before it was shipped off to the East. Now he decided that the offices would have to be more than buildings with safes in them. They would have to be actual banks.

He knew that not all miners wanted to sell their gold to the company. Some planned to take all or a portion of their dust home for everyone to see. Until then, they needed a place where it could be safely stored. Wells said that each company office would hold the gold dust for them, just as banks held money for their customers. The company would charge a small monthly fee for this service.

The system worked this way: A miner could store his dust in any Wells Fargo office. In return, he was given a slip of paper with the exact amount of the deposit written on it. He could then hand the slip in at any Wells Fargo office at any time and receive a like amount in gold. The company promised that it would be completely responsible for the deposit. If the gold were misplaced or stolen, Wells Fargo would make good the loss. The system proved so popular that the company was soon providing all types of banking services.

Stolen Gold!

Those two words haunted Wells throughout his trip and brought him to yet another decision. The company planned to have its offices place its gold in boxes that would be shipped down to San Francisco aboard stagecoaches and wagons. For much of the time, the shipments would be moving along wilderness trails. Those trails would make fine places for robberies.

Wells had good reason to fear robberies. The gold rush had attracted all types of men from over the world—from the very finest to the very worst. Among the latter were cutthroats, burglars, shady gamblers, and bandits. They had already robbed and cheated miners everywhere. The rich gold shipments were bound to be their next prey.

Wells set down two rules concerning the robberies that were sure to come. First, since much of the gold was to be shipped aboard stagecoaches, he issued orders to his drivers. If they were held up by bandits while carrying passengers, they were not to put up a fight. They were to hand over their "treasure boxes" without a word. This would protect the passengers. The passengers must always know that they were safe when traveling with Wells Fargo.

Second, no matter how small the amount taken, the company was to spare no expense in tracking down the robbers. By letting highwaymen know that they would pay dearly for their crimes, Wells hoped to discourage at least some robbery attempts.

Throughout its history, Wells Fargo never strayed from these rules. They made the company one of the most trusted firms of the day.

FIVE HUNDRED DOLLARS REWARD!

WELLS, FARGO & CO.

WILL PAY

FIVE HUNDRED DOLLARS,

For the arrest and conviction of the robber who stopped the Quincy Stage and demanded the Treasury Box, on Tuesday afternoon, August 17th, near the old Live Yankee Ranch, about 17 miles above Oroville.   By order of

J. J. VALENTINE, Gen'l Supt.

RIDEOUT, SMITH & CO., Agents.

Oroville, August 18, 1875.

Henry Wells and William G. Fargo

Meet the Author

Edward F. Dolan, Jr. began writing when he was twelve. By the time he was sixteen years old, he had published his first story. Now he has written over seventy books! Many of his books are about history, social studies, the environment, health, and law. He has also written about explorers, sports, and mysteries of nature, such as the Bermuda Triangle.

Theme Connections

Within the Selection

Record the answers to the questions below in the Response Journal section of your Writer's Notebook. In small groups, report the ideas you wrote. Discuss your ideas with the rest of the group. Then choose a person to report your group's answers to the class.

- What things did Wells and Fargo decide to do in their company that made their business a success?
- Why did Wells and Fargo decide to start a business in California?
- How did Wells and Fargo plan for possible robberies?

Across Selections

- Did Wells and Fargo follow the steps for new businesses outlined in "Starting a Business"?

Beyond the Selection

- Think about what "Henry Wells and William G. Fargo" tells you about the business world.
- Add items to the Concept/Question Board about Dollars and Sense.

Focus Questions Does a business always mean lots of work? When can it be fun to be in business?

Lemonade Stand

Myra Cohn Livingston
illustrated by Bob Barner

Every summer
under the shade
we fix up a stand
to sell lemonade.

A stack of cups,
a pitcher of ice,
a shirtboard sign
to tell the price.

A dime for the big,
A nickel for small.
The nickel cup's short.
The dime cup's tall.

Plenty of sugar
to make it sweet,
and sometimes cookies
for us to eat.

144

But when the sun
moves into the shade
it gets too hot
to sell lemonade.

Nobody stops
so we put things away
and drink what's left
and start to play.

PRICE
BiG 10¢
Small 5¢

LEMONADE

Focus Questions What makes a business successful?
Does everyone have what it takes to run a business?

Elias Sifuentes
Restaurateur

from *All in a Day's Work: Twelve Americans Talk About Their Jobs*
by Neil Johnson

I do it all. I open the restaurant in the morning and I
close it up at the end of each day. From the minute that
I open the door I do everything that has to be done
until I close the door. There are a thousand things that
have to be done in a restaurant.

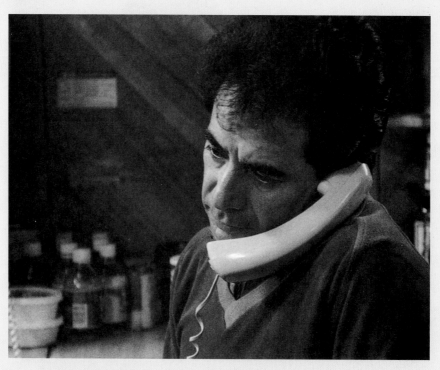

*Elias Sifuentes has run a Mexican restaurant for
almost ten years. After having other jobs and working
part-time in Mexican restaurants for many years, he
and a friend decided to start their own.*

146

I used to work at a General Electric factory. I was a punch-press operator. I was making good money, but working there frustrated me because I like to work with people, talk to people. And there, there was nobody to talk to. The only time I got together with others was during lunch or during meetings. And I said to myself, "I like the money. I like the benefits. But this is not what I want to do all my life."

I've worked part-time in Mexican restaurants for most of my life being a waiter, cook, dishwasher. Not because I was hungry for money, but because I told myself, "Someday I'm going to do something for myself and I want to learn the whole trade." While I was at GE, the restaurant where I was working part-time was closed down. So my partner and I got together, and I said, "What are you going to do?" He said, "I don't know." I said, "Let's get a place of our own! I'll do the cooking. You be the front man. What else do we need?" He liked the idea, and so we put the idea to work, and it works.

We started from scratch. In the beginning, we didn't get a paycheck. The only money we got was to buy groceries. My partner was kind of frustrated. Whatever we were making was going to pay our bills. I told him, "That's what it is. That's the way it goes. I like to have a payday, but we just can't do it right now." When we expanded the place, we got more customers, more business. We felt better because it finally started to pay off. We were very pleased. We saw more traffic and we started putting money in our pockets. We felt better. One hundred percent. The success has continued ever since.

In the beginning I was kind of shaky and afraid because I knew very little spoken English. I could more or less write in English. And to learn all the trade—that's a big step. In Mexico I took a year of business administration in college, so I had my year's training. It's not a whole lot, but it helped me when I needed it. I learned about supervising, expenses, administration. How to buy, how to spend, how to control, all these kinds of things.

But now I am learning on the job. I believe you learn a lot better when you exercise what you are doing. To me, I have no other choice but to learn——be forced to learn to do the job. Until now, I have been fortunate to do a good job. There are a good number of people depending on me, and I haven't let them down yet. My twenty-eight employees depend on me to be smart enough to continue the business for all of us——so all of us can make a good living. A lot of places come and go. Even big companies with big money and good managers——they are gone. Fortunately we have managed to stay.

To stay in business, I have to be aggressive. I have to fight. If I go by another Mexican restaurant and I see a line of people, I say to myself, "They are doing something right." If I go to my place and see nobody there, I say, "I am doing something wrong." So then I have to do something different. I must be more conscious of my customers and give them more attention. That's what I do best——pay attention to my customers. Talk to them. Meet them. Let them know who I am.

When customers complain, they keep me more aware. They open my eyes. I don't mind having a complaint once in a while. Nobody likes to have those, but if I do, I want to be sure that the same customer doesn't have the same complaint twice. I feel bad when a customer comes and tells me that he waited too long and never got service. I feel bad when a customer comes to tell me that a waiter has been rude. When a customer tells me that the food doesn't have enough seasoning, I feel bad. But I face the customer. It doesn't matter what happens, they always come to me. They say they want to see me. I say, "Fine, no problem." I take all kinds of complaints, which can get me down a lot.

I usually come to work at eight o'clock in the morning. Normally, I stay until two o'clock in the afternoon, doing the supervising, the purchasing, seeing the salesmen, seeing the advertisers. Then I go to my house to take a shower, and I come back at five o'clock. I stay until closing time at ten o'clock. We usually leave the place at eleven or twelve, after cleaning up.

When customers walk in my door, I receive them in the friendliest way I can. I see to it that they get service properly from my busboy, from my waitress, even from myself. If anything takes longer than it's supposed to, that is what I am there for——to take care of that kind of problem. Afterward, when the customer is finished, I come to the table again——maybe two, three more times. "Is everything OK? Everything satisfactory?" That's my job in the front of the restaurant. Then back in the kitchen, I see that everything comes out properly. I do that myself every morning. I taste everything, believe me! Chips, hot sauce, dressing, beans, Spanish rice, cheese sauce, you name it. I taste everything to see it is prepared right, before we open the doors. That keeps me going through lunchtime. Sometimes we stay so busy that I forget to sit down and have a meal.

A man who had come up from Mexico asked me the other day about opening a restaurant. He said to me, "If you did it, I can do it. " I said, "Yes, you can do it." Then he said, "You tell me how." I said, "Wait a minute. You just told me you can do it. You don't need my advice. You can do it! But if you don't have your heart in it, forget it."

Elias Sifuentes
Restaurateur

Meet the Author and Photographer

Neil Johnson lives in Shreveport, Louisiana. His articles and photographs have appeared in magazines and newspapers such as *Time*, *USA Today*, and *Louisiana Life*.

When Mr. Johnson decided to write about people at work, he looked for people who were enthusiastic, willing to talk, and didn't mind having their pictures taken. Elias Sifuentes fit all those things and more.

About photography, Mr. Johnson says, *"Photography . . . allows us to see things that cannot be put into words."*

Theme Connections

Within the Selection

Record your answers to the questions below in the Response Journal section of your Writer's Notebook. In small groups, report the ideas you wrote. Discuss your ideas with the rest of your group. Then choose a person to report your group's answers to the class.

- What experiences and skills did Elias Sifuentes have that helped him run his restaurant?
- How did Elias Sifuentes feel about customer complaints?

Across Selections

Did Elias Sifuentes plan his business the way "Starting a Business" suggests? What did he do differently?

Beyond the Selection

- Think about how "Elias Sifuentes, Restaurateur" adds to what you know about business.
- Add items to the Concept/Question Board about business.

Buffalo Newsboy. 1853. **Thomas LeClear.** Oil on canvas. 24 × 20 in. Albright-Knox Art Gallery, Buffalo, New York.

Poultry shop trade sign. Date unknown. Marble relief. Museo Ostiense, Ostia, Italy.

Incantation. 1946. **Charles Sheeler.** Oil on canvas. 24 × 20 in. The Brooklyn Museum, Brooklyn, New York.

Market Scene. Mid-20th century. **Rodrigue Mervilus.** Oil on canvas. Private Collection.

155

Focus Questions Are profits always the most important thing to a business? What business can you think of that could help your community?

Food from the 'Hood
A Garden of Hope

by Marlene Targ Brill

Sometimes horrible events turn into the most hopeful dreams. That's what happened to students at Crenshaw High School in South Central Los Angeles, California. In May 1992, riots destroyed the neighborhood surrounding their school. Businesses went up in flames. Hundreds of shopkeepers were left with nothing but ashes. Families, some too poor to afford gas money, were forced to travel from the city to the suburbs just to buy food.

Students in Tammy Bird's biology class felt awful. "This is where we all grew up," said Carlos Lopez. "The corner store in my neighborhood burned down. That was where we hung out."

Carlos and his classmates refused to let riots wreck their lives. They talked about different ways to help rebuild their community. Nothing seemed quite right. Then Ms. Bird remembered the weed-infested patch behind the football field. Perhaps the school would give them the quarter-acre plot of land for a garden. As a bonus, Ms. Bird offered extra credit to attract student gardeners.

Carlos and 38 of Ms. Bird's other students decided that planting was an important step toward restoring their neighborhood. The garden would be one green spot among the ashes. With Los Angeles's warm, sunny climate, crops could grow year round. Everyone agreed that their harvests should go to people unable to buy food.

Within weeks, the teenagers cleared the overgrown lot and planted seeds for collard greens, squash, tomatoes, and herbs. They grew vegetables organically, without chemicals that might hurt their bodies or the environment. Each day, they took turns watering and weeding the shoots during free time and before and after school. Adults from outside the community worked with the students as part of the city's overall plan to rebuild the riot-torn downtown.

The teenagers soon realized the community needed more than food to survive. It needed shops where people could easily buy everyday goods. Most of the burned-out stores had owners who lived outside the neighborhood. The money they made left South Central Los Angeles at the end of the workday. Students believed their community needed new business owners who were willing to put money back into the burned-out community. One adult volunteer, Melinda McMullen, suggested that the garden become that kind of business.

"We all wanted to give something back to the community, and this was a way to do it," Carlos remembered.

Melinda helped the students organize their business. First, they hunted for an office to house the company. They discovered an unused rabbit room behind the animal science lab and gave it a good scrubbing. Except for a few escaped rats eating electric wires, the room seemed perfect.

Then students met at lunchtime and after school to hammer out what the company would be like. Each volunteer became a student owner with an equal voice in making decisions. After several meetings, the owners agreed that the number-one reason for their business was to better their community. They wanted to prove that businesses could be kind and still make money, too. They pledged to create jobs for more teenagers. And they promised to use skills they learned from the garden to better the future for themselves and those around them.

Student owners named the company in much the same way as they planned——with respect for everyone's ideas. First, they brainstormed what the name should say about the business. They wanted a name that told people about the company's products in a general way. For now, products included organic foods. Who knew what the future would bring?

Everyone insisted that the name reflect who they were as people. This was a student-owned company, so the name should be catchy and fun. Moreover, students came from the inner city and were proud to live there. They represented many cultures, especially African-Americans, Latinos, and Asian Americans. The right name would celebrate these different groups working and living together.

For several hours, owners shouted out whatever name seemed to fit. Ms. Bird wrote 72 choices on the blackboard. Some sounded hip, such as *Food from the 'Hood,* and others unusual, such as *Straight Out 'the Garden.* Then everyone voted until five names remained. Over the next two weeks, students tested the five names on friends in class, at home, and throughout the neighborhood. They talked with strangers of all races, ages, and occupations.

Food from the 'Hood won thumbs-up. The name told about the products, which were different foods. And the name said where the company and its owners were from—the *'hood,* which was short for "inner-city neighborhood."

The only missing piece was the many cultures behind the business. To represent the different races, student artist Ben Osborne drew a company logo with white and brown hands reaching toward sun-lit buildings. He painted the logo and snappy name in bright colors on a mural behind the garden.

"People usually smile or laugh when they hear our company name," said student founder Ivan Lopez. "But they never forget us."

Slowly, a small garden turned into the nation's first student-run natural food company. Food from the 'Hood harvested its first crop two months after forming a business. They gave all the vegetables to a neighborhood homeless shelter. "Giving food to the needy really brought out the holiday spirit in us," said student owner Jaynell Grayson.

Now Melinda had another idea. The student owners proved they could grow a healthy garden and brighten the community. Why not sell some of the vegetables to raise money to help owners pay for college?

"We found the best way to give back to our community was to get a higher education," remembered Jaynell.

"We all got hooked on gardening. Then we decided to make money off of it. Then the scholarship idea kicked in," Carlos added.

In the summer of 1993, students took a supply of vegetables to the Santa Monica, California, farmer's market. Excited customers swarmed around the Food from the 'Hood table like bees. Customers couldn't buy fast enough. Within 30 minutes, the company sold $150 worth of vegetables. Student owners were amazed at their easy success.

Making enough money to build a scholarship fund proved more difficult, however. After one year in business, sales totaled only $600. Three graduating owners split the sum, which was a good start but not nearly enough to send anyone to college. "That hardly covered college book fees," Ben Osborne said.

After summer break, student owners met again. This time they talked about finding another way to raise money. A customer at a farmer's market suggested that they offer a factory-made product with the company's name on it. The product could sell more widely in stores than at a local farmer's market.

One student studied what buyers liked and disliked in new products. He found that people were more willing to try new salad dressings than other new products. "We thought, since we already grow lettuce, why not sell the topping?" Jaynell said.

Students experimented with salad dressing recipes in Ms. Bird's science class. They tasted different mixes of ingredients for the right balance. The dressing had to include plenty of basil and parsley because these were grown in their garden. Then students sent the formulas to outside food labs to test the ingredients. "Our community has a problem with heart disease, so we wanted a healthy, low-salt choice," Jaynell said.

After six months of testing mixtures, students agreed on a creamy Italian recipe. Ben designed a colorful label modeled after the garden mural. Then everyone voted on the name for their new line of dressing. The winner, Straight Out 'the Garden Creamy Italian Dressing, combined the runner-up company name with the dressing flavor.

Ms. Bird continued to supervise Food from the 'Hood at school. Melinda kept her ears open for different sources of money and aid. Other adult help came from unusual places.

Norris Bernstein, who ran the successful Bernstein Salad Dressings, read about Food from the 'Hood. After talking with student owners, Bernstein became hooked on their strong sense of pride and independence. He helped students connect with large chain stores that would sell their dressing.

basil

parsley

oregano

Another surprise visitor was Prince Charles from England. Carlos heard that the prince loved organic gardening, and he was visiting California. So Carlos wrote the British consul and asked if the prince would like to see Food from the 'Hood. "It was just something to do, just to see if it would really happen, and it really did," Carlos said later. The prince not only accepted, but he also ate lunch in the garden and later donated a van to help transport vegetables, herbs, and flowers to farmer's markets.

The city gave Food from the 'Hood $50,000. Some of the money went to supply an office to house the growing company. Students selected carpeting, a large meeting table, and furniture for five work stations. They ordered a telephone, answering machine, and computers.

Most money went toward making the first batch of salad dressing. Food from the 'Hood hired businesses to print labels, manufacture large amounts of salad dressing, and distribute the finished product to stores. "We wanted to work with other companies from poorer areas of Los Angeles. We especially looked for businesses run by minorities," student owner Mark Sarria said.

Food from the 'Hood chose women-owned company Sweet Adelaide to make and bottle the dressing. Skid Row Access, staffed by former homeless people of color, decorated banners. And herbs and spices came from small vendors rather than larger grocery store suppliers.

Some of the most difficult problems involved working together. Student owners took months to create a plan for dividing money the company earned. Finally, everyone agreed to a point system. Each owner earned points for hours spent in the garden and office.

Food from the 'Hood stands for good grades and going to college. Therefore, student owners received points for grades and for helping others improve their schoolwork. Owners learn to take care of each other. They share tips about how to study, complete college forms, and take college exams. For many, Food from the 'Hood is like family.

Although an adult watches over the office full-time now, student owners run every other part of the business. They produce and sell vegetables and salad dressing. They keep records, train new workers, pay bills, and answer telephones. Most importantly, they grow the garden, the heart of the business.

Hard work has paid off. Food from the 'Hood has added another salad dressing, Straight Out 'the Garden No-Fat Honey Mustard. More than 2,000 grocery stores carry the two dressings in 25 states. By 1996, the company awarded student owners a total of $27,000 to fund college.

Teachers claim that students improve in reading, writing, public speaking, and math after joining Food from the 'Hood. Many student owners discover talents they never knew they had. Sandra Raymond hated to talk in class before selling dressing and answering the office telephone. Now she feels confident enough to go into business. Similarly, Ben Osborne intends to study art in college as a result of designing the logo, mural, and salad dressing label.

"We showed that a group of inner-city kids can and did make a difference. We learn to take responsibility for our actions, how to sort out what's important, and how to be leaders instead of followers," Terie Smith, student founder, said.

Food from the 'Hood has become so successful that other schools asked to copy the program. In 1996 a high school group from Ithaca, New York, began using the name on applesauce. "We met with them in Washington, D.C., to talk about their applesauce idea, and we were very impressed," Terie said. Now three flavors of Food from the 'Hood East's Straight Out 'the Orchard are sold in Ithaca and are headed for New York City and other areas. Schools in Chicago, Illinois; Hawaii; and Oakland, California, hope to sell products that will help put kids through school.

The real success, however, is the garden, the center of giving. Half the total crop goes to community groups. Student owners vote which organizations receive the food. The idea is to help a balance of African-American, Latino, and Asian groups that reflects the company's——and community's——population.

New students apply to Food from the 'Hood each year. About 40 percent work other jobs in addition to going to school, but find time to garden. After more than five years, the business is here to stay. A small group of inner-city teenagers have proven that anyone can achieve success if they try.

"What comes from that garden is hope," said Carlos. "From anything——even the riots——amazing things can grow."

Food from the 'Hood
A Garden of Hope

Meet the Author

Marlene Targ Brill was born in Chicago, Illinois. She loved books from a very young age. Her parents read constantly, and she remembers being jealous of her older brother who had a room filled with books and records.

Ms. Brill had an active imagination. A favorite pastime was sitting in the window, watching people pass by, and making up stories about where they were going and what they were doing.

Brill says she loves all kinds and aspects of writing, especially research. She says, *"I feel like an explorer, delving into old newspapers, tracking down historical documents, and locating famous and not-so-famous people to interview. To me, research is an endless treasure hunt with many pots of gold."*

170

Theme Connections

Within the Selection

Record your answers to the questions below in the Response Journal section of your Writer's Notebook. In small groups, report the ideas you wrote. Discuss your ideas with the rest of your group. Then choose a person to report your group's answers to the class.

- Why did the students at Crenshaw High School decide to plant a garden?
- How did the students turn their garden into a business?
- How did the students decide on a name for their business?

Across Selections

In "Birth of a Baby Food," the Gerbers spent a year trying different recipes for baby food. How was their experience in creating a product to sell similar to the experience of the students in "Food from the 'Hood: A Garden of Hope"?

Beyond the Selection

- What needs do you see in your community that you and other students could help with? Could you start a business while helping your community like the students at Crenshaw High School? Discuss your ideas with the members of your group.
- Think about how "Food From the 'Hood: A Garden of Hope" adds to what you know about business.
- Add items to the Concept/Question Board about business.

BUSINESS IS LOOKING UP

Barbara Aiello and Jeffrey Shulman
illustrated by Diane Paterson

Renaldo Rodriguez, a visually impaired eleven-year-old, needs money to buy a special type of calculator for the blind. He decides he can earn the money by starting a business and shares his idea with his best friend, Jinx.

"Jinx!" I shouted when she answered the phone. I sure was excited about my business idea. "It's me! Renaldo. Renaldo Rodriguez!"

"Renaldo, you're the only Renaldo I know," Jinx said. "And you don't have to holler! I can hear you."

I explained the whole idea to her——"R.R. Stepcards" I called it. That was a pretty clever name, even I have to admit. I told her how I would make and sell cards for people who had stepfamilies: birthday cards, get well cards, Valentine cards——the list was endless!

"What do you think, Jinx? Am I going to be Woodburn's first millionaire?"

172

There was silence on the other end. I could tell Jinx was thinking about it. She always thinks about things before she gives her opinion. And she always thinks about what other people might think. "Opposing viewpoints," she calls them. Jinx does a lot of thinking.

"Well," she finally asked, "have you done any marketing research?"

"Marketing research?"

"Have you thought about your investment?"

"Investment?"

Jinx was on a roll. I felt doomed.

"Oh, how will you advertise?"

I felt it coming, but I couldn't stop it. "Advertise?" I said. "Just listen to me," I thought to myself, "Renaldo Rodriguez, the human echo!"

Research? Investment? Advertising? "Jinx," I said, "this is starting to sound like work! Explain this stuff to me."

I knew Jinx was excited. I could hear the excitement in her voice. "Look," she began, "marketing research is the first thing you do. You find out if someone else has already thought of your idea. You find out if there's such a thing as a stepcard. If there's not, then you can figure out your investment. That's how much money you want to spend to get the business started."

"Spend?" I said. "But I want to *make* money, Jinx."

"I know," Jinx said in her most patient voice. "But you can't get something for nothing. We will have to buy markers and paper, maybe even paints and stencils, too. That's our investment."

"*Our* investment? When did it become *our* investment?"

"Renaldo, this is an excellent idea," Jinx continued. "But there's a lot to do. You're going to need a partner." And I didn't even have the time to say "A partner?" before Jinx jumped in again. "Hmmmm . . . I do like the sound of it," she said. "Yes, 'R.R. and J.B. Stepcards.' I like the sound of it very much."

And you know what? So did I. With J.B. as my partner, I was more excited than ever——so excited that I couldn't get to sleep that night. I turned my pillow to the cold side a hundred times until I gave up trying to sleep. I got out my stylus and slate and started to write: "R.R. and J.B. Stepcards. For Your Favorite Stepfriend." There were stepfathers, stepmothers, stepbrothers, stepsisters, stepgrandmothers——the list went on and on. "For All Occasions." There were birthdays,

anniversaries, graduations, holidays—and so many more. I started counting our profits. I couldn't help it.

"Excuse me, Mr. Businessman," Josue said, hiding a big yawn. "Mom already came in here. She made me stop reading. We're supposed to be asleep, you know."

Josue was right. Mom doesn't let us read or write after lights out. But, you see, I don't have to sneak under the covers with a flashlight the way Josue does.

"I'm not reading," I told Josue. "This, my little brother, is marketing research—I think."

"It looks like reading to me. It's not fair. I ought to tell on you!" Josue climbed out of bed to get a better look. "Just what kind of business is this anyway?"

"None of *your* business," I said firmly. And I closed my slate. I wasn't taking any chances on someone stealing the business idea of the century, certainly not a nosy little brother. I turned my pillow over for the last time.

"Let's go to sleep."

The next day was Saturday, and with lots of kids from Woodburn, Jinx and I headed for the mall. We take turns delivering the "Woodburn Flyer" to the stores at the Woodburn Shopping Center. The "Flyer" is the free newspaper that tells about all the things happening at Woodburn. Then it's time for fun.

But this Saturday was different. Today, there were no video games, no french fries, no window-shopping. Today, we were all business.

I knew we were near Calloway's Cards and Gifts when I smelled the tempting aroma of cheese, tomato sauce, and special toppings. Polotti's Pizza Palace was just next door to the card store.

"I don't think I can do the marketing research on an empty stomach. How about a business lunch?" I was tapping my cane toward the sweet smell of Polotti's.

"Renaldo," Jinx said sternly, "we don't have much time."

"Okay. Okay," I said. "Give me your arm." Jinx was right. We really didn't have much time. "It will be faster for me to walk alongside you—and less temptation, too."

There must have been a thousand different kinds of cards in Calloway's, and each one was cornier or mushier than the last. One thing about those cards, though—they really cracked us up!

"Look at this one, Renaldo," Jinx said.

"*To My Daughter and Her Husband on This Special Day*," Jinx read. She described the card to me. "It's big," she said, passing it to me.

"It's almost the size of our spelling notebook," I said, feeling around the edges of the card.

"It has two pink hearts with bows on them. Two white doves are holding the ends of the ribbons in their mouths. It looks like the words *Happy Anniversary* are coming right out of their beaks," Jinx giggled.

I could feel the raised lines of the hearts, the bows, and the birds. "Yuk," I said, "it sounds pretty corny to me."

"Listen to this, Renaldo."

To My Daughter and Her Husband on This Special Day:
'Like two white doves are lovers true,
Like two pink hearts forever new.
I hope this day will always view
A ribbon of happiness just for you.'

"Double yuk," I said. "Who buys this mush?"

"Here's another one, Renaldo," Jinx said. "*Congratulations on Your New Baby!* It has a picture of a stork with a baby in a diaper hanging in its mouth."

"It must look so silly," I said, trying hard not to giggle too loudly.

"It gets worse." Jinx was cracking up. "When you open up the card, the stork drops the baby—plop!—right on somebody's doorstep!"

"It sounds like a wet diaper to me!" I squealed. Jinx was laughing, too. But then she suddenly stopped. I could tell she was really thinking.

"But, Renaldo," she said in a serious voice, "somebody buys these cards, and"—she was getting very excited—"there are no stepcards!"

Now I was getting excited, too. We did a high-five right there in Calloway's. "We're going to be rich!" we both shouted.

"C'mon, Renaldo," Jinx urged, "let's go home and get to work."

"Be sure to save an extra large pepperoni and sausage for Woodburn's youngest millionaires!" I shouted when we passed Polotti's.

Getting to work was not as easy as it sounded.

Jinx and I had to buy the paper for the cards. We put our money together for an investment of twelve dollars and thirty-two cents. ("That's a lot of french fries," I thought.) We had to decide what kind of cards to make. We had to think of designs for the front of the cards and messages to go inside. We had to find a way to let people know about "R.R. and J.B. Stepcards."

Let's face it: We had a lot to learn about starting a business.

When I have more questions than answers, I always turn to the expert—my Mom. "Mom," I said when she got home from work, "Jinx and I need to speak to an old hand in the business world."

"Good luck finding one," she replied as she started to take off the running shoes she wears to work.

"No, Mom," I explained, "I meant you."

"Oh," she said, looking up. "What can this 'old hand' do for you?"

My Mom knows about business, especially bad businesses. She works in an office helping people who bought things that don't work or aren't safe. I figured if she knew all about bad businesses, she could tell us how to start a good one.

Jinx and I explained our business idea. "How do we get started?" Jinx asked.

"How do we make lots of money?" (I guess you can figure out who asked that one!)

179

Mom thought for a while. Then she spoke slowly. "Jinx, Renaldo, starting and running a business is not so easy. It's more than just making money. A successful business needs a good product to sell or a useful service to offer. And a successful businessman—or businesswoman—thinks about the customer all the time. Ask yourself: 'What do they want?' 'How can my product or my service help them?' "

Jinx and I were trying to listen to all of this, but it wasn't easy. We *did* have a lot to learn.

"Now, you two have a good product," Mom continued. "I'm proud of you for coming up with this idea. But a good idea is not enough. You need to plan carefully."

"What do we do, Mrs. Rodriguez?" Jinx asked.

"Well," Mom said, "you need to figure out how much money you'll need to get started and where the money will come from. You need to decide who will do the work and, believe me, a business *is* work. Now, if you're still interested in 'R.R. and J.B. Stepcards,' let's make a plan!"

"Always ask the expert," I shouted. I could hear the rubber soles of Mom's shoes make that familiar squeegy sound. Mom wears business suits and running shoes every day to work. Dad says she's dressed for success from her head to her knees——but her feet are dressed for failure! That always makes me laugh.

With Mom's help we really got started. Jinx and I used our "investment" to buy paper, paints, markers, and stencils. We worked every day after school. We took turns with the stencils to make the designs. We'd take a small roller and dip it into a bright color of paint. When we'd smooth the roller over the stencil, there was a butterfly or flower or other designs. Jinx said they looked great!

I liked making up the words for our stepcards. I thought of some pretty good ones, if I must say so myself.

181

To My Stepfather:
'Getting to know you hasn't been half bad.
I'm glad Mom picked you to be my Stepdad!'

Well, I didn't say they were great cards.

To My Stepsister:
'You have two families, I know that's true.
But I want you to know that I love you, too!'

All right, so Renaldo Rodriguez has a mushy side. Don't rub it in!

At the end of just one week, Jinx and I had 34 cards ready to go.

"To go where?" I asked.

"Where else?" Jinx said. "Why, the Woodburn School and Community Center!" It was time to advertise, and Woodburn was the place to start.

The Woodburn School was the oldest school building in the city. It almost closed the year before. There just weren't enough kids to fill it up, I guess. That's why the school board decided to add a Community Center. Now there was a day-care room for little kids and an activity center for older people, too. Woodburn is like a little city all its own.

The first thing on Monday morning Jinx and I marched down to Woodburn and showed our cards to Mr. Mohammadi, the assistant principal. Boy, was he excited!

"A sound idea," he said. "A very sound business idea. And you'll get a real education in the bargain. A real education. How can I help?"

We explained that advertising "R.R. and J.B. Stepcards" was the next part of our business plan.

"Let's see now." Mr. Mohammadi was thinking out loud. "You can put advertisements in the school newspaper, posters in the Senior Center, flyers to go home. . . ." Mr. Mohammadi was pacing the floor and spouting new ideas faster than . . . faster than . . . well, faster than Jinx and I could write them down.

"This is going to be a snap," I predicted. "I should have started a business years ago. Think of all the time I've wasted in school!"

That stopped Mr. Mohammadi in his tracks. "Just a little business joke," I gulped.

If you want to start a business, take it from me: advertise! With Mr. Mohammadi's help, Jinx and I spread the word about "R.R. and J.B. Stepcards." Believe it or not, within one week, we sold 17 of our cards and had orders for 20 more. That's 37 cards! We'd make back all the money we spent on supplies. We'd even have some left over.

"Now that we'll have a little extra money, why not buy some stickers and glitter?" Jinx suggested. "Let's make the cards even prettier."

I was thinking about my calculator. I wanted to buy it as soon as I could. "But, Renaldo," Jinx said, "if we make our cards prettier, we'll sell more and make more money."

That made sense. Then I could buy the calculator and a new pair of soccer shoes.

"Don't forget," Jinx reminded me, "we have to pay to use the copying machine." We had to make copies of the advertisement Mr. Mohammadi was going to send home with the kids.

"And we need copies to take to the Senior Center, too," I told Jinx. I remember Mom saying, "You have to spend some money to make money." We thought that advertising was the best way to get more sales.

We thought right! Every day more orders came in the mail.

This was going to be a snap.

Jinx and I had to work every afternoon that week to fill the orders. And every day more orders came in.

Jeremy Kendall's stepsisters had their birthdays coming up, so he ordered two cards from "R.R. and

J.B. Stepcards," along with a special card for his stepmother. Mrs. Rothman (from the Senior Center) told us her son had just married a woman with twin boys, and she needed birthday cards for her stepgrandchildren. Roger Neville's stepfather was in the hospital, so he wanted a special get well card. And Joanne Spinoza's mother, Lena, wanted a stepcousin Valentine.

Phew! Jinx and I could hardly believe how well our business was going. We just didn't expect how happy people would be with our cards.

"You know, Jinx," I said, as I lined up the paint jars, "it's nice to give people something special."

Jinx agreed. "Jeremy told me that our card really helped him tell his stepmother how much he liked her."

"No kidding?"

"You know what else? He said she cried a little when she read it, and then she said she really liked him, too."

"Hey," I said, "making people happy is a pretty good way to make a living."

BUSINESS IS LOOKING UP

Meet the Authors

Barbara Aiello was eight years old when her mother had to spend several weeks in a hospital. While she was away, Barbara made a magazine for her filled with neighborhood news, a short story, a pet column, and want ads. That was the beginning of her writing career. In addition to being a writer, Ms. Aiello is also a teacher who has spent many years working in special education.

Jeffrey Shulman teaches English at Georgetown University in Washington, D.C., and has been writing children's books since 1986. *Business Is Looking Up* is Mr. Shulman's first and favorite book. He enjoys telling his daughters stories. *"I like to make up the stories as I go along. It keeps my imagination pretty busy."*

Meet the Illustrator

Diane Paterson has illustrated several books for children, including *The Christmas Drum* and *Marmee's Surprise*. She has also illustrated several books she wrote herself, such as the children's books *Someday* and *Smile for Auntie*. Ms. Paterson lives in southwest Florida with her husband, her dog, and over 50 orchids.

Theme Connections

Within the Selection

Record your answers to the questions below in the Response Journal section of your Writer's Notebook. In small groups, report the ideas you wrote. Discuss your ideas with the rest of your group. Then choose a person to report your group's answers to the class.

- How did R.R. and J.B. Stepcards know there was a need for their cards?
- What advice did Renaldo's mom give to Renaldo and Jinx about their business?

Across Selections

- "Starting a Business" tells how to analyze the business market. Did Renaldo and Jinx follow any of these steps while doing marketing research for their business?
- What other selections have you read in which students started a business?

Beyond the Selection

- Think of a product you could market to a small group of consumers. Create a way to advertise your product, and share your advertisement with the members of your group.
- Think about how "Business is Looking Up" adds to what you know about business.
- Add items to the Concept/Question Board about business.

SALT

Harve Zemach
illustrated by Margot Zemach

Long ago there lived a merchant who had three sons. The first was Fyodor, the second Vasily, and the third Ivan—Ivan the Fool.

This merchant was rich. He sent his ships over the ocean in all directions to trade goods in foreign lands. Once he loaded two ships with precious furs, wax, and honey, and sent them sailing with his two elder sons. But when Ivan asked for the same, the merchant refused, saying: "You would do nothing but sing songs to the moon, and try to make the fishes dance, and come home without your head."

However, when he saw how much his son wanted
to go, he gave him a ship with the very cheapest cargo
of beams and boards.

Ivan prepared for the journey, set sail, and soon
caught up with his brothers. They sailed together for a
day or two, until a strong wind came up and blew
Ivan's ship away into uncharted seas.

The wind blew Ivan and his crew to the north and
to the south. At last they reached an island. Ivan
stepped out upon the shore and found
a path which led to the top of a
mountain. There he discovered
that this mountain was not
made of rock, nor of sand,
nor of stone, but of salt—
pure Russian salt.

Without delay he ordered his sailors to throw away all the boards and beams, and to load the ship with salt. As soon as this was done, Ivan set forth once more.

After a long time or a short time, either nearby or far away, the ship arrived at a large city. Ivan went into the city to bow before the king and request permission to trade his merchandise. He took a bundle of the salt with him. The king greeted him in a friendly manner and heard his request.

"And what kind of goods do you sell?" asked the king.

"Russian salt, Your Majesty," said Ivan, showing him the contents of his bundle.

The king had never heard of salt. The people of his kingdom ate all their food without salt. When he saw what Ivan showed him, he thought it was only white sand.

"Well, little brother," he said to Ivan, "we have all we need of this. No one will pay you money for it."

Ivan turned away feeling very disappointed. Then he thought to himself: "Why don't I go to the king's kitchen and see how the cooks prepare the food and

what kind of salt they use." He went and watched the cooks running back and forth, boiling and roasting and pouring and mixing. But no one put a single grain of salt in the food.

Ivan waited his chance and then secretly poured the right amount of salt into all the stews and sauces.

When the first dish was served to the king, he ate of it and found it more tasty than ever before. The second dish was served, and he liked it even better.

Then the king called for his cooks and said to them: "In all the years that I have been king, you have never cooked me such a delicious meal. How did you do it?"

The cooks answered: "Your Majesty, we cooked the same as ever. But the merchant who asked your permission to trade was watching us. Perhaps he added something to the food."

"Send for him!" commanded the king.

Then Ivan, the merchant's son, was brought before the king. He fell on his knees and confessed his guilt.

"Forgive me, Your Majesty," he begged. "I put Russian salt in all the stews and sauces. That's the way we do it in my country."

"And what is the price of this salt?" asked the king.

Ivan realized his advantage and said: "Not very much—for two measures of salt, give me one measure of silver and one of gold."

The king agreed to this price and bought the entire cargo. Ivan filled his ship with silver and gold and made ready to sail for home.

Now the king had a daughter, a beautiful princess. Attended by her maidservants, she went down to the port to see the Russian ship. Ivan the Fool just then was strumming a tune. The melody reached the ears of the princess, and its sweetness entered her heart.

It was not long before Ivan and the beautiful princess stood together before the king to receive his blessing. To the sound of trumpets and the cheers of the king's subjects, Ivan and the princess departed from the city and sailed forth on a favorable wind.

For a long time, for a short time, Ivan and the princess sailed the sea. Then his elder brothers appeared across his path. They learned of his good luck and were very jealous.

They boarded his ship, seized him, and threw him into the sea. Then they divided the booty; Fyodor, the eldest brother, took the princess, and Vasily, the second brother, took the ship full of silver and gold.

Now it happened that when they flung Ivan from the ship, one of the boards that he himself had thrown into the sea was floating nearby. He grabbed hold of this board and for a long time was tossed upon the waves. Finally he was carried to an unknown island. No sooner had he landed on the shore than along came a gloomy giant with an enormous mustache, from which hung a huge pair of mittens, drying after the rain.

"What do you want here?" asked the giant. Ivan told him everything that had happened.

The gloomy giant sighed and said: "Come along, I will carry you home. Tomorrow your eldest brother is to marry the princess. Sit on my back."

The giant lifted Ivan, set him on his back, and raced across the sea. Soon Ivan could see his native land ahead, and moments later they arrived. The giant put him down, saying: "Now promise not to boast to anyone about riding on my back. Don't try to make fun of me. If you do, I shall grab you up and toss you back into the sea."

Ivan, the merchant's son, promised not to boast, thanked the giant, and went home.

He arrived just as the wedding procession was about to enter the church. When the princess saw him, she cried aloud and tore herself away from Fyodor, the eldest brother.

"This is the one I must marry," she said, "and not the other."

"What's that?" asked the father.

Ivan told him everything——how he had traded the salt, how he had won the favor of the princess, and how his brothers had thrown him into the sea.

The father got very angry at his elder sons, called them scoundrels, and married Ivan to the princess.

There now began a joyful feast. The guests ate and drank and made merry. The men began to boast, some

about their strength, some about their riches, some about their beautiful wives. And Ivan the Fool happily boasted too: "Listen to this! I really have something to boast about! A giant carried me piggyback across the sea!"

As soon as he said these words, the giant appeared at the gate.

"Ah, Ivan!" said the gloomy giant. "You promised not to boast about me. Now what have you done?"

"Forgive me!" cried Ivan. "It was not really I that boasted, but my happiness."

"Come, show me what you mean," said the giant. "What do you mean by happiness?"

Then Ivan took up his mandolin, and played and danced the best he knew how. And his playing and dancing was so filled with happiness that all the

guests danced and clapped their hands. And soon the gloomy giant let himself smile and kept time to the music with his feet.

"Well, Ivan," he said at last, "now I know what happiness is. You may boast about me all you like."

So the wedding feast continued, and the giant departed, and Ivan the Fool and the beautiful princess lived happily ever after.

SALT

Meet the Author

Harve Zemach was born in New Jersey. He was a philosopher and a social science teacher. While in college, he met Margot Zemach in Vienna, Austria, and they were married two years later.

Harve did not plan to be a writer. He was a teacher. But Margot really wanted to draw illustrations for children's books. She finally convinced him to write a book so she could illustrate it. He wrote a story about a boy in Vienna, and the book was a success. Harve kept teaching, but after that he also wrote a book every year for Margot to illustrate.

Meet the Illustrator

Margot Zemach was born in Los Angeles, California. By the time she was five, she was involved with the theater. Her mother was an actress and her stepfather was a director and dancer. Margot watched from backstage where she also drew pictures and made up stories.

"I have always drawn pictures, all my life. It seems necessary for me to draw. It really is where I live. I was a poor file clerk, a messy confused messenger girl, a very bad salesgirl, and I cannot add. Thank goodness I can draw."

Theme Connections

Within the Selection

Record your answers to the questions below in the Response Journal section of your Writer's Notebook. In small groups, report the ideas you wrote. Discuss your ideas with the rest of your group. Then choose a person to report your group's answers to the class.

- How did Ivan convince the King that salt was valuable?
- Why did Ivan throw away the boards and beams on his boat to load the salt?

Across Selections

What do the Gerbers in "Birth of a Baby Food" have in common with Ivan?

Beyond the Selection

- Think about how "Salt" adds to what you know about business.
- Add items to the Concept/Question Board about business.

Focus Questions Do dreams always come true for businesspeople? How can a small business grow into a larger one?

The Milkmaid and Her Pail

Aesop
illustrated by Valerie Sokolova

A farmer's daughter finished milking the cows and was carrying her pail of milk upon her head. As she walked along, she started to daydream: "The milk in this pail will provide me with cream. I will make the cream into butter and take it to the market to sell. With the money, I will buy some eggs, and these will hatch into chickens. Then I'll sell some of the chickens, and with the money I'll buy myself a beautiful new dress, which I will wear to the dance. All the young fellows will admire me and want to dance with me, but I'll just toss my head and have nothing to say to them." At this, she forgot all about the pail on her head, and imagining herself at the dance, she tossed her head. Down went the pail, the milk spilled out all over the ground, and all her fine plans vanished in a moment!

Do not count your chickens before they are hatched.

The Milkmaid and Her Pail

Meet the Author

Aesop lived, historians believe, sometime during the sixth century B.C. He was born a slave and, while working as a slave, began telling his stories. Because he was so witty and skillful with words, his master set him free. Many phrases from his stories are now widely used expressions such as "out of the frying pan and into the fire" and "actions speak louder than words."

Meet the Illustrator

Valerie Sokolova was born in Lvov, Ukraine, and later moved to Minsk, Belarus, where she graduated from the Belarus State Academy of Arts in 1986. She has illustrated more than thirty picture books in Russia, as well as a number of books in the United States, including *The Magic of Merlin* and *The Golden Books Treasury of Christmas Joy*. Ms. Sokolova presently lives in Brooklyn, New York.

Theme Connections

Within the Selection

Writer's Notebook

Record your answers to the questions below in the Response Journal section of your Writer's Notebook. In small groups, report the ideas you wrote. Discuss your ideas with the rest of your group. Then choose a person to report your group's answers to the class.

- What was the milkmaid's business plan?
- Why is the phrase "Do not count your chickens before they are hatched" good business advice?

Across Selections

Both Ronaldo, from "Business is Looking Up," and the milkmaid had good ideas for making money. Why was one more successful?

Beyond the Selection

- Have you ever had an idea for a business like the milkmaid? Was your idea successful? Why? Why not?
- Think about how "The Milkmaid and Her Pail" adds to what you know about business.
- Add items to the Concept/Question Board about business.

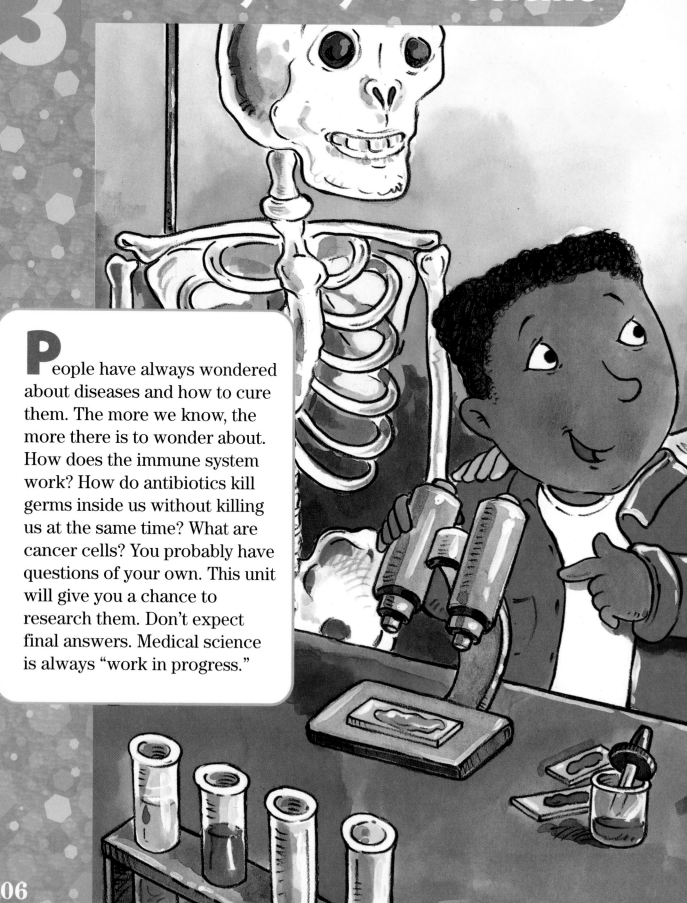

People have always wondered about diseases and how to cure them. The more we know, the more there is to wonder about. How does the immune system work? How do antibiotics kill germs inside us without killing us at the same time? What are cancer cells? You probably have questions of your own. This unit will give you a chance to research them. Don't expect final answers. Medical science is always "work in progress."

Medicine:
Past and Present

André W. Carus

illustrated by Jim Roldan

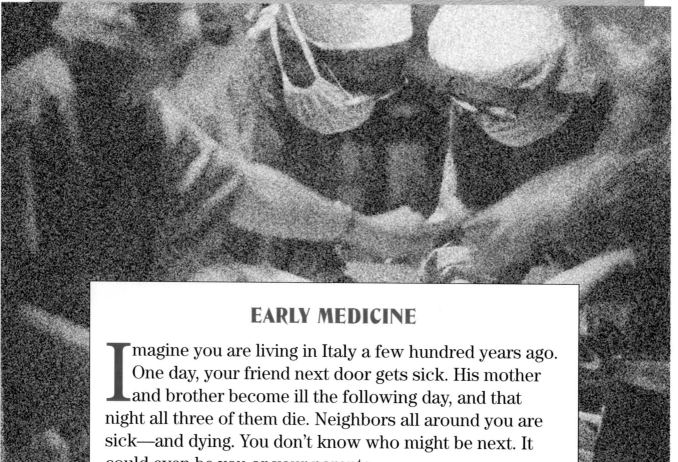

EARLY MEDICINE

Imagine you are living in Italy a few hundred years ago. One day, your friend next door gets sick. His mother and brother become ill the following day, and that night all three of them die. Neighbors all around you are sick—and dying. You don't know who might be next. It could even be you or your parents.

In those days, this nightmare is what life was like. In the middle of the fourteenth century, an epidemic called the Black Plague swept across Europe, Asia, and Africa. It killed about 75 million people, wiping out more than a third of Europe's population. While the disease spared some towns and villages, it killed nearly everyone in others. There was little warning, and those who caught the disease were dead within a few days.

Getting sick was always scary, not just during epidemics like the Black Plague. Death was never far away. People could fall ill and die at any moment, and no one would know why. Most people did not live to be very old. The average life expectancy was only thirty or forty years, about half what it is now in the United States.

For most of human history, people did not know what caused diseases. They could not see germs, so they didn't realize germs existed. Even after germs were discovered, it took a long time to connect them up with various diseases. It took even longer for people to understand how to keep germs from making people sick.

Before people knew about germs, they had other ideas about what caused diseases. Mostly, these ideas involved some kind of magical powers. It is easy to understand why people would believe such ideas. Diseases were terrifying and mysterious. Often there seemed to be no pattern to them. Why did some people die young and others get old? Why did some wounds get infected and others heal? Why did epidemics kill some people and not others? Without knowing about germs, it was easy to believe anything that might make a difference and possibly save a life.

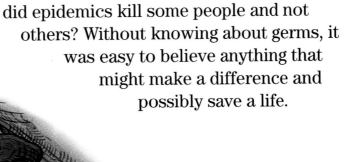

2500–300 B.C.
Chinese practice acupuncture and the use of herbal treatments to remedy illnesses.

So, it was a new idea when a few people suggested, in Greece about 2,500 years ago, that the human body is predictable and that diseases have natural causes and reasonable explanations. Hippocrates is the best known of these people. Because this basic idea is so important, he is called the Father of Medicine. Hippocrates was sure that he could find reasons for illness by closely studying the human body and observing diseases. He also thought that people could understand the way the body worked.

We now know that Hippocrates was on the right track. But when he lived, and for a long time afterwards, his idea was no more than a guess. And often it didn't seem like a very good guess (Hippocrates had lived nearly 2,000 years before the Black Plague and his beliefs still had very little support). So most people went on believing their old ideas and attempting to use magic to cure diseases. Sometimes the things they did had good results, even though the ideas about why these things worked were wrong. For example, when the ancient Chinese used herbs and the ancient Egyptians used moldy bread on wounds, they found that infections healed. Some Native-American people knew that chewing willow tree bark would help reduce pain. And many people knew that a doctor could help just by soothing patients and taking good care of them.

460–377 B.C.
Hippocrates learns through observation and examination of patients. Living in Greece, he is a great medical teacher and creates the Hippocratic oath, a code of medical ethics still in use today.

A.D. 1220–1280
Venetians first use eyeglasses to correct poor vision.

But Hippocrates' basic idea went on being not much more than a guess for a long time. Around 1600, things began to change. An Englishman named William Harvey discovered that blood in human and animal bodies doesn't just sit there. It moves, or circulates, all through the body every few minutes. And the heart is the pump that makes it move. This was an important breakthrough because it made sense of many things that had long been known about the heart and blood, but had never been pulled together. So it was an important step toward making Hippocrates' guess look more reasonable. A lot of seemingly mysterious and unrelated facts turned out to have a simple and natural explanation.

1334
The Plague spreads across Europe. Three fourths of the European and Asian populations die in a twenty-year period.

1628
The English doctor, William Harvey, discovers blood is circulated throughout the body by the heart. He realizes the heart works like a pump to keep the blood in constant motion.

DISCOVERING GERMS

The discovery of germs and how they cause diseases took much longer. The first step was to realize that there were animals so tiny that they couldn't be seen by the naked eye. This step was taken by a Dutchman named Anton van Leeuwenhoek in 1674. After he heard of microscopes that magnified small objects, he made himself a very powerful one. He used it to look at water from a nearby pond and was amazed to find tiny animals swimming around in it. No human being had ever seen them before! He found many different kinds of microbes, as these tiny animals are called today, and became famous for this discovery. Ever since 1300, people had sometimes thought that such tiny living things might cause diseases. But Leeuwenhoek did not know of this idea. He did not suspect that the microbes he saw could cause the diseases that kill people. But now people knew that microbes really existed.

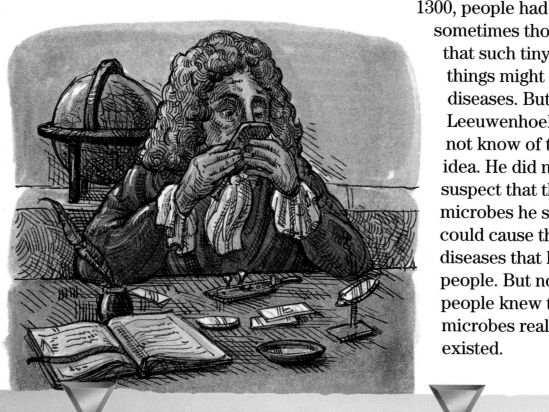

1674
Anton van Leeuwenhoek studies life under the microscope and is able to achieve 160 times magnification.

1735
English surgeon Claudius Amyan successfully completes the first surgery to remove the appendix.

Another big step was taken around 1800 by an English doctor named Edward Jenner. He believed Hippocrates' guess; he was sure that diseases had natural causes. One particularly terrifying disease at that time was smallpox, which killed most people who got it. The few who recovered were left with scars on their faces and bodies but never got the disease again. Jenner guessed that the body developed some means to fight the disease, so that if it were invaded by smallpox again, the infection could not survive. He tried to think of a way of getting the body to develop these antibodies (as they are now called) to attack the disease without having to get smallpox first.

He knew that among cattle there was a disease called cowpox, which was similar to the human disease of smallpox. Humans could also get cowpox, but it rarely killed them and left no permanent scars. Jenner heard it said among country people in some parts of England that if you got cowpox, you would never get smallpox. Jenner

1753
James Lind discovers that lemons and limes can cure scurvy, a vitamin C deficiency. Sailors, who frequently suffer from this disease on long ocean voyages, welcome his findings and drink lime juice.

1780
Benjamin Franklin invents a bifocal lens.

213

decided to find out if this was true. He guessed that once the body developed antibodies to cowpox, the same antibodies would be able to fight off smallpox. He infected some people with cowpox, waited until they recovered, and then tried to infect them with smallpox. (This test was dangerous. Such experiments wouldn't be tried today!) The people didn't get ill. They had developed the antibodies, and they would not catch smallpox. They were immune to the disease.

So, Jenner had discovered a way of preventing smallpox. For the first time ever, doctors could do something to prevent a disease. And they had evidence that whatever caused smallpox could be defeated by something the body developed for itself. But they still didn't know what actually caused the disease. For centuries, people had been guessing that microbes, or germs, caused smallpox. No one made the actual connection between germs and disease until Louis Pasteur, a French chemist, conducted some experiments in the mid-1800s.

1796
Edward Jenner experiments with cowpox vaccinations against smallpox.

1860
The French scientist Louis Pasteur demonstrates the presence of airborne bacteria.

MAKING THE CONNECTION

While Pasteur was doing his experiments, other scientists were discovering many different microbes. One kind of very small microbe, shaped like a rod or stick, was called bacterium, after the Greek word for stick. Pasteur carefully followed these discoveries and learned a lot about different types of bacteria. But before he could make the connection between these bacteria (or germs) and diseases, he had a more difficult job. Pasteur had to dispel, or prove wrong, an old belief that was standing in the way of his research.

Many people believed that living things could grow from nonliving things. They thought that rats grew from pieces of cheese, rotting meat turned into worms, and animals grew out of water. This idea, called spontaneous generation, seems silly to us now. But, it is easy to see why people believed it. When Anton van Leeuwenhoek discovered microbes under his microscope, no one had an explanation for how they got into the water. So it seemed likely that the water must have turned into these animals. Pasteur thought this idea was wrong. He conducted several experiments to make sure.

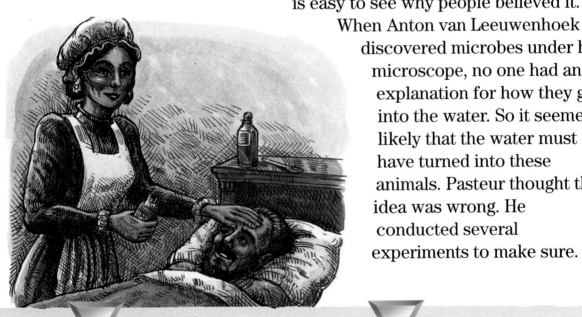

1860
Florence Nightingale establishes the Nightingale School for Nurses, the first of its kind in the world. An English nurse, Nightingale was the founder of modern nursing.

1881
Louis Pasteur vaccinates animals against anthrax.

In a previous series of experiments, Pasteur had learned that certain bacteria made wine spoil. When he heated the wine, the bacteria were killed. (This process of heating to kill bacteria became known as pasteurization.) In another set of experiments, Pasteur heated a flask of water to kill all the bacteria. He took samples of the water and showed under the microscope that the water contained no microbes. He then opened the flasks so that dust could get into the water. He took another sample of the water, looked at it under the microscope, and found bacteria in it. This proved that the bacteria was carried into the water by the dust particles. The bacteria had not grown out of the water.

Once people believed that all living things came only from other living things, it was easier for Pasteur to prove that diseases were caused by living things. While conducting his experiments on wine, Pasteur had wondered if bacteria might also cause diseases in humans.

1885
Louis Pasteur develops a vaccine for rabies.

1886
Louis Pasteur creates a process of sterilization known as pasteurization.

Pasteur began conducting experiments on animals with anthrax, a disease common in sheep and cattle. While looking under the microscope at blood samples from the sick animals, Pasteur discovered bacteria that were common to all of the infected animals. He knew that if he could inject healthy animals with this bacteria, and they got anthrax, it would prove that the bacteria caused the disease. Pasteur injected healthy rabbits and guinea pigs with a solution that contained the bacteria. All the animals became sick and died, proving the bacteria caused the disease. Using this information, Pasteur was able to develop a vaccine for anthrax.

1893
Daniel Hale Williams performs first successful heart surgery.

1895
Wilhelm Conrad Röntgen discovers X-rays.

FIGHTING GERMS

Pasteur's work made people aware that bacteria, or germs, caused diseases and infections. Joseph Lister, a Scottish surgeon who was a friend of Pasteur's, began to sterilize all his equipment before an operation to get rid of germs. He made sure that only clean gloves were used by his assistants. He disinfected wounds with carbolic acid to kill germs. Sure enough, his patients rarely died of infections, and other surgeons began to use his methods.

1899
The drug aspirin is first used to relieve pain.

1929
Alexander Fleming discovers mold contains a substance that will kill bacteria. He names it penicillin.

Although doctors could take steps to prevent germs on the outside of the body from spreading or infecting people, they had no way to kill the germs once they were inside the body. This important step in fighting diseases took place less than fifty years ago when Alexander Fleming discovered a substance that would kill bacteria. Quite by accident, Fleming noticed that one of his lab experiments on bacteria was contaminated with mold. Instead of just throwing the ruined experiment away, Fleming studied it carefully. What he found was extraordinary. The mold destroyed the bacteria. Fleming then tested the mold on other types of bacteria and found it had the same effect on many of them. Years of testing confirmed Fleming's observations. The substance Fleming found was penicillin, modern medicine's first antibiotic. Since its discovery, penicillin has saved hundreds of thousands of lives. Many infections that once killed people are now easily treated.

1939
Howard Florey uses penicillin, extracted from mold juice, to treat a patient for the first time.

1953
Jonas Salk develops a polio vaccine.

It is only within the last hundred years that most people in the United States have come to believe that Hippocrates' guesses are true. All medical research now assumes that the human body is part of nature, and that diseases have explanations just like everything else in nature. As the natural causes of diseases are discovered, scientists are able to find ways of stopping those diseases. More and more diseases can be prevented or cured. There has been tremendous progress in the last hundred years.

1958
Swedish doctor Ake Senning invents the first cardiac pacemaker.

1975
Smallpox is eliminated through a mass vaccination sponsored by the World Health Organization.

But there is a great deal that we don't know. We still cannot cure many diseases. We don't understand why some people get cancer or heart disease. Millions of people, however, are involved in research on these diseases and on the drugs to cure them. They all accept that Hippocrates was right. But, his idea is still just a guess. And while we think there must be natural causes for these diseases, we don't know what they are. When someone gets cancer today, we are almost as mystified and helpless as people were about any disease a few hundred years ago. If you become a doctor or a medical researcher you may be one of the heroes, like Jenner or Pasteur, who have dispelled some of that fear.

1985
"Keyhole" surgery is created, named so because it is less invasive.

1997
Stanley Prusiner is awarded a Nobel Prize for his discovery of prions, the cause of several serious brain diseases.

Medicine:
Past and Present

Meet the Author

André W. Carus was the boss at the time the editors were putting together this book. They had trouble finding a short article about the history of medicine. The editors knew Mr. Carus had studied history, so they asked him to write an article. Said Mr. Carus, *"Writing is hard, but it's satisfying to get something down on paper. Running a company never gives you a sense of completion like that."*

Meet the Illustrator

Jim Roldan received a box of crayons, his first memorable gift as a child. He drew pictures of cartoon characters, animals, comic book heroes, dinosaurs and spaceships. He studied art at the Rhode Island School of Design. After a few years of working in a graphic design studio, Mr. Roldan started his own business illustrating advertisements, magazines, posters, books, and cartoon characters. He currently lives and works in New Hampshire, where he shares a house with his wife and their two cats.

Theme Connections

Within the Selection

Record your answers to the questions below in the Response Journal section of your Writer's Notebook. In small groups, report the ideas you wrote. Discuss your ideas with the rest of your group. Then choose a person to report your group's answers to the class.

- What did people think caused diseases years ago?
- What was the first step in discovering how germs cause diseases?
- Whose work made people aware of how germs cause diseases?

Beyond the Selection

- Based on the information you read in this selection, what do you think is the most important discovery in the history of medicine? Why?
- Think about how "Medicine: Past and Present" adds to what you know about medicine.
- Add items to the Concept/Question Board about medicine.

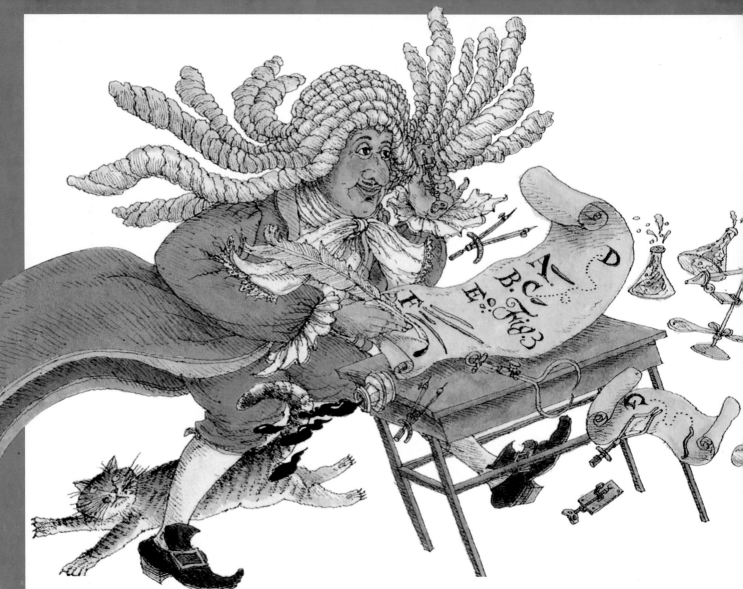

Focus Questions What would medicine be like if everyone
was too frightened to try new things? Why haven't
people always known about microbes?

The
Microscope

Maxine Kumin
illustrated by Robert Byrd

Anton Leeuwenhoek was Dutch.
He sold pincushions, cloth, and such.
The waiting townsfolk fumed and fussed
As Anton's dry goods gathered dust.

He worked, instead of tending store,
At grinding special lenses for
A microscope. Some of the things
He looked at were:

   mosquitoes' wings,
the hairs of sheep, the legs of lice,
the skin of people, dogs, and mice;
ox eyes, spiders' spinning gear,
fishes' scales, a little smear
of his own blood,

   and best of all,
the unknown, busy, very small
bugs that swim and bump and hop
inside a simple water drop.

Impossible! Most Dutchmen said.
This Anton's crazy in the head.
We ought to ship him off to Spain.
He says he's seen a housefly's brain.
He says the water that we drink
Is full of bugs. He's mad, we think!
They call him *Dummkopf,* which means dope.
That's how we got the microscope.

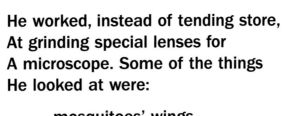

Sewed Up His Heart

from *Sure Hands, Strong Heart:
The Life of Daniel Hale Williams*
by Lillie Patterson
illustrated by Leslie Bowman

July 9, 1893, was hot and humid in Chicago. The
scorching heat wave wrapped the city like a sweltering
blanket and blistered the sidewalks. Rising
temperatures sent thermometers zooming toward one
hundred degrees.

The heat and high humidity took a heavy toll on young
and old, animals and people. Horses pulling carts and
streetcars dropped in their tracks. People fainted from heat
prostration and sun strokes. No relief was in sight.

Doctors and hospitals were kept busy. The new Provident
Hospital was no exception. Dr. Dan kept close watch on his
patients. Making his rounds, he looked as immaculate as
always, despite the heat. After his late-afternoon rounds
were over, he retired to the closet-like room he used for
his office.

Suddenly, a young student nurse burst into the room, her
long starched skirt rustling as she ran.

"Dr. Dan!" she gasped. "An emergency! We need you."

Without a word Dr. Dan dropped the report he was
reading and hurried to the room set aside for emergency
cases. The lone hospital intern, Dr. Elmer Barr, came
running to assist.

The emergency case was a young man. He had been brought in by his friend, who gave sketchy information. The patient's name: James Cornish. His age: twenty-four years. His occupation: laborer. The illness: he had been stabbed in the chest.

The frightened friend tried to explain what happened. James Cornish had stopped in a neighboring saloon on his way home from work. The heat and a few drinks caused an argument among the customers. A fight broke out. When it ended, Cornish lay on the floor, a knife wound in his chest.

"How long was the knife blade?" Dr. Dan asked as he began his examination. This would give a clue to the depth and seriousness of the wound.

The victim had not seen the knife blade. Nor had his friend. Action in the fight had been too fast and furious.

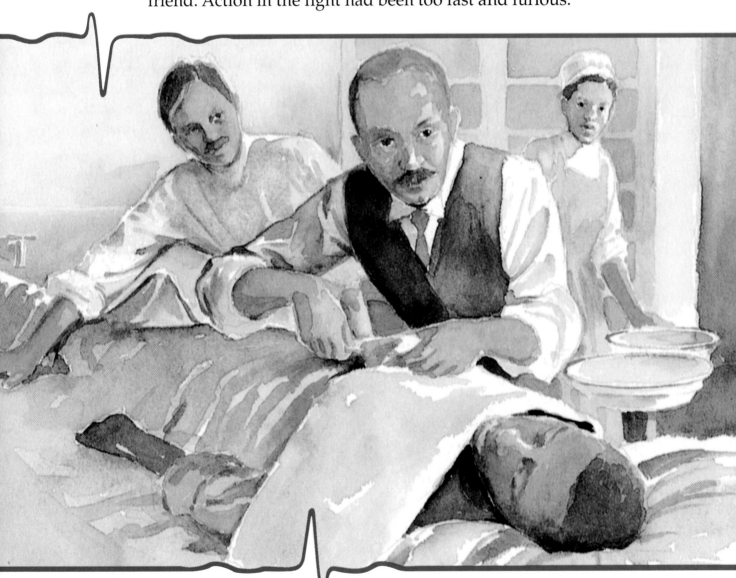

Dr. Dan discovered that the knife had made an inch-long wound in the chest, just to the left of the breastbone. There was very little external bleeding. Nevertheless, Cornish seemed extremely weak, and his rapid pulse gave cause for concern. The X ray had not yet been invented, so there was no way to determine what was happening inside the chest.

Dr. Dan knew from experience that such cases could develop serious complications. James Cornish must be kept in the hospital, he decided. And he must be watched closely.

That night Dr. Dan slept in the hospital. He did this often when there were serious cases. As he had feared, Cornish's condition worsened during the night. He groaned as severe chest pains stabbed the region above his heart. His breathing became labored. A high pitched cough wracked his sturdy frame. The dark face on the pillow was bathed in perspiration.

Dr. Dan watched the wounded man carefully all night. The next morning, as he took the patient's pulse, he voiced his concern to the intern. "One of the chief blood vessels seems to be damaged," he said to Dr. Barr. The knife must have gone in deep enough to cut the internal mammary artery, he explained. The heart itself might be damaged.

James Cornish showed symptoms of lapsing into shock.

Both doctors knew that something had to be done, and done quickly. Otherwise Cornish would surely die within a matter of hours.

But what?

The only way to know the damage done would be to open the chest and look inside. In 1893, doctors considered this highly impracticable. For surgery, the chest was still off limits.

Standing beside the patient's bed, the barber-turned-doctor faced the situation squarely. Later he would recall how he weighed the risks of that moment. Thoughts tumbled through his mind as furiously as flurries in a wintry Chicago snowstorm.

He knew that medical experts repeatedly warned against opening the thorax, the segment of the body containing the heart and lungs. Heart wounds were usually considered fatal. As a medical student, Dr. Dan had read a quote from an eminent physician-writer. "Any surgeon who would attempt to suture a wound of the heart," the surgeon wrote, "is not worthy of the serious consideration of his colleagues."

So far, doctors had followed this cautious advice.

The risks were there for him and for Cornish. If he did not attempt an operation, Dr. Dan reasoned, the patient would die. Nobody would blame the doctor. Such cases often died.

On the other hand, if he opened the chest and Cornish died anyway, there would be certain condemnation from medical groups. His reputation as a surgeon would be questioned, perhaps lost.

The odds were against both him and Cornish. But Daniel Hale Williams had never allowed the odds to intimidate him.

Dr. Dan lifted his chin, the way he did when he faced a challenge. The storm of doubts suddenly swept away, leaving his mind clear and calm as a rain-washed April morning.

The surgeon quietly told his decision to the intern. Two words he spoke. "I'll operate."

The word spread quickly through Provident hospital. Like a small army alerted to do battle, student nurses rushed to get the operating room ready and prepare the patient. They knew Dr. Dan's strict rules regarding asepsis, or preventing infection. The instruments, the room, furniture; everything that came in contact with the patient must be free of microbes that might cause infection.

Meanwhile, Dr. Dan sent a hurried message to a few doctors who often came to watch him operate. The intern, a medical student, and four doctors appeared. Dr. George Hall of Provident's staff was there. So was Dr. Dan's friend, Dr. William Morgan. The circle of watchers gathered in the operating room; four white, two black.

Dr. Dan scrubbed his hands and arms thoroughly. Then, with a nod toward his colleagues, he walked over and looked down at Cornish, now under the effects of anesthesia. Strong shafts of sunlight slanted through a window, giving the doctor's curly red hair a glossy luster. His thin, sensitive mouth drew taut with concentration.

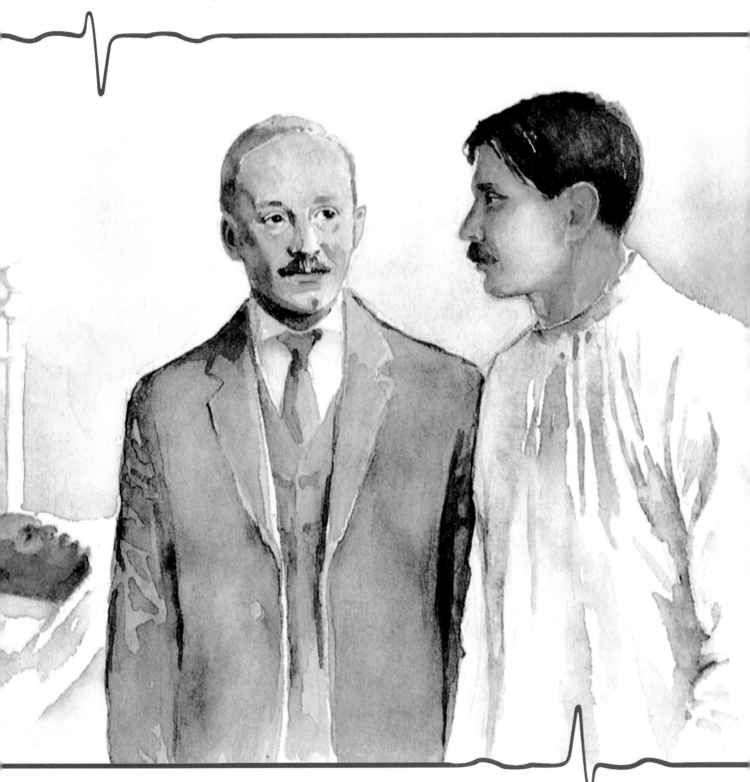

The surgical nurse, proud of her training, stood at attention.

Scalpel!

A loud sigh escaped one of the doctors when the light, straight knife touched Cornish's bare skin. After that there was silence from the onlookers.

None of them knew what would happen next. How would the body react when air suddenly hit the chest cavity? Would vital chest organs shift too far out of place? Dr. Dan could not benefit from the experiences of other doctors. No paper had been written, no lectures given to guide him. Dr. Dan was pioneering in an unexplored territory. He was on his own.

The surgeon worked swiftly. He had to. The surgeon of 1893 did not have a variety of anesthetics or artificial airways to keep the patient's windpipe open. Blood transfusion techniques were unknown. Penicillin and other infection-fighting drugs had not been discovered.

Quickly, Dr. Dan made the incision, lengthening the stab wound to the right. Expertly, he cut through the skin and the layers of fat beneath it. Now he could see the breastbone and the ribs. He made another cut to separate the rib cartilage from the sternum.

Long years of studying and teaching human anatomy gave his every movement confidence. Working with precision, he made his way through the network of cartilages, nerves, blood vessels. A few inches from the breastbone he cut through the cartilage to make a little opening, like a trapdoor.

Bending his head close to the patient's chest, he peered through the opening he had made. Now he could examine the internal blood vessels.

Now he could see the heart!

The tough bundle of muscles throbbed and jerked and pulsated, sending food and oxygen through the body. Dr. Dan examined the pericardium, the fibrous sac that protected the pear-shaped heart and allowed it to beat without rubbing against other parts of the body.

At each step, Dr. Dan reported his findings to the group of observers. The vital pericardium was cut——a tear of about an inch and a quarter in length. He probed further. Yes, there was another puncture wound, he reported, about one-half an inch to the right of the coronary artery. Had the knife moved a fraction of an inch, Cornish would have bled to death before he reached the hospital. Also——Dr. Dan paused——the left mammary artery was damaged.

As the problems were ticked off, the atmosphere in the room grew more tense. The temperature rose above one hundred degrees. Yet not one doctor reached to wipe the perspiration that poured down hands and faces. No one took note of the time. It seemed as though the moment were somehow suspended in history, awaiting results.

Dr. Dan kept on talking and working. The small wound in the heart itself should be left undisturbed, he advised. It was slight. The tear in the pericardium was a different matter. That had to be repaired.

Now the surgeon's hands moved with a rhythm born of knowledge, practice, and instinct. Strong hands; flexible enough to pluck tunes from guitars and violins. Sure hands; steady enough to string high telephone wires. Quick hands; made nimble from years of cutting hair and trimming beards and mustaches.

These hands now raced against time to save a life. Dr. Dan tied off the injured mammary artery to prevent bleeding.

Forceps!

Now he had to try to sew up the heart's protective covering. Meticulously, he irrigated the pericardial wound with a salt solution of one hundred degrees Fahrenheit. There must be no chance of infection after the chest was closed.

Using the smooth forceps, he held together the ragged edges of the wound. Against his fingers the fist-sized heart fluttered and thumped like a frightened bird fighting to fly free.

Sutures!

Despite the rapid heartbeats, the master surgeon managed to sew up the torn edges of the pericardium. For this he used a thin catgut. After that he closed the opening he had made, again using fine catgut.

Another kind of suture would be used for the skin and cartilages, he informed the circle of watchers. He changed to silkworm gut, using long continuous sutures. This allowed for quick entry if infection or hemorrhage developed later. Over the outer sutures he applied a dry dressing.

The operation was over. James Cornish was still alive.

Dr. Dan straightened his aching back. Only then did he stop to wipe the perspiration from his face.

Like figures in a fairy tale suddenly brought to life by magic, the circle of doctors began to move and talk. They rushed to congratulate the surgeon. "Never," said one, "have I seen a surgeon work so swiftly, or with so much confidence."

Each of them dashed from Provident to spread the news. Daniel Hale Williams had opened a man's chest, repaired the pericardium, closed the chest; and the patient's heart was still beating.

How long would Cornish live? Worried watchers waited in suspense. Had the doctor repaired the heart but killed the patient?

During the hours that followed the operation, Dr. Dan scarcely left Cornish's side. Alarming symptoms developed, and he made careful notes. The patient's body temperature rose to 103 degrees. His pulse raced at 134 beats a minute. Heart sounds became muffled and distant. Seizures of coughing shook his frame.

Dr. Dan shared his fears with Dr. Barr. Fluid had collected in the pleural cavity. This meant another operation.

He waited a few more days to give Cornish more time to gain strength. Three weeks after the first operation, Cornish was again rolled into the operating room. As before, Dr. Dan made an incision, this time between the seventh and eighth ribs. Through this opening he drew five pints of bloody serum.

Thanks to his careful adherence to antiseptic surgical techniques, there was no infection, and there were no further serious complications. Fifty-one days after James Cornish entered Provident with little chance of living, he was dismissed—a well man.

A news reporter from Chicago's *Inter Ocean* newspaper came to Provident to interview the surgeon and get the story first-hand. He found Dr. Dan more anxious to talk about his interracial hospital and the program for training nurses than to talk about the historic operation. The reporter had to coax details from him.

Nevertheless, the reporter's story came out with an eye-catching headline: "SEWED UP HIS HEART!" Another heading read: "DR. WILLIAMS PERFORMS AN ASTONISHING FEAT. . . ."

The *Medical Record* of New York later carried Dr. Dan's own scientific account of the techniques and procedures he had used during the operation. His case created worldwide attention, for it was the first recorded attempt to suture the pericardium of the human heart.

His pioneering operation gave courage to other doctors to challenge death when faced with chest wounds. Dr. Dan's techniques were copied by other surgeons, step by step.

The phrase "Sewed Up His Heart" became closely associated with the name of Daniel Hale Williams. The historic operation on James Cornish helped to advance the progress toward modern heart surgery.

Sewed Up His Heart

Meet the Author

Lillie Patterson grew up on Hilton Head, South Carolina. She spent most of her time with her grandmother who was a great reader and singer. *"From my grandmother I captured a sense of the power of words. It was natural that I would follow a career in library media services, and later in writing."*

Ms. Patterson became a children's librarian and a popular storyteller. She also helped to develop radio and television shows for children.

When she gets an idea for a book, Ms. Patterson spends a great deal of time doing research. She finds as much information as possible. Then she rereads everything until she feels she has captured "the spirit" of her subject.

Meet the Illustrator

Leslie Bowman grew up in Connecticut. She started drawing when she was about four years old. She says she never wanted to be anything but an artist. She got lots of encouragement, especially from her mother who was a painter herself.

Ms. Bowman started illustrating children's books in 1986. Since then she has illustrated several books and also worked for *Cricket Magazine*. She says, *"When I work on the illustrations for a book, I read the story over and over until I see the pictures in my head. Then I do sketches of what I see."* She does any research she needs, like finding out what clothes people wore at the time of the story. She adds these details to her sketches, and from these she produces her final illustrations.

Theme Connections

Within the Selection

Writer's Notebook

Record your answers to the questions below in the Response Journal section of your Writer's Notebook. In small groups, report the ideas you wrote. Discuss your ideas with the rest of your group. Then choose a person to report your group's answers to the class.

- Why did Dr. Dan decide to operate on James Cornish's heart?
- Why did Dr. Dan have to perform the heart surgery quickly?

Across Selections

Compare Dr. Dan with Mrs. Frisby in "Mrs. Frisby and the Crow." How are they alike? How are they different?

Beyond the Selection

- Think about how "Sewed Up His Heart" adds to what you know about medicine.
- Add items to the Concept/Question Board about medicine.

Surgeons Must Be Very Careful

Emily Dickinson
illustrated by Robert Byrd

Surgeons must be very careful

When they take the knife!

Underneath their fine incisions

Stirs the culprit,—Life!

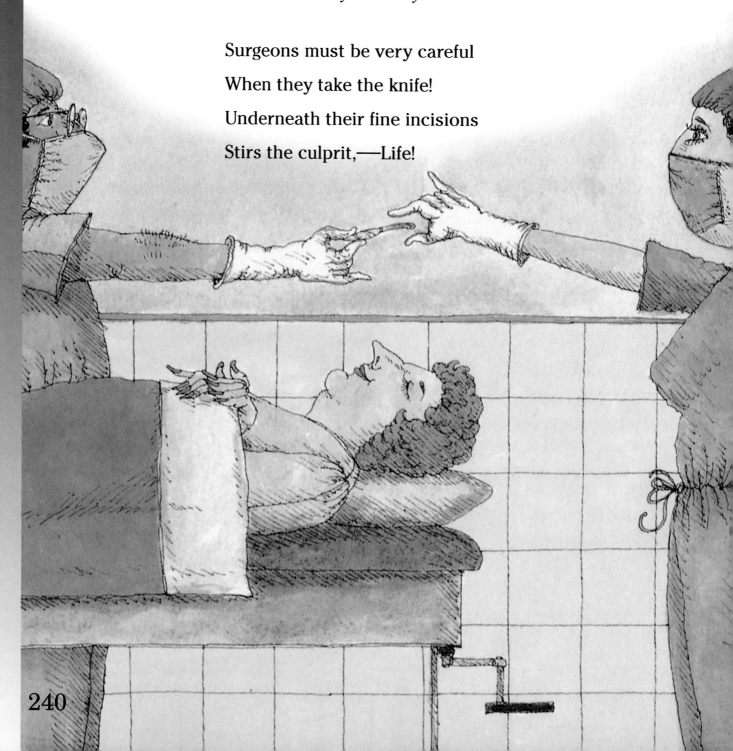

240

The Germ

Ogden Nash

illustrated by Robert Byrd

A mighty creature is the germ,
Though smaller than the pachyderm.
His customary dwelling place
Is deep within the human race.
His childish pride he often pleases
By giving people strange diseases.
Do you, my poppet, feel infirm?
You probably contain a germ.

241

The Bridge Dancers

Carol Saller

illustrated by Gerald Talifero

ama gives the comb a yank through the mess of Callie's long, wild hair, and Callie gives a yell like you've never heard before. That's not to say I've never heard it before; I've heard it plenty. Callie says when she grows up she's going to the city to live, where she'll start a new style. All the ladies will come to her and pay a lot of money to get their hair tangled up in knots, and she'll get rich and never comb her hair again.

I'm not a lot like Callie. My hair doesn't fly around much, and I like it combed, and I don't often think about leaving this mountain. Callie's going to be thirteen soon. I'm only eleven, and I've never even been across the bridge.

242

When Callie's all combed, we go down the path to the bridge. It's our favorite place to play when our chores are done. The dirt path is steep from our house down the twisty old hill. We like to run down fast, bouncing off the little trees in a crazy zigzag, but when we reach the edge of the gorge, the path levels off and we run alongside it. To folks way down below on the river we must look like two little pokeberries, up high on the mountain's edge.

What we call the bridge isn't the real bridge, where horses and buggies can get across, that's a few miles off along the path. Our bridge is just a shaky old skeleton, a tangle of ropes and boards that ripples and swings in the breeze. Our house is the closest one to this bridge. The next nearest is the Ketchums' place, another mile up the mountain. Most of our neighbors live across the gorge; Mama says there are seven houses within the first half hour's walk. Mama often has to cross the bridge, but we're not allowed.

On this day, the wind is strong and the bridge is rocking like a boat in a storm. We make clover chains and toss them into the gorge, watching them blow away and then down, down. We count the seconds till they hit the water far below. Callie stays by the edge, but I spy some yellow-eyed daisies growing up the hill a ways, and I know Mama will want them. If you boil daisies——stalks, leaves, and all——it makes a tea that's good for coughs, or a lotion for bruises and sores. Mama doctors most of the folks on this mountain, and we always keep a store of dried plants for medicine. I pull the best ones and put them in my apron pocket.

Later, when the sun is behind the mountain and I'm getting cold and hungry, I start back up the path, but Callie doesn't want to go. "Maisie! I dare you to stand on the bridge!" she calls, just like she does every time we're here. I don't answer, but I stop and turn to look. She knows the thought of it scares me.

Now she skips up the hill a little ways and stands on her toes like a dancer, her skirt ballooning in the wind. In the gloomy light of sundown she is ghostlike and beautiful. "Announcing . . . Calpurnia the Great!" She twirls and leaps and strikes a pose with one toe pointed forward: "Calpurnia——the Daring Bridge Dancer!"

I laugh. I'm pretty sure she's only teasing. Callie dances toward the bridge, humming a tune that she imagines sounds like a circus. When she gets to the part of the bridge that sits on land, she holds onto one post and points her foot out

toward the gorge, leaning back in a swoop. Then she grabs both posts and slides both feet out onto the bridge. She starts to slip, but before I can cry out, she turns back, laughing. My heart is jumping. I'm getting ready to run and pull her away from the bridge when she skips aside quick as lightning and starts chewing a piece of clover. In a second I see why.

Mama is huffing down the path. She's lugging her doctoring bag and has to watch her step. If she'd seen Callie fooling around on the bridge we'd both have caught it. "Girls, I've got to attend to Mrs. Gainie," Mama says, putting her bag down for a rest. "She thought the baby would come last night, but tonight's the full moon. It'll come tonight." She looks us over and frowns across the gorge. "I might be gone till sunup, so get yourselves some supper, and don't forget to bolt the door, you hear?" She points at some dark clouds moving fast across the sky. "Hurry on up. I've already made a fire——there's a storm blowing." We nod. She starts for the bridge.

"Mama?" I call, and she stops and turns. "Is Mrs. Gainie going to be all right?" Mama nods. "She's a strong woman." She reaches for the bridge rail with one hand.

"Wait!" I call.

Mama stops again. "What is it, Maisie?"

"Have you got the tansy I picked?" I ask. Tansy is supposed to help a baby come, but if it doesn't do that, at least it keeps the bugs away.

Mama says, "I've got it, but I don't expect to need it this time." She smiles at me. "I'll mind my steps on the bridge, Maisie." Mama knows I'm afraid.

When Mama crosses the bridge, I never let go of her with my eyes. She's a big, heavy woman, and when she steps off the land part, the whole bridge from one side to the other dips into a sharp V with Mama at the bottom point. She goes slow, holding the ropes with one hand and her bag with the other, and she walks in a careful rhythm, giving the bridge time to bounce just right between steps. Callie says, "She won't fall if you look away," but I never look away. On the other side it's already dark, but we can just see Mama turn and wave. We wave back, and Mama disappears around the side of the mountain down the path to the Gainies'.

"Come on, Callie," I say, starting up the path. I know that there's supper to get and more wood to gather and plenty else to do. But Callie isn't of a mind to work. She throws her blade of grass to the wind and runs ahead of me, her arms flung wide. "Burst into jubilant song!" she cries. "The everlasting chains are loosed and we are free!" Callie gets a lot of big words from reading the Bible. "Let us soar into the heavens, never to be enchained again!"

With that, she scampers off the path into the brush, and is soon just a flutter of white in the dusk, dancing and dodging among the trees. I feel the first drops of rain, and in a moment Callie is back.

"Maisie, I know what let's do," she says, blocking the path. She has to raise her voice now against the wind.

"What?" I ask with a frown. Callie's smile looks like it's hiding a bad idea, and I'm not sure I want to know.

"Let's get the ax and split a log for the fire," she says, wrapping her skirt around her and skipping along beside me. "There's a big storm coming. Let's have a fire that will last us all night."

I'm not sure. A fire would be good on a cold, stormy night, and I know there's only kindling left in the box. But Mama's the one who chops the wood. She takes down that big old ax from its pegs high on the wall and tells us to stand away. She's never told us not to touch it, but I have a feeling that we're not supposed to. I shake my head. "Callie, I don't hardly think you could even lift that ax. You're likely to get yourself killed." But my words blow away with the wind, and Callie is already halfway up to the house. I start to run, too, but I've never yet stopped Callie from doing what she wants to do. I figure the best I can do is be there when she needs help.

When I get to the door, Callie has the lantern lit and is dragging the rocking chair over to the wall. "Don't stand on that——it's too tottery!" I cry, and I run to hold the rocker while Callie climbs up and waits for the wobbling to stop. When the

chair is still, she reaches up both hands to lift the ax from its pegs. It's heavy, all right; I can see by the way Callie's muscles stand out on her arms. Just when she's got it lifted off the pegs, the wind blows the door shut with a powerful "bang!" and we both jump with fright. The rocker pitches, and Callie falls.

For a long moment it seems like nothing happens. My thoughts stop; even my heart seems to stop. Then Callie is crying out with pain and fear. It's her leg, cut deep by the ax. She clutches hold of my arm, tight, and gasps with the force of the pain. "Maisie, hurry and get Mama!" she whispers. "Callie . . ." I start to say, thinking about the wind, the dark, the bridge. Callie sees how I don't want to go, and she looks at me, begging with her eyes. "Maisie, I'm sorry——but you've got to go! You're the only one who can help me!"

I don't want to think about what Callie is saying. Instead I grab one of the clean cloths Mama uses for straining her herb medicines, and with shaky fingers, tie it tight around Callie's

leg. I take a quilt from the bed and put it over her, then run to the kindling pile and throw an armload of sticks on the fire. Callie is crying; the wind is crying. I light another lantern and wonder how I can cross the bridge, in the night, in the storm.

Outside, the wind and trees are whipping at the sky. I hold my skirt in one hand, the lantern in the other, and stumble in the quivery light down the path to the bridge. With my whole heart I wish there was some other way to fetch Mama. I think of Mama with her jars and packets, her sure hands and her healing ways. She'll stop the bleeding with a poultice of yarrow; she'll make an herb tea that will help Callie sleep. But Mama is far across the valley——how will I ever cross that bridge . . . Near the bottom of the hill, I can hear it before I see it, ropes groaning and boards creaking, as it tosses in the storm.

I stand at the edge of the gorge, my lantern lighting the first few steps of the rain-slicked bridge. The fear in me is so powerful it stings my eyes, and I know I don't have the courage for even the first step. But I remember what Callie said——"Maisie, you're the only one who can help me"——and I step onto the bridge with both feet.

The bridge pitches and plunges. I grab for the ropes, and the lantern flies from my hands. "No!" I shriek, as it rolls away and drops into the darkness. On my hands and knees, I crawl back to the edge of the gorge, sobbing in the terrible black night, crying for Callie, crying for Mama. How can I cross the bridge . . . how can I help Callie . . . think what to do, Maisie, think what to do. With my face near the ground, I make myself take slow breaths. I can smell clover, damp with rain.

Suddenly, I know what to do. I pick myself up and start back up the path, feeling my way in the darkness, guided by the small light in the house at the top of the hill. I remember all the times I've watched Mama with her bag, with her poke leaves for burns, her chickweed for tummyache. It's the yarrow plant that stops someone bleeding, and I can make the poultice myself. Near the top I begin to run.

When I burst in through the door, I see that Callie's face is pale. "Maisie——Mama!" she says, weakly. "There, Callie, don't fret; it's going to be fine," I comfort her. "I know what to do. Mama will come later, but I know just what to do."

My hands shake a little as I set the kettle on to boil——the fire is still burning strong. Then I go to Mama's cupboard of crushed and dried plants. I find some yarrow and wrap it in a clean muslin cloth to make the poultice. My fingers are sure now——Mama does it exactly so. Then I take a handful of dried feverfew and put it in a pot, for tea. Callie is moaning, so I sit by her and talk. "Yarrow is just the thing——and I remember I picked this myself! It has such pretty little flowers, and so many funny names: thousand-leaf, angel flower, bunch-a-daisies, sneezewort. It won't take but a minute, once that water's boiled. Don't you worry, Callie. Maisie can take care of you."

When the water is boiling, I pour some into the teapot with the feverfew and put it near the window to cool. Then I put the wrapped-up yarrow into the kettle and put the kettle back on the fire——not too long, just long enough for the water to soak in and soften the yarrow. Then I scoop out the poultice with a ladle, and after a minute, while it's still hot, I put it carefully on Callie's leg. I know it will hurt, so I keep talking. "Listen to that rain! It's really starting to pour now. You know, this is a pretty bad cut, Callie, and it hasn't stopped bleeding yet. This poultice will stop it. Can you smell how sweet?" But Callie yells when the poultice touches her leg.

When the tea is cool, I pour some into a cup, and hold up Callie's head for her to drink. "That's good," I tell her. "This will ease the pain. Maybe you can sleep a little; sleep till Mama comes." I rest her head in my lap, leaning my back against the wall. Rain thrashes the roof as I stroke her hair, all tangled and wild. I talk on and on, about ox-eye daisies and Queen Anne's lace, chickweed and tansy, the names like song words, lulling her to sleep at last.

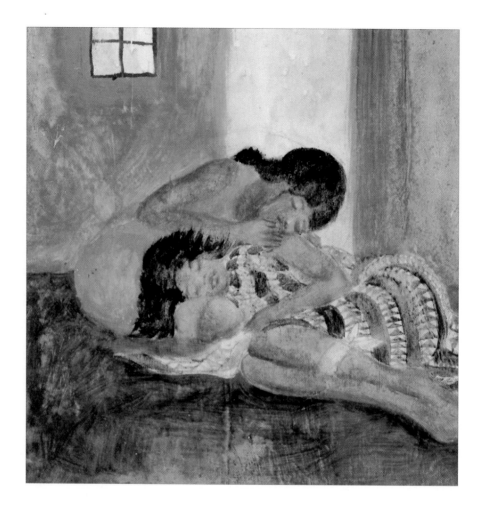

When Mama came home early the next morning, she found us sleeping on the floor. She unwrapped the cloths and washed out the cut——Callie hollered like anything——and said I'd done just what she'd have done herself. She never scolded about the ax——she knew there was no need——but she did ask why I hadn't come to fetch her. I was ashamed, telling Mama how I'd been too afraid to cross the bridge. "You've got good sense, Maisie," she answered. "I guess there's more than one way to cross a bridge."

It's been three months since Callie was hurt, and she's healed as much as she ever will. There's a fearsome scar on her leg, but Callie says that when she goes to live in the city she'll wear long pants like the men and no one will ever know.

Ever since I took care of Callie, Mama has let me help her with the doctoring. From the time I was little, I've helped her find and dry the flowers, but now I go along and watch when she tends to sick folks. When Callie talks about the city, I sometimes think I might visit her there. But for me, I think the mountain will always be my home. I like the way the mountain needs Mama. Someday I think it's going to need me, too.

The Bridge Dancers

Meet the Author

Carol Saller is a writer and editor who lives in Chicago, Illinois. She gets ideas for some of her stories from her two sons, John and Ben, who love to read.

When she's not working, Ms. Saller enjoys quilting and finding recipes for her husband to cook.

The Bridge Dancers is Ms. Saller's first book.

Meet the Illustrator

Gerald Talifero was born in Detroit, Michigan. Today he lives in Santa Barbara, California, where he works as an artist, designer, musician, and teacher.

Gerald Talifero is a multimedia artist who works in watercolor, pencil, and ink. In addition to art, he also works with troubled and disadvantaged children. His goal is to help children *"explore and develop their inner resources by outwardly coming in contact with nature."* Mr. Talifero and his "children" enjoy sailing, scuba diving, biking, and mountain climbing.

Theme Connections

Within the Selection

Record your answers to the questions below in the Response Journal section of your Writer's Notebook. In small groups, report the ideas you wrote. Discuss your ideas with the rest of your group. Then choose a person to report your group's answers to the class.

- What did Mama use for medicine?
- How did Callie hurt herself?
- How did Maisie help Callie?

Across Selections

In "Medicine: Past and Present" you read about the history of medicine. How is the way Maisie helped Callie's cut similar to the medical treatments used by other people?

Beyond the Selection

- How was Maisie's treatment of Callie's cut the same as a doctor's would be? How was it different?
- Think about how "The Bridge Dancers" adds to what you know about medicine.
- Add items to the Concept/Question Board about medicine.

Fine Art

From Mystery to Medicine

Louis Pasteur in His Lab. 1885. **Albert Edelfelt.** Oil on canvas. Musée d'Orsay, Paris, France. Photo: ©Erich Lessing/Art Resource, NY.

Medicine, hexagonal relief from the Campanile. Mid-13th century. **Andrea Pisano.** Museo dell'Opera del Duomo, Florence, Italy. Photo: Nicolo Orsi Battaglini/Art Resource, NY.

The Shop of the Druggist. **Pietro Longhi.**
Accademia, Venice, Italy. Photo: SCALA/Photo
Resource, NY.

*Interior of a Hospital with Doctors Tending
Patients.* **Gaddiano Manuscript 247.** Biblioteca
Laurenziana, Florence, Italy. Photo: SCALA/Art
Resource, NY.

Emily's Hands-On Science Experiment

by Hugh Westrup

Emily Rosa looks nothing like what you would expect a scientist to look like. She doesn't carry around a calculator or wear a lab coat with a pocket protector. Still, the 11-year-old Colorado schoolgirl is the youngest person ever to publish the results of a scientific experiment in the *Journal of the American Medical Association*.

"Age doesn't matter," said George Lundberg, editor of the journal. "It's good science that matters, and this is good science."

Controversial science, too. Emily's experiment, a test of a widely used healing practice known as *therapeutic touch* drew angry responses when it was published in 1998.

Therapeutic touch (TT) doesn't actually involve touching. Instead, TT practitioners hold their hands several inches above a patient's body and move the hands back and forth.

The theory behind TT is that the practitioner's hands can sense a patient's energy field. That field, according to one longtime TT practitioner, feels to the touch like "warm gelatin or warm foam." By pushing the field around until it is in "balance," the therapist can supposedly make the patient feel better. Touch therapists claim they can treat cancer, ease asthma, and reduce pain and nausea, among other things.

One day, while Emily and her mother Linda were watching a videotape about therapeutic touch at home, an idea struck Emily: Why not do a scientific investigation of TT?

"My parents are skeptics, but I wanted to see for myself," said Emily.

Emily designed an experiment to test TT as a project for her school's annual science fair. She began by drawing up a *hypothesis*—an assumption that can be tested. Emily's hypothesis was this: If a human energy field exists, then trained touch therapists should be able to detect it.

Emily asked 21 practitioners of TT to be *subjects,* or participants in her experiment. She had them sit, one at a time, at a specially designed table. Positioned in the center of the table was an upright cardboard screen with two holes near the bottom. Each subject was asked to sit behind the screen and put his or her hands, palms up, through the holes.

Next, Emily flipped a coin and held one of her hands over the subject's left or right hand. The subject was then asked to identify which of his or her hands was near Emily's hand—in theory, by feeling her energy field.

In 280 *trials*, or repetitions of the experiment, the subjects correctly specified which hand Emily held above their own less than 44 percent of the time. In other words, the subjects performed no better than they would have simply by guessing.

When Emily's experiment was published in April 1998, the responses were sharp and immediate. "I do hope it's an April Fool's joke," said Dolores Krieger, a nursing professor at New York University. Krieger developed TT 26 years ago and says she has trained about 47,000 practitioners.

"The way [Emily's] subjects sat is foreign to TT, and our hands are moving, not stationary. You don't just walk into a room and perform—it's a whole *process,*" contended Krieger.

Several scientists praised Emily's work, however, and said that it cast doubt on the existence of a human energy field. *Journal* editor Lundberg urged touch therapists to reveal the results of Emily's study to potential patients. "Patients should save their money unless or until additional honest experimentation demonstrates an actual effect," said Lundberg.

Though Emily's experiment was a significant study, more work must be done to back up her findings. Like other first-time scientific experiments, Emily's must be *replicated*—done again by an independent investigator—to confirm or challenge her results. Further investigations could also modify Emily's experiment in various ways, in response to the criticisms of Krieger and other TT practitioners. A body of research on TT would then emerge.

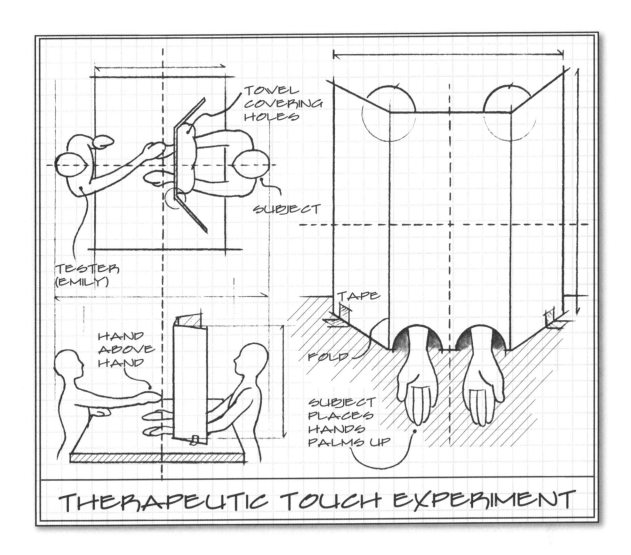

THERAPEUTIC TOUCH EXPERIMENT

Labels in figure: TOWEL COVERING HOLES; SUBJECT; TESTER (EMILY); HAND ABOVE HAND; TAPE; FOLD; SUBJECT PLACES HANDS PALMS UP

Because TT is a medical treatment, further *clinical trials* could also be conducted. A clinical trial is one that tests the effectiveness of a medical therapy on actual patients.

Numerous clinical studies of TT have actually been done already, said Donal O'Mathuna, a professor of bioethics and chemistry from Columbus, Ohio. Reviewing more than 100 clinical studies of TT, O'Mathuna found little evidence that TT helps patients.

Meanwhile, Emily continues her scientific pursuits. For her next experiment, she plans to test another popular form of alternative medicine: healing with magnets.

"Emily has always learned better by doing [things] herself," said Linda Rosa. "She is very curious, and it's a constant challenge to make sure she's involved in an active learning experience."

Emily's Hands-On Science Experiment

Meet the Author

Hugh Westrup was born and raised in Canada, receiving his Master's degree in psychology at York University. Mr. Westrup's scientific training helps him write nonfiction books for children. Some of the books he has written are *Maurice Strong: Working for Planet Earth*, *The Mammals*, *Bite Size Science*, and *Bite Size Geography*. He has also worked as an editor for *Current Science Magazine*, where his article about Emily's experiment was published.

Theme Connections

Within the Selection

Record your answers to the questions below in the Response Journal section of your Writer's Notebook. In small groups, report the ideas you wrote. Discuss your ideas with the rest of your group. Then choose a person to report your group's answers to the class.

- What was Emily's hypothesis?
- How did Emily test her hypothesis?
- Why were TT practitioners critical of Emily's experiment?

Across Selections

Emily designed an experiment to test her hypothesis about therapeutic touch. Who in "Medicine: Past and Present" also designed an experiment to test a hypothesis?

Beyond the Selection

- Emily designed an experiment and drew up a hypothesis to test whether a human energy field exists. Think of a hypothesis you would like to test. Share your hypothesis with the members of your group.
- Think about how "Emily's Hands-On Science Experiment" adds to what you know about medicine.
- Add items to the Concept/Question Board about medicine.

The New Doctor

from ***You Can Hear a Magpie Smile***
by Paula G. Paul
illustrated by Roberta Collier-Morales

Manuelita's house seemed unusually quiet as Lupe approached it. She wasn't sure why at first, then she realized that it was because she did not hear Noche screeching, cawing, and chattering. Maybe Manuelita was not at home. Lupe ran the last few steps up to the front and knocked on the door.

Still no sounds came from inside the house, but soon the door opened noiselessly, and Lupe saw Manuelita standing in front of her. Noche was perched on her shoulder, his long tail hanging down her back. Manuelita said nothing, but stepped aside for Lupe to enter.

"I thought you weren't home," Lupe said.

"In a few more ticks of the clock, we would not have been," Manuelita said.

As Lupe walked into the kitchen, she saw several small cloth bags lying on the table and a large knapsack beside them. Manuelita began gathering up the bags and putting them inside the knapsack.

"You are going to gather herbs," Lupe said. She had seen Manuelita make these preparations before.

Manuelita nodded. She turned toward the cupboard to check the contents of a glass jar. Noche almost lost his balance with the turn and fluttered his wings to keep his position on Manuelita's shoulder. He seemed to know that Manuelita was

going out and was making sure he stuck close beside her so that she would not leave him behind.

"You will look for summer herbs along the river? May I go with you?" Lupe asked eagerly.

"No," Manuelita answered. "I am going into the mountains."

"The mountains?" Lupe asked puzzled. There was a bigger variety of herbs along the river than in the mountains.

"Yes," Manuelita answered. "I will need more osha."

"But I just brought you some. Remember? I gathered it when Maria and I were lost, and——"

"Yes," Manuelita said. "But I will need more. Much more. There is nowhere else in the whole country that osha is as plentiful and as strong as it is in these mountains here."

Lupe wondered why Manuelita thought she would need so much of the herb. She thought of all the things it was used for. The root could be boiled for upset stomach and headaches, or ground to a powder and mixed with flour to paste on the chest of someone who had a cold, or placed on a sore spot on the body to aid healing. The green leaves could be cooked with meat or beans and eaten regularly, just to stay healthy.

Maybe Manuelita thought there was going to be a lot of sickness in the village. But with the new doctor's popularity, many people would no doubt go to her with their complaints. Manuelita must know that, too. It didn't make sense.

Oh, well, Lupe thought, at least Manuelita doesn't seem unhappy. She is still going about her work as usual. She is being her old dependable self. Maybe that is a good sign.

Still, Lupe wanted to be with her friend.

"I will go with you into the mountains," she said. "I will have to ask Mama, of course, but I'm sure if she knows you are going, she will——"

"No." Manuelita's voice was firm. "I must go alone."

"But——"

Manuelita reached toward Lupe and held her shoulders. "I will go alone," she said, looking deep into Lupe's eyes, "but when I come back, you must come to me."

Lupe searched Manuelita's face, trying to understand. "Yes, of course, I will come," she said.

"Then go and play now. There is still time for that."

Lupe thought that was a strange thing for Manuelita to say, but Manuelita said many strange things. She didn't have time to ask her about it, however, because Manuelita had finished packing her knapsack and was ushering her out the door.

As Lupe started through the brush toward the village, she looked back to see Manuelita, carrying the knapsack and with Noche clinging to her shoulder. The bird was not making a sound but was acting as if he dared not be naughty for fear he would be left behind.

By the time Lupe reached the village, her friend Maria had found someone else to play hopscotch with her. They were too far along with the game to add a newcomer, so Lupe walked away from the sandy spot, looking for something else to do.

She walked past the school and saw several children on the playground, but she didn't feel like joining them. She just kept walking, and before she realized it, she found herself in front of the new temporary clinic building.

There didn't seem to be any cars around it, and the only activity going on was at the noisy construction site for the permanent building nearby. Lupe decided to walk up to the temporary building and peek inside for another look. Since the front door was open just a crack, she tried to see through it. At first, she couldn't see too clearly, so she leaned closer to the door. Just as she did, the door opened from the inside, and Lupe tumbled forward, sprawling on the floor and looking at a pair of sandals. The feet inside the sandals were webbed by gossamer-thin nylon hose.

"Well, what have we here?" said a voice from above. Lupe looked up and saw that both the feet and the voice belonged to Dr. Johnson. The doctor came down to her knees and looked at Lupe. "Are you hurt?" she asked.

"No!" Lupe said. She jumped up quickly and dusted herself off.

"I didn't mean to make you fall. I opened the door to get a breath of fresh air, and I had no idea you were leaning against it."

Lupe ducked her head to hide her burning cheeks.

"Oh, look," the doctor said. "You've scraped your knee on the threshold. Let's see what we can do about that."

Dr. Johnson led Lupe into the examination room. She took her to the sink and washed the knee with warm soapy water, then rinsed and dried it. Next, she took a bottle of red liquid from a shelf and dabbed some of the liquid on the scraped spot. The red medicine caused Lupe's knee to burn furiously, but she did not cry out, and she swallowed hard to keep the tears from her eyes.

The treatment was very much the same as Manuelita would have given. She would have washed the area and dried it. Sometimes she even used the fiery red medicine you could buy at the grocery store, but more often, she would dab on a plaster made from the osha.

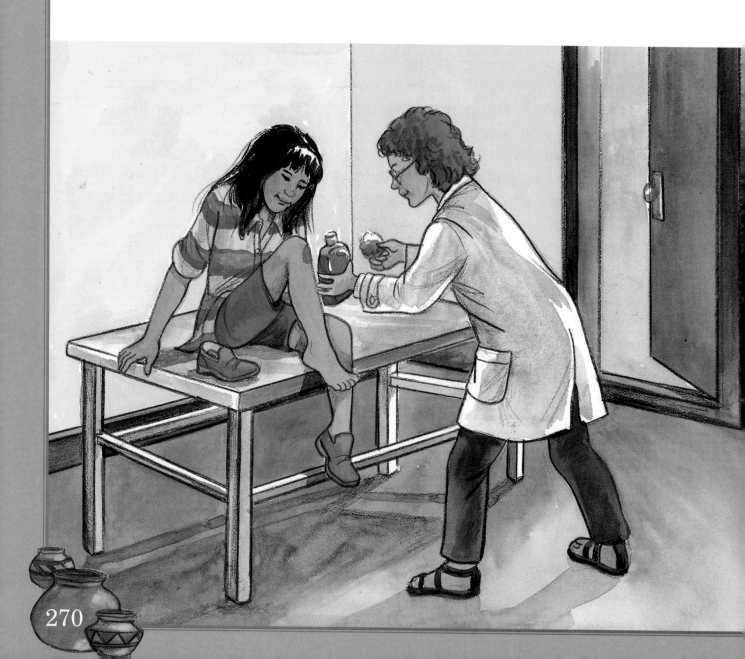

"There," Dr. Johnson said, putting the bottle of medicine away. "You have been my first patient, and you have come even before the clinic is officially open. It is to open tomorrow, you know. And I've spent all day today trying to get things organized and put away." The doctor sat down at her desk and faced Lupe. She smiled and said, "Now tell me, what can I do for you? Did you come for something special?"

"Nothing special," Lupe said, her voice very low.

"Perhaps you were just curious."

Lupe nodded her head.

"I can understand," Dr. Johnson said. "You have never had a clinic here before, and I suppose you wanted to see what it is like. I would have been the same way at your age. I was curious about just about everything—always poking my nose into something, and often getting into trouble."

Lupe looked up at the doctor, surprised. She was trying to imagine her as a little girl, poking her nose into things. The doctor was laughing at her memories, and the short curls on her head bounced as she laughed. Lupe found herself laughing with her.

"What is your name?" Dr. Johnson asked.

"Lupe Montano."

"I'm Dr. Eleanor Johnson. Did I meet you at the reception? I'm sorry I don't remember, but there were a lot of people there."

Lupe shook her head. "I wasn't there," she said. Lupe let her eyes roam around the room. Dr. Johnson had placed many things on the shelves and counters. There were bottles and jars which Lupe thought must contain medicines, but she didn't know what all the strange-looking tools were for.

"What are those for?" Lupe heard herself asking. She was surprised at her own question. She hadn't meant to ask anything, but her curiosity was stronger than her shyness.

This?" Dr. Johnson asked, picking up a piece of cloth attached to ropes and dials. "This is for taking blood pressure. Look, I'll show you how it works." The doctor wrapped the cloth around Lupe's arm. She put something in her own ears and placed the end of it to Lupe's arm also.

"When I listen here"——Dr. Johnson pointed to the thing in her ears——"and look at this" she pointed to the dial——"it helps me find out a little about your body, and maybe whether you are well or sick."

"What do you hear with that?" Lupe asked, pointing to the thing in the doctor's ears.

"This is a stethoscope, and I can hear your heartbeat," the doctor said, and she let Lupe listen to her own heartbeat.

"We will also have X rays, and on certain days of the week, we will have people come here to help me with them. An X ray takes pictures of the inside of your body."

Lupe had heard about X rays in school, although she had never seen one. Taking a picture, from the outside, of the inside of a person's body seemed more like witchcraft to her than anything Manuelita had ever done.

She looked up at the shelves full of bottles. "You have many remedies," she said. "It must have taken you a long time to mix them all."

"Oh, I didn't make them myself." The doctor laughed.

"Then where did you get them?" Lupe asked.

"Why, I bought them, from companies that sell medicines. There are many companies that know how to make medicines much better than I could."

Lupe looked at her silently. She wondered how she knew the medicines were good if she did not make them herself.

"I'll have a lot of advantages to share with you," Dr. Johnson said. "You won't have to travel all the way to Albuquerque when you are sick, or rely on home remedies you make yourself, that don't work most of the time. I'm looking forward to bringing that to all of you, and I'm looking forward to being your friend."

Dr. Johnson reached her hand toward Lupe's, but Lupe pulled her hand away and jumped up from her chair.

"I've got to go now," she said. "I forgot to tell my mother where I would be."

Lupe ran out of the building and down the road toward her house. She did not want to be friends with the new doctor, because the new doctor could not be Manuelita's friend. The new doctor would not want to have anything to do with a person who mixed her own medicines and did not know how to take pictures of people's insides.

Manuelita was gone for several days. Lupe began to worry about her. Manuelita had gone out searching for herbs and stayed far into the night and even overnight before, but never had she been gone this long. Lupe was also concerned because so many people had been going to the clinic. She was afraid they had abandoned Manuelita completely.

Worst of all, Lupe felt disloyal and guilty about the amount of time she, herself, had spent at the new clinic. She couldn't seem to help herself, though. She was fascinated by all the new medicines and strange instruments and, although she did not like to admit it, by the new doctor herself.

One day, when she couldn't talk Maria into going with her, Lupe decided to walk over to the clinic alone. She told herself she only wanted to see how the new building was coming along and perhaps catch a glimpse of Alonzo working with the big machines she'd heard him talk about. But before long, she was seated on the ground in front of the temporary mobile-home clinic, watching people coming and going. Occasionally, if it was someone she knew well enough, she would ask what their ailment was before they went in and what the treatment had been as they came out.

Manuelita had been right. The new doctor's medicine was often very different from hers.

Finally, when the sun was quite low on the horizon, Dr. Johnson herself came to the door. She took off her white coat and held it across her arm. She was wearing a summer dress made of a pretty blue material. It looked nice with her sandals.

"Hello, Lupe," she said. "Someone told me you were out here. Would you like to come in?"

Lupe shook her head.

"Oh, you needn't be shy," Dr. Johnson said. "You seem to be very interested in medicine. Wouldn't you like to talk? I enjoy talking to you."

"It's getting late. It will soon be time for supper," Lupe said, and she ran toward home.

The next time Lupe saw the doctor was in the grocery store. Lupe had gone there to get some flour for her mother to make *tortillas*. A few of the village men were standing around inside the store talking, and Dr. Johnson was talking to Mr. Baca, the owner of the store. She held a can of something in her hand and read the label.

"I don't know," she said. "I do hate to use this. I don't like these poisons, but the bugs are getting to be a problem at the clinic, and I've got to do something."

"You could try calabasilla leaves," Lupe blurted out.

"What?" Dr. Johnson turned around with a surprised look on her face. "Oh, hello, Lupe. I didn't know you were here. Seems you're always surprising me."

"I can bring you some leaves," Lupe said.

"Some what?"

"Leaves. Dried calabasilla leaves. If you sprinkle them around the edges of the rooms, it will keep the bugs out."

"Really? I've never heard of that."

"Works good," said one of the villagers in the store.

"Sure does," said another.

"Lupe knows," said still another.

"I'll bring you some tomorrow," Lupe said. She put the money for the flour on the counter.

Dr. Johnson had a funny look on her face, as if she didn't believe the dried leaves would work. But if she said anything in reply, Lupe didn't hear her over the noise of Mr. Baca's ancient cash register.

Lupe walked out of the store as quickly as she could. She would go back to the clinic just one more time, to deliver the leaves, she told herself. That would be her way of repaying Dr. Johnson for fixing her scraped knee. Every time Lupe thought of that incident, her heart sank. What would Manuelita think if she ever found out that her friend, Lupe Montano, had been the new doctor's first patient!

The day after Lupe had seen Dr. Johnson in the grocery store, she and Maria went down to the sandy spot to play hopscotch. While they were playing, Lupe heard a familiar cawing sound and looked up to see Manuelita walking through the brush toward her house. Noche, as usual, was perched on her shoulder.

"Manuelita's back!" Lupe said to Maria.

"Are you going to stop the game and go see her?" Maria asked, sounding disappointed.

"No," Lupe said. She stood on one foot and bent to pick up her pebble, then hopped to the end of the series of squares and circles. No matter how glad she was that Manuelita was back, she knew she wouldn't have time to go see her. It was getting late, and she still had to take the calabasilla leaves to Dr. Johnson.

When the game was over, Lupe went home to get the dried leaves. Maybe the doctor doesn't really want them, Lupe thought. She certainly didn't act as if she were anxious to have them. But Lupe was anxious to show her how well they worked, so she went to the pantry and took a jar from a shelf. It was too bad, she thought, to take the last jar, and one that Manuelita had given her family at that. But Lupe knew she could always gather the leaves from the sprawling gourd vines herself, when she found the time. They grew profusely along the river and on the mesas.

Lupe told her mother what she planned to do before she left the house.

"That's very nice of you, Lupe," Mama said. "It is always a good thing to welcome a newcomer with a gift."

When Lupe reached the clinic, there was no one in the waiting room. She was glad, because she didn't want to meet anyone who might say something to Manuelita about her being there. That was one of the reasons she had waited so late to come. She was surprised, however, to hear voices coming from inside the office as she walked up to the door. Two men's voices were speaking rapidly and excitedly in Spanish, and Dr. Johnson's voice was pleading in English.

"Please, please," Lupe could hear the doctor say. "Speak more slowly. My Spanish is not good. I can't understand you."

Lupe walked quietly into the office and saw Uncle Pedro and Cousin Josefa's husband.

"Lupe!" Dr. Johnson said as soon as she saw her. "Maybe you can help. Something's wrong, and these two men are too excited to speak English. Can you tell me what they're saying?"

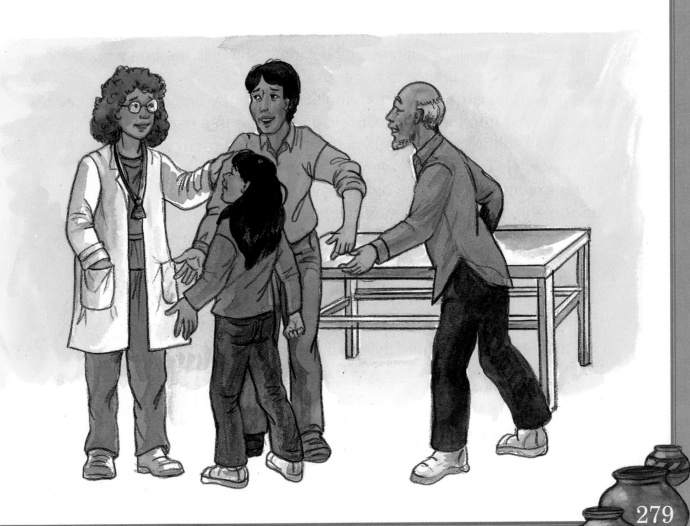

Lupe questioned the men, who answered her in breathless Spanish. Lupe turned to the doctor.

"It is my Cousin Josefa," she said. "They want you to go to her."

"Josefa?" The doctor seemed puzzled for a moment. "Oh, yes. The woman who is going to have a baby!"

"Yes," Lupe answered. "The men say it is time. They are very excited."

"Of course," Dr. Johnson said with a little laugh. She gathered some things into a bag. "I daresay your cousin will be much calmer than these men are. Come on," she said, motioning to the men. "I'll have to go to her. I have no more facilities for delivering a baby in this temporary building than you'll have at home."

The men followed the doctor out to her car, and everyone, including Lupe, got in. No one seemed to expect Lupe not to go, and she certainly hated to miss the excitement. Maybe it was a good thing she did go along, she decided. She was the one who had to direct the doctor to her cousin's house.

When they arrived, the men took the doctor by one arm each and led her into the house. Cousin Josefa was in a bedroom near the front of the house. Lupe waited in the living room with the family while Dr. Johnson went inside to examine Josefa. That was exactly as Manuelita would have done it, Lupe thought. Soon, the doctor came out of the bedroom. She was smiling.

"Josefa is in fine shape," she said. "It will only be a short wait before the baby is born."

In a little while, Dr. Johnson went back to see about Josefa again.

"She is doing very well," the doctor said when she came out of the bedroom, but her smile had vanished.

The next time the doctor went in to examine Josefa, she looked even more concerned when she emerged.

"She is doing very well, physically, but something is making her unhappy. She kept asking for someone named Manuelita. Is that her friend? Or perhaps her mother?"

"I can get her for you," Lupe said quickly.

"No! No!" said Uncle Pedro.

Just then Josefa called from the bedroom. "Is that Lupe's voice I hear? Let me talk to her."

Dr. Johnson turned to Lupe. "I don't know," she said. "You really shouldn't. . . . "

"Lupe! Let me talk to Lupe!" Josefa called.

Dr. Johnson's brow wrinkled into a frown. She bit her lower lip. "Oh . . . very well," she said. "Come with me." She led Lupe into the bedroom.

"Lupe!" Cousin Josefa said happily from her bed. "The little curandera." She spoke to Lupe softly in Spanish. She could also speak English very well, as could her husband and Uncle Pedro, but, as with most people in the village, when she was excited or had something very special to say, Spanish seemed the best language for saying it. When she had finished talking, Lupe turned to the doctor and told her what Cousin Josefa had said.

"Josefa says that her father, my Uncle Pedro, wants you to help with the baby because he thinks only the new modern ways are good enough for his grandchild, but she says she wants Manuelita to help her, because she is sure Manuelita knows all the right things to do. She says perhaps you know too, but with Manuelita she is certain."

"Who is Manuelita?"

"A curandera."

"A what?"

"A curandera."

"Oh, yes," Dr. Johnson said. "I seem to remember . . . a healer. Yes, I've heard of them. Sometimes associated with witchcraft, aren't they? No, I won't have that."

"Manuelita does not use witchcraft," Lupe said. "That is what Uncle Pedro thinks, but it is not true."

Josefa, who had heard the conversation, began to cry.

"Now, now," Dr. Johnson said, turning to her. "You mustn't be upset."

"I have seen that your kind of medicine is good, but Manuelita's is good, too," Lupe said. "Perhaps you could learn from each other."

"Superstition has no place at a time like this," Dr. Johnson answered.

Josefa was crying softly. "Lupe is a little curandera," she said in English. "She knows the good way."

"You, a curandera?" Dr. Johnson asked. "What does she mean?"

"Manuelita has taught me many things," Lupe said.

"Well, I guess that explains your interest in medicine. Lupe, I welcome you to come talk to me as often as we can find the time. Maybe I can undo some of the wrong ideas you may have."

"But——" Lupe started to protest.

"We don't have time to talk about it now," Dr. Johnson said. "Josefa's baby will be here soon."

Josefa was still crying. "It is only that I want the best for my baby," she said.

"The best thing for you and the baby both is for you to remain calm."

But Josefa only cried harder and clutched at her middle. Dr. Johnson spoke as if she were talking to herself. "She was handling it so well at first."

"Maybe Manuelita could at least help you," Lupe insisted.

"I could use some help," Dr. Johnson said, "but a curandera . . . no." She looked again at the sobbing Josefa.

Dr. Johnson's not going to give in, Lupe thought. She watched as the doctor fussed around Josefa, holding her hand and talking to her softly.

"It's not going to be a good birth if she is so upset," Dr. Johnson said to no one in particular. She turned to Lupe. "Maybe it wouldn't hurt anything for this, this Manuelita just to be here. . . . All right, Lupe, go get the healer."

Lupe ran from the house as fast as she could, still clutching the jar of calabasilla leaves she had forgotten to give to Dr. Johnson. She was breathless when she reached Manuelita's house, but she managed to explain what was happening and to tell her that the new doctor was with Josefa.

She was surprised at how fast the elderly Manuelita was able to get to Josefa's home. Noche flew ahead, circling and returning to Manuelita and Lupe, screeching and talking nonsense. As usual, he was left outside when Manuelita entered the patient's house.

Uncle Pedro stood up to protest as soon as he saw Manuelita.

"What's she doing here?" he asked.

Manuelita did not look at Uncle Pedro, or speak to him. He tried to follow Manuelita into the bedroom, but she slammed the door in his face, almost catching his nose between the door and the wall.

Lupe could hear many noises coming from the bedroom while she waited in the living room with the men.

"The doctor will see that it is done right," Uncle Pedro said, over and over again, to reassure both himself and his son-in-law.

The noises in the bedroom ceased. The silence was brief, interrupted by the cry of a tiny voice. Both of the men jumped from their seats. Dr. Johnson opened the bedroom door.

"Josefa and her husband have a beautiful daughter," she said.

She let everyone go into the room for a few minutes to see Josefa. First Josefa's husband went in, then Uncle Pedro, then Lupe.

Lupe saw Cousin Josefa holding her baby and smiling, and Manuelita standing beside them. Dr. Johnson walked toward Manuelita and held out her hand.

"Thank you," the doctor said. "I . . . I guess I have a lot to learn."

Manuelita took the doctor's hand in hers, but she did not speak.

The New Doctor

Meet the Author

Paula G. Paul grew up on a farm in Texas. Her family had no electricity, no television, no telephone, and the nearest town was 30 miles away. She was very good at entertaining herself and finding things that interested her. Even today she says, *"I am a person who is never bored."*

Ms. Paul says this about writing: *"The most important thing a person needs to be a good writer is perseverance, because it's not always easy. Even though we may be full of stories, what we need to learn is how to tell those stories in a way that is easy to read and understand. You have to learn how to tell the story. You have to believe in yourself."*

Meet the Illustrator

Roberta Collier-Morales admits that while she loved to draw, dance, sing, and play the piano as a child, she had a difficult time learning to read. She encourages others who are having problems with certain subjects to seek help and talk about what they are experiencing. *"The important thing is not to give up on yourself,"* she says. Ms. Collier-Morales studied art at Colorado State University, graduating in 1971. She is currently continuing her education in graduate school and lives with her two children, her parents, and her pets.

Theme Connections

Within the Selection

Record your answers to the questions below in the Response Journal section of your Writer's Notebook. In small groups, report the ideas you wrote. Discuss your ideas with the rest of your group. Then choose a person to report your group's answers to the class.

- How was the treatment Lupe received from Dr. Johnson similar to the treatment she would have received from Manuelita?
- What medical information did Lupe learn from Dr. Johnson?

Across Selections

- Both Manuelita in this story and Maisie's mother in "The Bridge Dancers" practiced medicine. How were their ways of healing similar?
- In "Where does Medicine Come From?" we learned where many of the medicines we use today come from. How is the medicine used by Manuelita similar to the medicine found in most pharmacies?

Beyond the Selection

- Think about how "The New Doctor" adds to what you know about medicine.
- Add items to the Concept/Question Board about medicine.

The Story of
Susan La Flesche Picotte

from ***Homeward the Arrow's Flight***
by Marion Marsh Brown
illustrated by Diane Magnuson

*Susan La Flesche Picotte was the first female
Native-American doctor in the United States.
After completing medical school she returned to her
home and began work as the doctor at the
reservation school. In this excerpt, her first
weeks as not only the school doctor but doctor
for the whole reservation are told.*

288

Susan wrote a letter of application on the very night that she told Rosalie, her sister, she wanted the position of reservation physician. Then she waited anxiously for a reply.

At last the letter arrived. She tore it open eagerly. "Well, finally," she sighed. She carried it to the kitchen where her mother was preparing supper. "I got the appointment," she said. "I don't get any more money though."

Her mother looked up. "So much more work and no more pay?" she asked.

"That's what the letter says: 'As there are no funds available except for your present salary as physician to the government school, we will be unable to pay any additional monies for your additional services as reservation physician.' Well, anyway I have the title. Now to see what I can do with it."

That same night, the first snow of the winter fell. Susan was soon inundated with a siege of colds, grippe, and pneumonia. It was as if the first snowstorm had been a signal for winter illnesses to attack.

She had laid her plans carefully before entering into her new contract to do two jobs for the price of one. She would spend mornings at the school and make house calls in the afternoons. The only problem, she soon discovered, was that there weren't enough hours in the day.

"I don't know why babies always want to get born in the wee hours of the morning," she said to Rosalie, stopping at her sister's house one day on the way to school. She'd been up since midnight and would not have time to go home before she was due at school. She was glad to have a place to clean up and get a cup of coffee.

"Sue, you can't go on this way," her sister said. "You'll ruin your own health."

Susan sighed. "But what else can I do, Ro?"

It was a bad winter, one of the worst Nebraska had seen in many a year. The north wind blew in icy gusts, finding its way around poorly fitted window frames and under ill-hung doors into the Omahas' houses. Many of the houses were getting old and they had not been kept in repair.

When Susan rode up to one in which a windowpane was out, the hole stuffed carelessly with old rags, anger flared in her. Inside, she knew, lay a child on the verge of pneumonia.

"Tom," she said, when she had entered, "there's no excuse for that." She pointed at the window. "When you get your next allotment, buy a piece of glass and some putty and replace that pane."

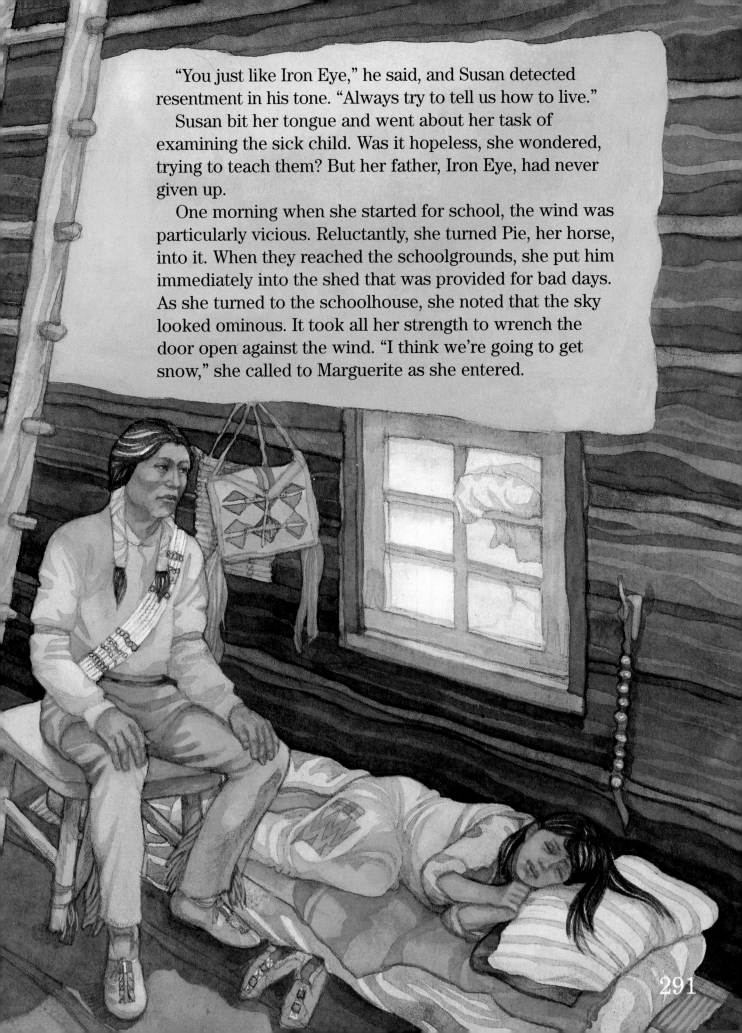

"You just like Iron Eye," he said, and Susan detected resentment in his tone. "Always try to tell us how to live."

Susan bit her tongue and went about her task of examining the sick child. Was it hopeless, she wondered, trying to teach them? But her father, Iron Eye, had never given up.

One morning when she started for school, the wind was particularly vicious. Reluctantly, she turned Pie, her horse, into it. When they reached the schoolgrounds, she put him immediately into the shed that was provided for bad days. As she turned to the schoolhouse, she noted that the sky looked ominous. It took all her strength to wrench the door open against the wind. "I think we're going to get snow," she called to Marguerite as she entered.

Marguerite turned back, and Susan saw the worried look on her face. "Oh, dear, I hope not. Charlie's sick again. He has an awful cough, Sue, and he was so hot last night, I know he has fever. And he went out to look after the stock this morning. I was hoping you could go by and see him this afternoon."

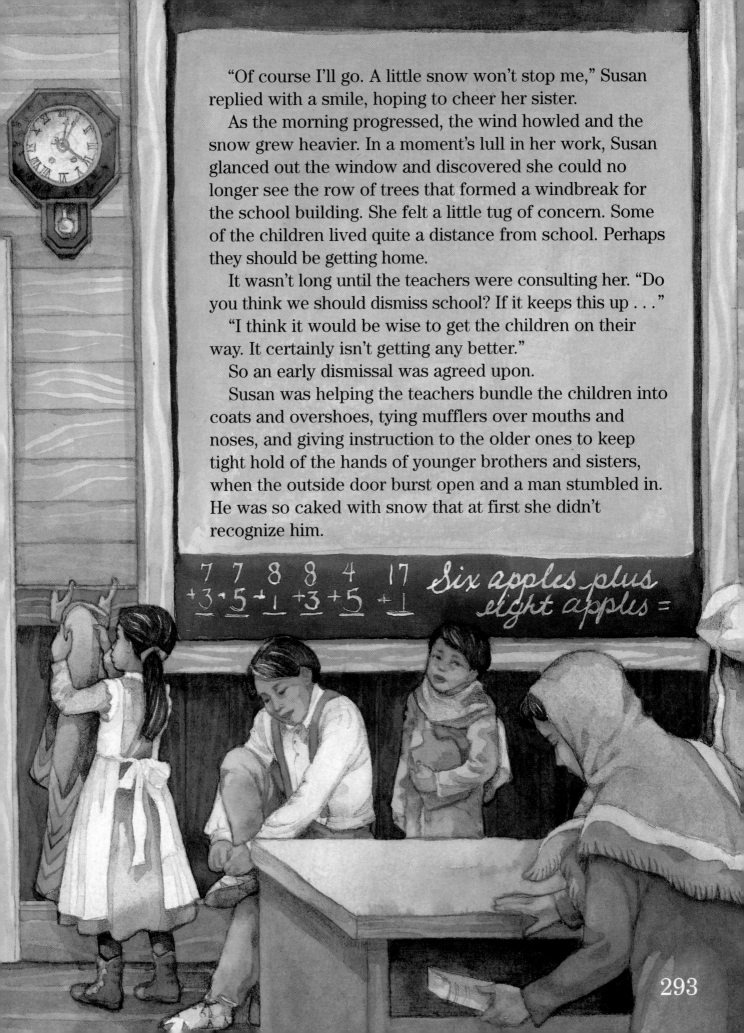

"Of course I'll go. A little snow won't stop me," Susan replied with a smile, hoping to cheer her sister.

As the morning progressed, the wind howled and the snow grew heavier. In a moment's lull in her work, Susan glanced out the window and discovered she could no longer see the row of trees that formed a windbreak for the school building. She felt a little tug of concern. Some of the children lived quite a distance from school. Perhaps they should be getting home.

It wasn't long until the teachers were consulting her. "Do you think we should dismiss school? If it keeps this up . . ."

"I think it would be wise to get the children on their way. It certainly isn't getting any better."

So an early dismissal was agreed upon.

Susan was helping the teachers bundle the children into coats and overshoes, tying mufflers over mouths and noses, and giving instruction to the older ones to keep tight hold of the hands of younger brothers and sisters, when the outside door burst open and a man stumbled in. He was so caked with snow that at first she didn't recognize him.

$$7 \quad 7 \quad 8 \quad 8 \quad 4 \quad 17$$
$$+3 \quad +5 \quad +1 \quad +3 \quad +5 \quad +1$$

Six apples plus eight apples =

"Dr. Susan!" he cried. "Come quick! My Minnie . . ."

"Oh, it's you, Joe," she said. "Has your wife started labor?"

He nodded. "But she's bad, Doctor. Not like before."

"Come on in and warm up, then go home and put lots of water on the stove to heat. I'll be along shortly."

Joe didn't linger. As soon as the children were on their way and she had straightened up her office, Susan sought out Marguerite. "I'll have to wait to see Charlie until after I deliver Minnie Whitefeather's baby. Joe says she's having a bad time, so I may be late."

"All right. Be sure to bundle up," Marguerite said. "It looks like the storm's getting worse."

"That I will. I always come prepared!" Susan assured her. She pulled her stocking cap down over her ears and donned the heavy wool mittens her mother had knit for her.

"I hope you'll be all right," Marguerite said. "It's a long way over there."

"Don't worry. You can depend on Pie!" Susan waved a cheery good-bye and plunged out into the storm. She had to fight her way to the shed. Already drifts were piling high. "I hope the children are all safely home by now," she thought. Her pony was nervous. "Good old Pie," she said, patting the sleek neck as she mounted. "When you were a young one and we went racing across the hills, you didn't think you were going to have to plow through all kinds of weather with me when you grew old, did you?"

The Whitefeathers lived on the northernmost edge of the reservation. Susan turned Pie onto the road, and he plodded into the storm. "Good boy!" she said encouragingly. But she couldn't hear her words above the violent shrieking of the wind. Nor, shortly, could she tell whether they were following the road; she could only trust Pie.

It seemed to her that the storm grew worse by the minute. Suddenly Pie stopped, turning his head back as if asking Susan what he should do. She tried to wipe the caked snow from her eyes to see what was wrong and found that her fingers were stiff. But she saw Pie's problem. A huge drift lay across their path. "We'll have to go around it, Pie." She pulled him to the left until they reached a point where the drift tapered off. Pie moved around it, and Susan thought, "Now can we find the road again—if we were on the road?" She pulled on the right rein. But she couldn't tell whether they were going north, for now the storm seemed to be swirling around them from all directions.

Soon another drift blocked their way. But this time Pie wallowed through with a strange, swimming motion. How did he know he could get through that one and not the

other, she wondered. Suddenly, having maneuvered the drift, the pony stopped.

"Get up, Pie! We have to go on!" she urged. He did not move. She slapped the stiff reins on his neck, but to no avail. She tried kicking his sides with feet she discovered were numb. "We'll freeze to death! Go on!" Still Pie refused to move.

At length she dismounted. If she could walk on her numb feet, perhaps she could lead him. Stumbling, she made her way to Pie's head.

Then she saw, and she caught her breath in terror. For Pie stood with his head directly over a bundle in the snow—a bundle that she knew instantly was a child.

"Oh, my!" she cried. She lifted the bundle into her arms. It was a boy, one of the little ones they had turned out of school to find his way home. "What were we thinking of?" Susan railed at herself. "Jimmy! Jimmy!" she cried, shaking the child. She scooped the snow off his eyelids. He stirred, and then his eyelids lifted. "Jimmy! It's Dr. Sue. You were asleep, Jimmy. You have to wake up now." She hoisted him in front of her on the pony, and holding him close to give him warmth from her body, she beat on his arms.

The minute she was back in the saddle, Pie moved on. "Pie! Bless you. You probably saved Jimmy's life."

As Pie pressed on, she continued to talk to Jimmy, working on him as she talked—rubbing his hands, cradling his face against her. "We have to warm up your nose," she told him. He began to cry. "You mustn't cry. Your tears will make cakes of ice!"

She strained her eyes ahead, but she could see nothing against the driving snow. She had no idea how long they had been in this frozen white nightmare. Surely if they were going in the right direction, they should have reached the Whitefeathers' by now. "Pie's going to take us to where it's nice and warm," she soothed Jimmy. And to herself she said, "If he doesn't, it's the end of all of us, you and me and him. And maybe Minnie Whitefeather too."

She tried to keep the child awake, finding to her consternation that she herself was growing drowsy.

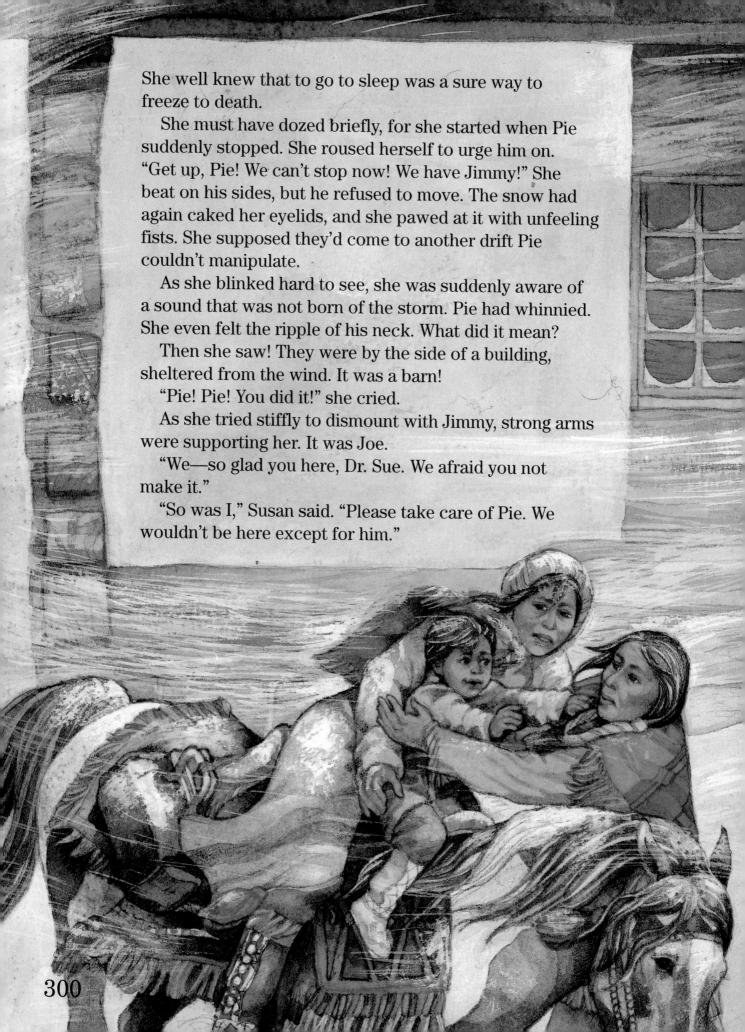

She well knew that to go to sleep was a sure way to freeze to death.

She must have dozed briefly, for she started when Pie suddenly stopped. She roused herself to urge him on. "Get up, Pie! We can't stop now! We have Jimmy!" She beat on his sides, but he refused to move. The snow had again caked her eyelids, and she pawed at it with unfeeling fists. She supposed they'd come to another drift Pie couldn't manipulate.

As she blinked hard to see, she was suddenly aware of a sound that was not born of the storm. Pie had whinnied. She even felt the ripple of his neck. What did it mean?

Then she saw! They were by the side of a building, sheltered from the wind. It was a barn!

"Pie! Pie! You did it!" she cried.

As she tried stiffly to dismount with Jimmy, strong arms were supporting her. It was Joe.

"We—so glad you here, Dr. Sue. We afraid you not make it."

"So was I," Susan said. "Please take care of Pie. We wouldn't be here except for him."

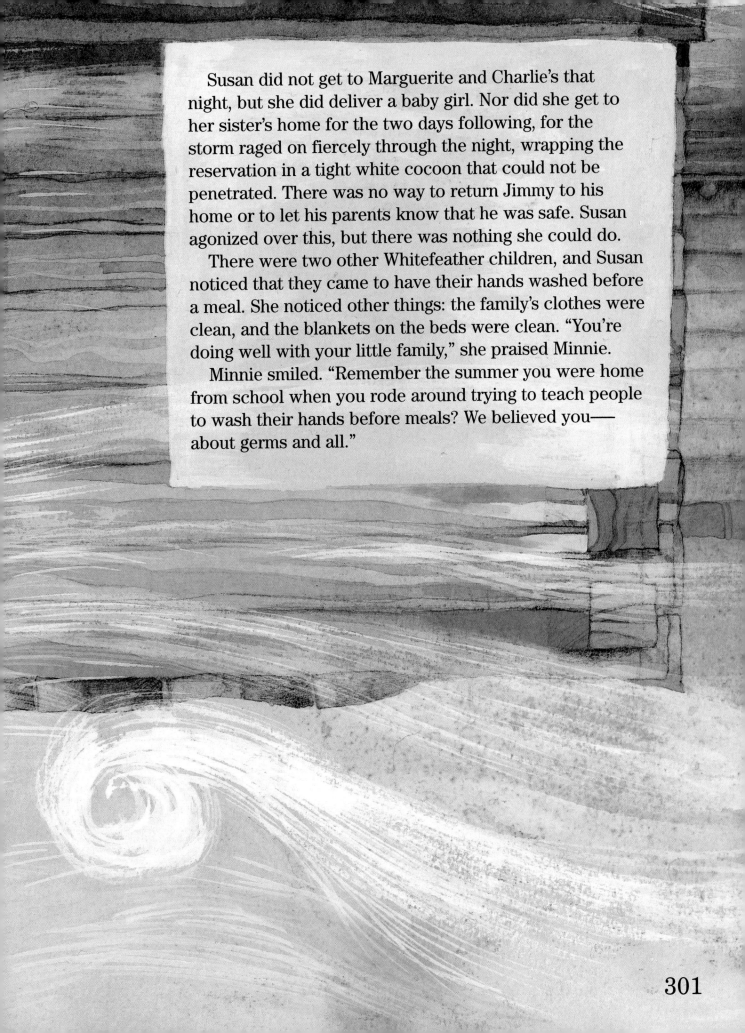

Susan did not get to Marguerite and Charlie's that night, but she did deliver a baby girl. Nor did she get to her sister's home for the two days following, for the storm raged on fiercely through the night, wrapping the reservation in a tight white cocoon that could not be penetrated. There was no way to return Jimmy to his home or to let his parents know that he was safe. Susan agonized over this, but there was nothing she could do.

There were two other Whitefeather children, and Susan noticed that they came to have their hands washed before a meal. She noticed other things: the family's clothes were clean, and the blankets on the beds were clean. "You're doing well with your little family," she praised Minnie.

Minnie smiled. "Remember the summer you were home from school when you rode around trying to teach people to wash their hands before meals? We believed you— about germs and all."

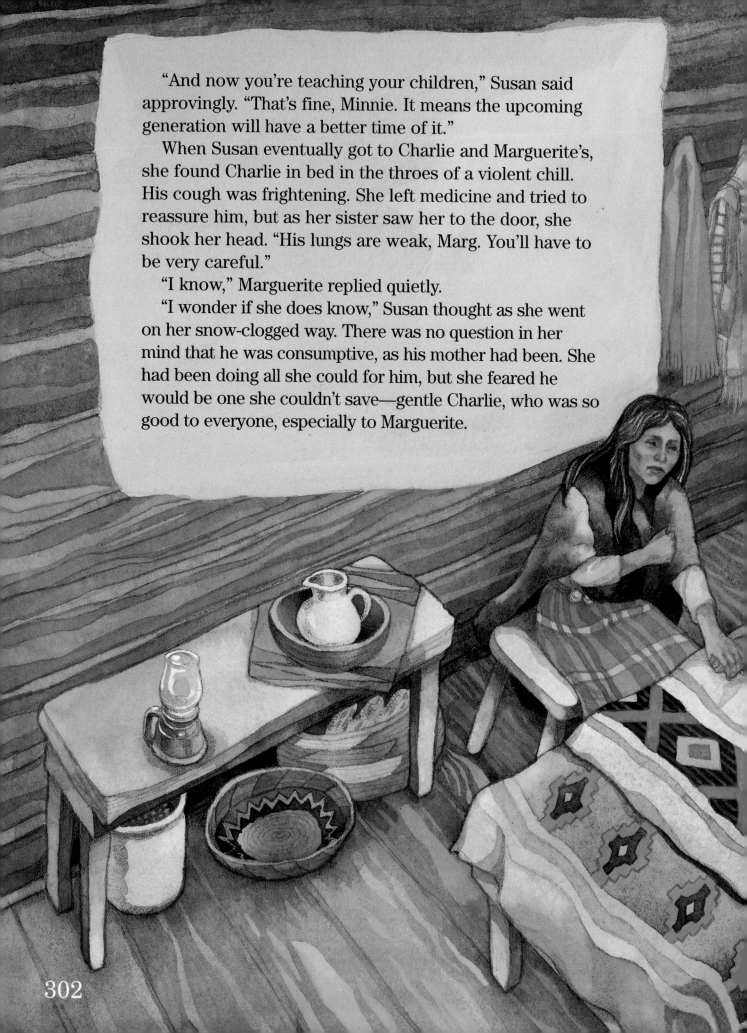

"And now you're teaching your children," Susan said approvingly. "That's fine, Minnie. It means the upcoming generation will have a better time of it."

When Susan eventually got to Charlie and Marguerite's, she found Charlie in bed in the throes of a violent chill. His cough was frightening. She left medicine and tried to reassure him, but as her sister saw her to the door, she shook her head. "His lungs are weak, Marg. You'll have to be very careful."

"I know," Marguerite replied quietly.

"I wonder if she does know," Susan thought as she went on her snow-clogged way. There was no question in her mind that he was consumptive, as his mother had been. She had been doing all she could for him, but she feared he would be one she couldn't save—gentle Charlie, who was so good to everyone, especially to Marguerite.

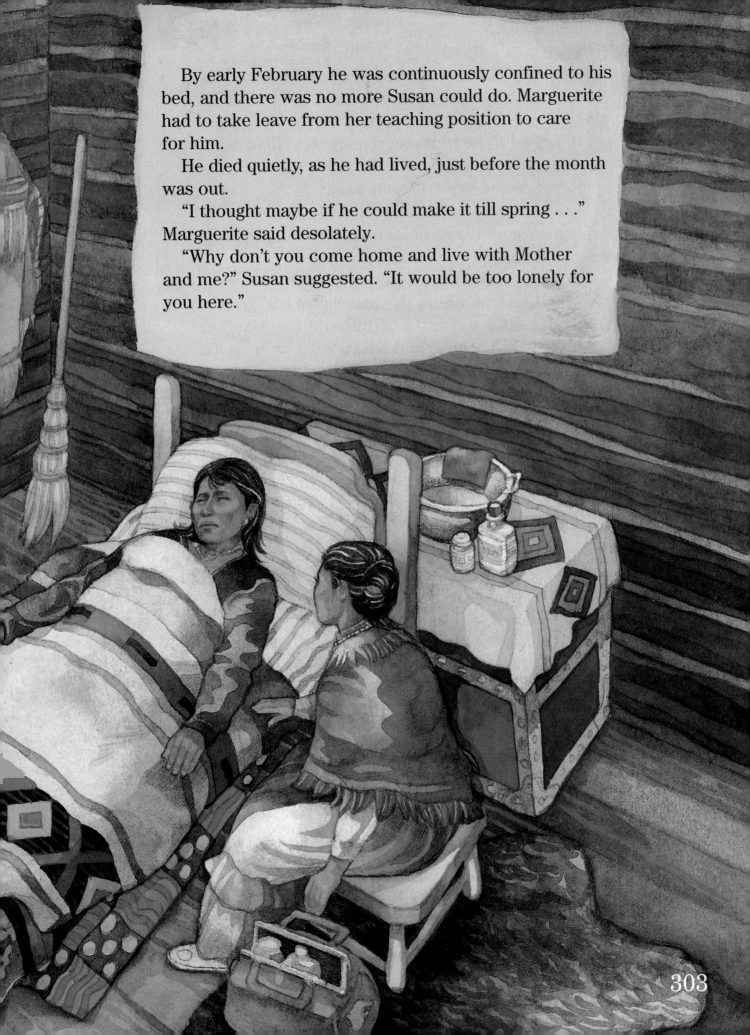

By early February he was continuously confined to his bed, and there was no more Susan could do. Marguerite had to take leave from her teaching position to care for him.

He died quietly, as he had lived, just before the month was out.

"I thought maybe if he could make it till spring . . ." Marguerite said desolately.

"Why don't you come home and live with Mother and me?" Susan suggested. "It would be too lonely for you here."

They sent word of Charlie's death to his family in Dakota, and his brother, Henry, came. "We wanted the family represented at his funeral," he said.

"Henry's different," Susan remarked to Rosalie. "Yet he reminds me of Charlie. Sort of a gayer edition!"

"He's more worldly," Rosalie said.

Susan smiled. It took Ro, who had had less "worldly" exposure than the rest of them, to see straight through to the point. "Yes, you're right," she agreed.

With the funeral over, Henry gone, and Marguerite back in the home where she and Susan had grown up, things settled down into a certain routine. Marguerite went back to teaching, and Susan went on with her doctoring.

"It's like the old days," Susan said one evening when she and Marguerite and their mother sat down to supper.

"Only different," Marguerite said.

"Yes," Susan agreed, thinking of how it had been when Nicomi, her grandmother, and Iron Eye and Rosalie had been at that table. "Things don't stay the same, do they, Mother?"

Her mother shook her head.

"We have to learn to accept change. That was one of the things Father tried to teach us long ago."

Spring was late that year, but when it finally came, it was so beautiful that Susan at times thought she couldn't bear it. Sometimes when she was riding home from a call in early evening, she would dismount and let Pie graze while she gazed down on the greening willows that fringed the river like a band of chartreuse lace. If it weren't too late, she would venture into the woods to look for violets and Dutchman's-breeches and the shy lady's-slipper.

"What a wonderful place to live," she thought. And more and more she could see that her work was bearing fruit. "I'm not accomplishing miracles," she told Rosalie one evening, "but I am beginning to see some of the results of better hygiene and health habits. And we're losing fewer babies and fewer cases to infection."

"You don't need to convince me," Rosalie said. "I can see it on every hand. How pleased Father would be."

The Story of
Susan La Flesche Picotte

Meet the Author

Marion Marsh Brown was born in Brownville, Nebraska. She grew up on a farm where she said she *"never lacked for interesting things to do."* She enjoyed riding horses, picking berries, climbing trees, swinging in a hammock, playing with the animals, and building tunnels through the haystack. Of all those things, reading was her favorite.

"I had to find out if I could write things too," she said. *"When I was ten, I saw my first story in print. It was on the children's page of the Sunday newspaper. I still remember the prize I received for it—a book called* I Wonder Why. *That was a good book for me to have, for I wondered 'Why?' about a lot of things then, and still do today, and I believe this is an essential trait for an author to have."*

Meet the Illustrator

Diane Magnuson has a degree in art and German and a master's degree in illustration. She has lived in many different places, but she began illustrating historical stories and Native American legends while living in the Northwest United States for 15 years. While they lived there, her husband was involved with Native American tribes, and his involvement in political issues brought many visitors and interesting discussions to their home.

Ms. Magnuson says of her work, *"Once the research and compositions are organized, I love to disappear into the painting, to become part of it and know the people in it."*

Theme Connections

Within the Selection

Record your answers to the questions below in the Response Journal section of your Writer's Notebook. In small groups, report the ideas you wrote. Discuss your ideas with the rest of your group. Then choose a person to report your group's answers to the class.

- What were some of Susan La Flesche Picotte's accomplishments?
- Susan La Flesche Picotte tried to improve the health conditions in her community. What changes was she trying to make?

Across Selections

How are Susan La Fleshe Picotte and Mae Jemison in "Mae Jemison: Space Scientist" similar?

Beyond the Selection

- What differences and similarities do you see between Dr. Picotte and a modern doctor?
- Think about how "The Story of Susan La Fleshe Picotte" adds to what you know about medicine.
- Add items to the Concept/Question Board about medicine.

Shadow of a Bull

from *Shadow of a Bull*
by Maia Wojciechowska
illustrated by Ramon Gonzalez Vicente

*Manolo Olivar is the son of Spain's most famous
bullfighter. Although his father died after being gored by a bull,
Manolo is expected to follow in his father's footsteps. Everyone
expects him to be Spain's next great bullfighter. But, Manolo
lacks* afición, *or desire. He knows he does not want to be a
bullfighter, but he is unsure what he will become. One day
while visiting a fighter who has been gored, Manolo
realizes what he must do.*

On the way to the gored boy's house, Manolo listened to them
tell about how bulls can hurt.

"The horn enters cleanly. If only it would exit that way. But either
the man or the bull or both are moving at the time of the goring,
and that's why the wounds are so bad."

"The horn tears into the body, ripping the muscles."

"And there is always the danger of infections. The horn is
dirty, and before penicillin, it was almost always either
amputation or death from infection."

"As far as the bullfighters are concerned, penicillin was the
greatest invention of man."

"Poor devils! When they get gored in small towns there is never a doctor."

"And that's where they usually get gored."

"Even here in Arcangel, there is only one doctor who will touch a horn wound. Only one who knows anything about them, and he is getting old; when he is gone, maybe there will be no one."

"If you must get gored, be sure it's in Madrid."

"In Madrid they have a dozen doctors."

"I knew a doctor once who got rich on bullfighters. And then one day, he took his money and went to a printer and had millions of pamphlets printed. The pamphlet was called 'Stop the National Suicide'."

The men had never said anything before about pain, the amount of it a bullfighter had to endure. And Manolo had never thought before about pain. Now, listening to them, he thought that it would not be of dying that he would be afraid, but of the pain.

'El Magnifico,' lying on sheets that were as white as his face, looked to be about eighteen. The first thing Manolo noticed about him were his lips. They were pale, but he had been biting them. Drops of blood stood out in a row marking the places where the lips had been bitten. Without anyone having to tell him, Manolo knew that the boy was in great pain.

When they came into the room, 'El Magnifico' tried to hide his bloodied lips behind his hand. He did not say much, just that he was feeling all right. When he looked away from the men, he did not look out of the window, but at the wall where there was nothing but a stain. And when he turned back to them, his lips had fresh drops of blood on them.

"I was terrible," the boy said, trying to smile.

"You weren't there long enough," one of the men said, "to let us see how terrible."

"I would have been very bad," 'El Magnifico' said, fighting back tears.

"You might have been fine. It was a good little bull. You were too brave, and sometimes it's silly to be too brave. You don't let the people see how long your courage is, just how wide."

The boy's mother came into the room. She was a big woman with strong hands and a face that seemed carved from a rock.

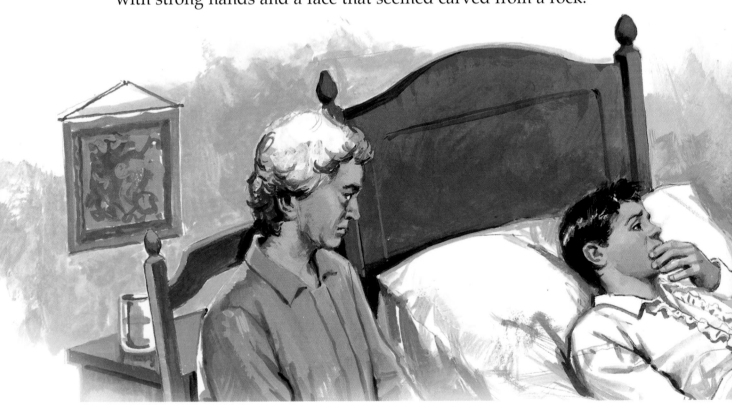

"The doctor's coming," she said, not looking at the men but looking hard at her son. She waited for him to say something. He said nothing.

"Hasn't the doctor seen you?" one of the men asked.

The boy moaned and coughed to hide the sound of his pain.

"He was out of town," the mother said, looking now at them for the first time, her eyes accusing.

"The barber then, he took care of you in the infirmary?" the man wanted to know.

"Yes," the boy said, "he did the best he could."

"The barber's only a barber," the mother said angrily and left the room.

"He's in great pain. He doesn't show it, but he is in great pain," one of the men said softly to Manolo.

"It never hurts right after the goring. But when it starts hurting, it hurts for a long time," another added.

They heard footsteps outside. They were slow in reaching the door. The doctor was an old man. He shuffled when he moved from the door to the boy's bed. He looked tired. A shock of white hair fell listlessly over his wrinkled forehead as he bent over the boy.

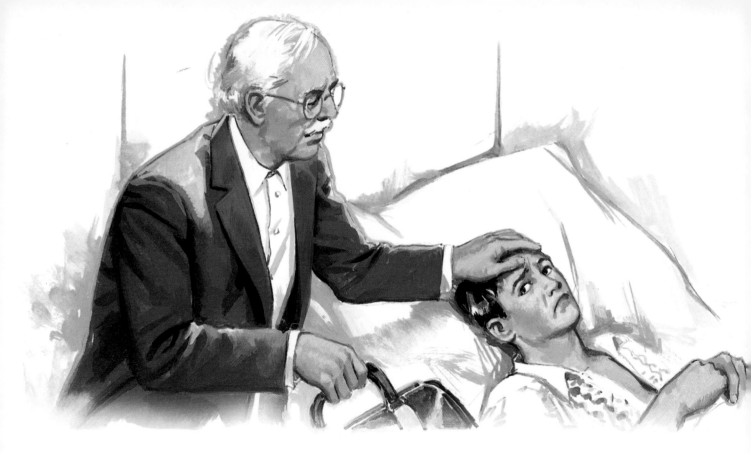

"*Olá.* How goes it?" He smiled at the boy and passed his hand over the boy's forehead. He did not greet the men, nor did he seem to notice Manolo.

"The barber cleaned it and bound it," the boy said feebly, raising on his elbow and then falling back on the pillows.

The men began to move towards the door.

"Stay," the doctor said not looking at them, taking the light blanket off the boy's bed and reaching into his bag for a pair of scissors. "I want Olivar's son to see what a goring looks like. Come here," he commanded, and Manolo moved closer, his heart beating loudly. "Look!" The doctor had cut the bandage and the gauze and pushed them aside. A flamelike, jagged tear, a foot long and several inches deep ran straight from the boy's knee up his thigh. Manolo caught his breath at the sight of it. "Bend down and look here," the doctor said. "Those are puddles of clotted blood. There are about seven different reds beside, all meat. The muscles are purple. The wound is always narrower where the horn enters and wider where it exits. Not pretty, is it?"

Manolo moved away feeling sick; but the voice of the doctor brought him back, and with its sound, so sure and matter of fact, the feeling of sickness left him.

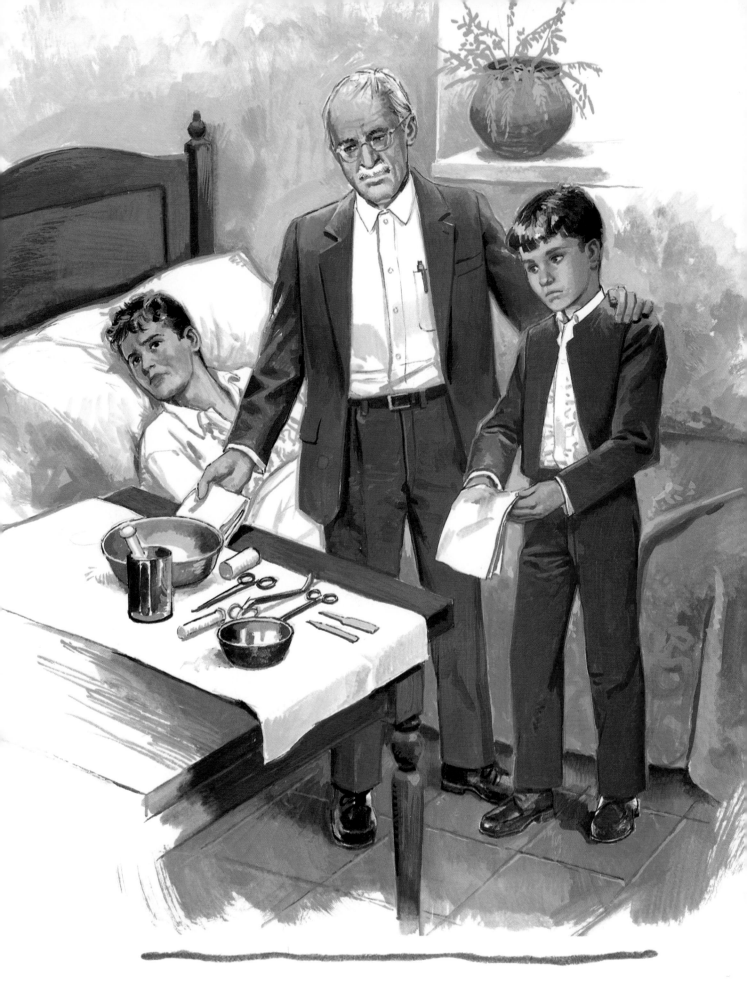

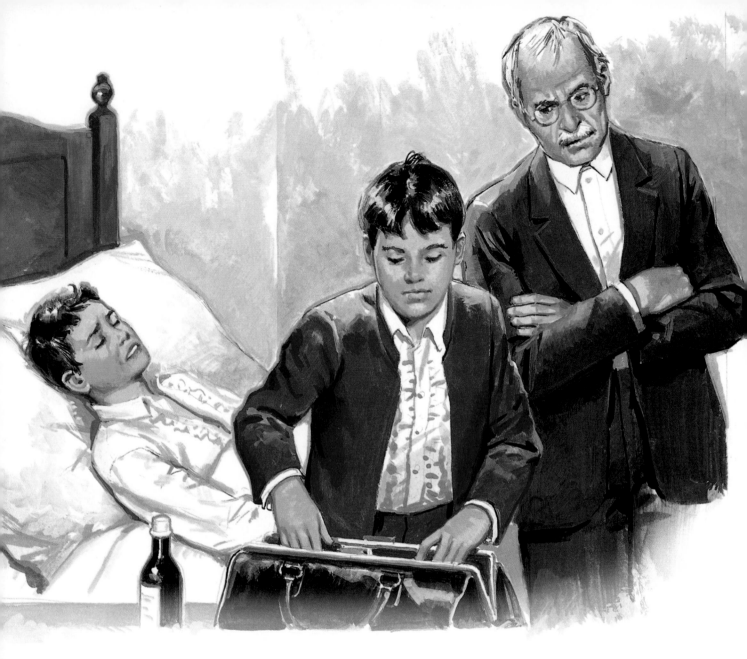

"I'll need your help," the doctor said, still looking at but not touching the wound. "It's a good, clean tear. The barber did his work well. He took the dirt out and cut off the dead flesh."

When he walked to the washbasin, his feet were not shuffling. He scrubbed his hands thoroughly. He put the surgical towel on the bedside table, took some instruments from the bag, put them on the towel, and then reached for a package of gauze pads and put those next to the instruments.

"Hand me those gloves," the doctor said to Manolo, pointing to a pair of rubber gloves in a plastic bag. "Let's see how good a nurse you'd make," he added. "Open the bag without touching the gloves and hold them out to me." Manolo did as he was told.

Manolo watched fascinated, as the doctor's hands moved surely into the wound, exploring the inside of it.

"The horn stayed away from the thigh bone," the doctor said. "He's a lucky boy. What I am doing now," he explained, speaking to Manolo, "is looking for foreign matter: dirt, pieces of horn, or dead flesh. But as I said before, the barber did a very good job of taking all those out of the wound. There is no danger of infection."

The admiration Manolo felt for the doctor was growing with each word, each gesture. No sound came from the pillow. With tenderness the doctor looked away from his work.

"He's fainted," he said with a smile. "Get the bottle of ammonia," he motioned towards the bag, "and a wad of cotton. Moisten the cotton and hold it under his nose."

Again Manolo did as he was told. When he opened the bottle, the strong odor of ammonia invaded his nostrils and spread through the entire room. He bent over the boy and passed the cotton directly under his nose. The boy coughed and jerked his head away.

"Good!" the doctor said watching, "he's not in shock. Just passed out from the pain. He will be fine. What he's got is one of those lucky gorings." His gloved hand pointed to the straight line of the torn flesh. "It's as good a goring as you could wish for, if you were wishing for a good goring. The bad ones are the ones that tear in and change angles. Those are the messy ones, the dangerous ones. But I don't want you to think this is nothing. It's the result of foolishness. Not the beast's, but the man's. The beast is led into the ring, the man walks in himself."

The doctor finished cleaning the wound and then stitched the flesh. Manolo was not asked again to help. He wished the doctor would once more request him to do something. As he watched the magic way the man's hands brought torn flesh together, he thought that what the doctor was doing and had done was the most noble thing a man could do. To bring health back to the sick, to cure the wounded, save the dying. This was what a man should do with his life; this, and not killing bulls.

"It will heal nicely. This one will. But then what?" The doctor walked to the wash basin and began washing the blood off the rubber gloves. "He," he pointed with his head to the boy, "will go on trying to prove that he can be good. And he isn't. But it's a point of honor with him. He will go on trying, and they will give him chances to try because he's fearless and the paying customers know that they will see a goring each time 'El Magnifico' is on the bill. But the tragedy is not that some people are bloodthirsty. The tragedy is that boys like him know of nothing else they want to do. I've grown old looking at wasted lives."

He walked over to Manolo and patted his head.

"The world is a big place," he said gently.

He seemed to want to add something, but he said nothing more. Silently, he put his instruments back in the bag and snapped it shut.

"Thank you for your help," the doctor said to Manolo, but his voice was tired now. The shuffle came back into his steps, and before he reached the door, he looked once again like a very old, very tired, man.

Walking back with the men, Manolo decided that if only he did not have to be a bullfighter he would be a doctor. He wanted to learn how to stop the pain and how to stop the fear of it. If only his father had been a doctor, a famous one, a bullfighters' doctor, then they would expect him to be one, too. And he would study hard. It would not be easy, but he would be learning to do something worthwhile.

He wondered if he were to tell the men, the six men, what he thought he would like to be, if they would listen to him. He looked at the men walking alongside him, talking once again about what they always talked about; and he knew that he would not tell them. He was who he was. A bullfighter's and not a doctor's son, and they expected him to be like his father. Maybe someday he could tell them.

Shadow of a Bull

Meet the Author

Maia Wojciechowska has lived an exciting, adventurous life. She was born in Warsaw, Poland, and came to the United States in 1942. Her jobs have included such things as detective, motorcycle racer, bullfighter, tennis player, and translator. In one year, she had 72 jobs!

Many of Ms. Wojciechowska's books are about the problem of trying to fit in with the rest of the world, but not fitting so well that you lose yourself. She said, "Shadow of a Bull *was mostly about pride and being locked in. . . . The word* pride *encompasses so much—honor and dignity and self-esteem. That sort of pride sometimes—most of the time—makes life harder than it needs to be. But without pride life is less.*"

Meet the Illustrator

Ramon Gonzalez Vicente was born in Salamanca, Spain, where he also studied art. Later, he went to Barcelona, which is also in Spain, where he worked as an artistic director and illustrator for a publisher. Mr. Vicente has also illustrated for publishers in the United States, England, Germany, and other European countries. He has created illustrations for many books, but his favorite subject is children's literature.

Theme Connections

Within the Selection

Record your answers to the questions below in the Response Journal section of your Writer's Notebook. In small groups, report the ideas you wrote. Discuss your ideas with the rest of your group. Then choose a person to report your group's answers to the class.

- What would Manolo have been afraid of if he became a bullfighter?
- Why did Manolo decide that he wanted to become a doctor?
- Why did Manolo choose not to tell the men he wanted to become a doctor?

Across Selections

How are Dr. Dan from "Sewed Up His Heart" and the doctor in "Shadow of a Bull" alike?

Beyond the Selection

- Think about how "Shadow of a Bull" adds to what you know about medicine.
- Add items to the Concept/Question Board about medicine.

Sometimes life gets very hard. People live through natural disasters and wars and terrible accidents. How do they do it? What helps them to survive all of these things?

I'm still having diff
finding fresh water
Luckily there har
been enough wil
berries to hold m
over. I don't kr
what to do for
now that the
have run out.
cloudy tonigh
Maybe it w
tomorrow.
I can't gir
after all, I'v

Island of the Blue Dolphins

from *Island of the Blue Dolphins*
by Scott O'Dell
illustrated by Russ Walks

With the help of the white man's ship, Karana's people have fled their island to escape the Aleuts, their enemies. In their haste Karana is left behind on the island. As she waits for a ship to return to rescue her, Karana's hopes begin to fade.

Summer is the best time on the Island of the Blue Dolphins. The sun is warm then and the winds blow milder out of the west, sometimes out of the south.

It was during these days that the ship might return and now I spent most of my time on the rock, looking out from the high headland into the east, toward the country where my people had gone, across the sea that was never-ending.

Once while I watched I saw a small object which I took to be the ship, but a stream of water rose from it and I knew that it was a whale spouting. During those summer days I saw nothing else.

322

The first storm of winter ended my hopes. If the white men's ship were coming for me it would have come during the time of good weather. Now I would have to wait until winter was gone, maybe longer.

The thought of being alone on the island while so many suns rose from the sea and went slowly back into the sea filled my heart with loneliness. I had not felt so lonely before because I was sure that the ship would return as Matasaip had said it would. Now my hopes were dead. Now I was really alone. I could not eat much, nor could I sleep without dreaming terrible dreams.

The storm blew out of the north, sending big waves against the island and winds so strong that I was unable to stay on the rock. I moved my bed to the foot of the rock and for protection kept a fire going throughout the night. I slept there five times. The first night the dogs came and stood outside the ring made by the fire. I killed three of them with arrows, but not the leader, and they did not come again.

On the sixth day, when the storm had ended, I went to the place where the canoes had been hidden, and let myself down over the cliff. This part of the shore was sheltered from the wind and I found the canoes just as they had been left. The dried food was still good, but the water was stale, so I went back to the spring and filled a fresh basket.

I had decided during the days of the storm, when I had given up hope of seeing the ship, that I would take one of the canoes and go to the country that lay toward the east. I remembered how Kimki, before he

had gone, had asked the advice of his ancestors who had lived many ages in the past, who had come to the island from that country, and likewise the advice of Zuma, the medicine man who held power over the wind and the seas. But these things I could not do, for Zuma had been killed by the Aleuts, and in all my life I had never been able to speak with the dead, though many times I had tried.

Yet I cannot say that I was really afraid as I stood there on the shore. I knew that my ancestors had crossed the sea in their canoes, coming from that place which lay beyond. Kimki, too had crossed the sea. I was not nearly so skilled with a canoe as these men, but I must say that whatever might befall me on the endless waters did not trouble me. It meant far less than the thought of staying on the island alone, without a home or companions, pursued by wild dogs, where everything reminded me of those who were dead and those who had gone away.

Of the four canoes stored there against the cliff, I chose the smallest, which was still very heavy because it could carry six people. The task that faced me was to push it down the rocky shore and into the water, a distance four or five times its length.

This I did by first removing all the large rocks in front of the canoe. I then filled in all these holes with pebbles and along this path laid down long strips of kelp, making a slippery bed. The shore was steep and once I got the canoe to move with its own weight, it slid down the path and into the water.

The sun was in the west when I left the shore. The sea was calm behind the high cliffs. Using the two-bladed paddle I quickly skirted the south part of the island. As I reached the sandspit the wind struck. I was paddling from the back of the canoe because you can go faster kneeling there, but I could not handle it in the wind.

Kneeling in the middle of the canoe, I paddled hard and did not pause until I had gone through the tides that run fast around the sandspit. There were many small waves and I was soon wet, but as I came out from behind the spit the spray lessened and the waves grew long and rolling. Though it would have been easier to go the way they slanted, this would have taken me in the wrong direction. I therefore kept them on my left hand, as well as the island, which grew smaller and smaller, behind me.

At dusk I looked back. The Island of the Blue Dolphins had disappeared. This was the first time that I felt afraid.

There were only hills and valleys of water around me now. When I was in a valley I could see nothing and when the canoe rose out of it, only the ocean stretching away and away.

Night fell and I drank from the basket. The water cooled my throat.

The sea was black and there was no difference between it and the sky. The waves made no sound among themselves, only faint noises as they went under the canoe or struck against it. Sometimes the noises seemed angry and at other times like people laughing. I was not hungry because of my fear.

The first star made me feel less afraid. It came out low in the sky and it was in front of me, toward the east. Other stars began to appear all around, but it was this one I kept my gaze upon. It was in the figure that we call a serpent, a star which shone green and which I knew. Now and then it was hidden by mist, yet it always came out brightly again.

Without this star I would have been lost, for the waves never changed. They came always from the same direction and in a manner that kept pushing me away from the place I wanted to reach. For this reason the canoe made a path in the black water like a snake. But somehow I kept moving toward the star which shone in the east.

This star rose high and then I kept the North Star on my left hand, the one we call "the star that does not move." The wind grew quiet. Since it always died down when the night was half over, I knew how long I had been traveling and how far away the dawn was.

About this time I found that the canoe was leaking. Before dark I had emptied one of the baskets in which food was stored and used it to dip out the water that came over the sides. The water that now moved around my knees was not from the waves.

I stopped paddling and worked with the basket until the bottom of the canoe was almost dry. Then I searched around, feeling in the dark along the smooth planks, and found the place near the bow where the water was seeping through a crack as long as my hand and the width of a finger. Most of the time it was out of the sea, but it leaked whenever the canoe dipped forward in the waves.

The places between the planks were filled with black pitch which we gather along the shore. Lacking this, I tore a piece of fiber from my skirt and pressed it into the crack, which held back the water.

Dawn broke in a clear sky and as the sun came out of the waves I saw that it was far off on my left. During the night I had drifted south of the place I wished to go, so I changed my direction and paddled along the path made by the rising sun.

There was no wind on this morning and the long waves went quietly under the canoe. I therefore moved faster than during the night.

I was very tired, but more hopeful than I had been since I left the island. If the good weather did not change I would cover many leagues before dark. Another night and another day might bring me within sight of the shore toward which I was going.

Not long after dawn, while I was thinking of this strange place and what it would look like, the canoe began to leak again. This crack was between the same planks, but was a larger one and close to where I was kneeling.

The fiber I tore from my skirt and pushed into the crack held back most of the water which seeped in whenever the canoe rose and fell with the waves. Yet I could see that the planks were weak from one end to the other, probably from the canoe being stored so long in the sun, and that they might open along their whole length if the waves grew rougher.

It was suddenly clear to me that it was dangerous to go on. The voyage would take two more days, perhaps longer. By turning back to the island I would not have nearly so far to travel.

Still I could not make up my mind to do so. The sea was calm and I had come far. The thought of turning back after all this labor was more than I could bear. Even greater was the thought of the deserted island I would return to, of living there alone and forgotten. For how many suns and how many moons?

The canoe drifted idly on the calm sea while these thoughts went over and over in my mind, but when I saw the water seeping through the crack again, I picked up the paddle. There was no choice except to turn back toward the island.

I knew that only by the best of fortune would I ever reach it.

The wind did not blow until the sun was overhead. Before that time I covered a good distance, pausing only when it was necessary to dip water from the canoe. With the wind I went more slowly and had to stop more often because of the water spilling over the sides, but the leak did not grow worse.

This was my first good fortune. The next was when a swarm of dolphins appeared. They came swimming out of the west, but as they saw the canoe they turned around in a great circle and began to follow me. They swam up slowly and so close that I could see their eyes, which are large and the color of the ocean. Then they swam on ahead of the canoe, crossing back and forth in front of it, diving in and out, as if they were weaving a piece of cloth with their broad snouts.

Dolphins are animals of good omen. It made me happy to have them swimming around the canoe, and though my hands had begun to bleed from the chafing of the paddle, just watching them made me forget the pain. I was very lonely before they appeared, but now I felt that I had friends with me and did not feel the same.

The blue dolphins left me shortly before dusk. They left as quickly as they had come, going on into the west, but for a long time I could see the last of the sun shining on them. After night fell I could still see them in my thoughts and it was because of this that I kept on paddling when I wanted to lie down and sleep.

More than anything, it was the blue dolphins that took me back home.

Fog came with the night, yet from time to time I could see the star that stands high in the west, the red star called Magat which is part of the figure that looks like a crawfish and is known by that name. The crack in the planks grew wider so I had to stop often to fill it with fiber and to dip out the water.

The night was very long, longer than the night before. Twice I dozed kneeling there in the canoe, though I was more afraid than I had ever been. But the morning broke clear and in front of me lay the dim line of the island like a great fish sunning itself on the sea.

I reached it before the sun was high, the sandspit and its tides that bore me into the shore. My legs were stiff from kneeling and as the canoe struck the sand I fell when I rose to climb out. I crawled through the shallow water and up the beach. There I lay for a long time, hugging the sand in happiness.

I was too tired to think of the wild dogs. Soon I fell asleep.

Island of the Blue Dolphins

Meet the Author

Scott O'Dell was born in Los Angeles, California. His father was a railroad worker and so the family moved often, but they always lived by the ocean. One of their homes was on Rattlesnake Island, near Los Angeles, where they lived in a house on stilts. From the house they could watch sailing ships go by.

Island of the Blue Dolphins is based on a true story. The rest of it, according to Mr. O'Dell, *"came directly from the memory of the years I lived at Rattlesnake Island and San Pedro. From the days when, with the other boys of my age, I voyaged out on summer mornings in search of the world."*

Theme Connections

Within the Selection

Writer's Notebook

Record your answers to the questions below in the Response Journal section of your Writer's Notebook. In small groups, report the ideas you wrote. Discuss your ideas with the rest of your group. Then choose a person to report your group's answers to the class.

- On Karana's first night on the canoe, she could not tell the difference between the sky and the sea. How did Karana survive, stay on course, and not get lost?
- How did Karana survive on the sea when her canoe began to leak?

Across Selections

How is Karana's situation similar to "Voyage of the Frog"? How is it different?

Beyond the Selection

- If you were left behind on an island like Karana, what would you do to survive? Would you look for food or shelter? Would you leave the island?
- Think about how "Island of the Blue Dolphins" adds to what you know about survival.
- Add items to the Concept/Question Board about survival.

Focus Questions What makes it easier to survive in some places than in others? What steps would you take to survive in the Arctic?

Arctic Explorer:

THE STORY OF MATTHEW HENSON

by Jeri Ferris

Matthew Henson was the first African-American explorer to reach the North Pole. Before he made this famous expedition, he went on several trips to the arctic region with Robert Peary. During these trips, Henson learned the skills that would make him a great explorer. In this excerpt about Henson's first arctic journey, Peary has planned an expedition to North Greenland. He has little money and has asked Henson to help him without pay. Henson is eager to go. His job is to learn the survival techniques used by the Eskimos as they face the harsh, cold climate.

Members of the 1891–1892 North Greenland Expedition (left to right): Cook, Henson, Astrup, Verhoeff, and Gibson. Josephine and Robert Peary are standing in back. John Verhoeff fell into a crevasse in Greenland in the spring of 1892 while exploring and was never seen again.

"It was in June 1891," Matt Henson wrote, "that I started on my first trip to the Arctic regions, as a member of what was known as the 'North Greenland Expedition.' "

America's newspapers predicted disaster. A small group of inexperienced men trying to survive in a frozen place that had killed better men than they? Impossible. Then reporters learned that a woman was going too—the new Mrs. Peary. "Now we know he's crazy!" said one newspaper about Peary.

Josephine Peary listed the expedition members in her diary: "Dr. Cook, Mr. Gibson, Mr. Astrup, Mr. Verhoeff, and Mr. Peary's faithful attendant in his surveying labors in Nicaragua, Matt Henson." The ship, *Kite*, was so small that the people and supplies barely fit. They were going to be gone for a year and a half, so they needed a lot of supplies. There were crates of food (enough for two and a half years, just to be safe) and cans of pemmican, the beef-fat-raisin mixture that the men and dogs would eat while crossing the ice cap. There were skis and snowshoes, guns and ammunition, sledges, woolen clothing, a stove, pots and pans, and camera equipment. And after the last one hundred tons of coal was piled on deck, Matt could hardly find a place to set down his hammer and nails while he put together the wood frame for their base camp house.

The *Kite* plunged on through the Atlantic, rolling and pitching and sending all the passengers except Henson and Peary to bed seasick. On June 21 Matt saw Greenland for the first time. Its steep, wild cliffs rose straight up from the icy water. As the *Kite* steamed north through Baffin Bay, Matt saw hundreds of icebergs—gleaming blue and white chunks of ice—from the size of small sailboats to that of enormous floating mountains. In the valleys of Greenland, Matt saw glaciers that looked like thick flowing cream, frozen into white walls. And on the very top of Greenland lay the five hundred thousand square miles of silent ice cap. Matt couldn't see it yet, but he knew it was there, waiting.

The *Kite* pushed farther north into heavy ice, which floated on the water like a field of white. There were splits and cracks in the ice, and through these cracks (called leads) the *Kite* forced its way. Sometimes there were no leads at all, and the captain would shout for more steam power. The *Kite* would dash forward and smash against the ice. Sometimes the ice would break, and the ship could continue. Sometimes it would not, and the ship would have to back up and try another way.

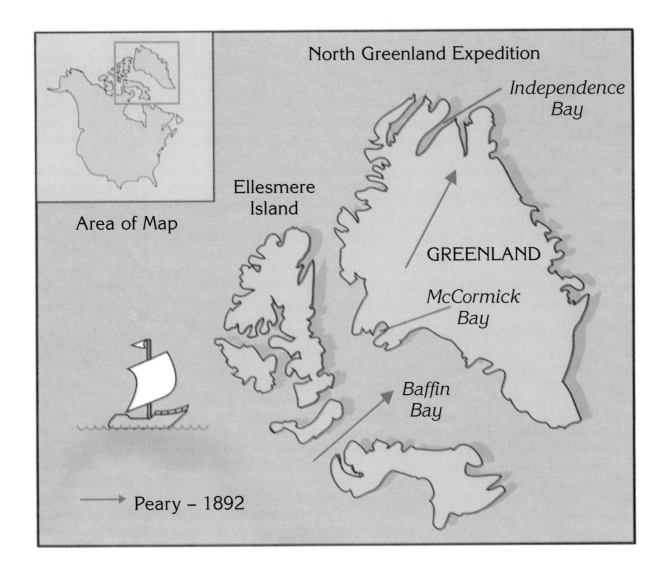

North Greenland Expedition

Independence Bay

Area of Map

Ellesmere Island

GREENLAND

McCormick Bay

Baffin Bay

Peary – 1892

When the *Kite* was as far north as it could go, it dropped anchor in McCormick Bay, Greenland, and the crew unloaded the supplies. At the end of July, the *Kite* sailed for home, leaving Matthew Henson, the Pearys, and the other four men to survive the arctic winter. (A ship could only get through the ice in the summer, and the long, dangerous trip over the ice cap could only be started in the spring with the return of 24-hour sunlight. So the men had to wait in the Arctic through the dark winter months.) Matt immediately began putting up their sturdy house, to make sure they would survive.

August 8 was Matt's 25th birthday. For the first time in his life, he had a birthday celebration. Mrs. Peary fixed mock turtle soup, stew of little auk (a bird the size of a robin) with green peas, eider duck, baked beans, corn, tomatoes, and apricot pie. Matt remembered the delight of that dinner long after the tin plates were put away. Seventeen years later he said of that day, "To have a party given in my honor touched me deeply."

While Matt finished the small wooden house, the other men went to find Eskimos to join their group. (The men would have to use sign language because none of them spoke Eskimo.) Peary needed Eskimo men to help hunt polar bears and seals and walruses and reindeer and caribou and foxes for furs and meat. He needed Eskimo women to chew the furs and sew them into pants and coats. The thickest wool coat from home would be useless in the Arctic; they had to have clothing made of the same fur that kept the arctic animals warm. In exchange for their work, Peary would give the Eskimos pots and pans, needles, tools, and other useful items.

Matt and an Eskimo friend return from a hunting expedition.

On August 18 the men returned, and with them were four Eskimos: Ikwa, his wife, and their two children. The Eskimos walked slowly up to Matt and the Pearys. Then Ikwa stepped closer to Matt and looked at him carefully. His brown face lit up with excitement as he spoke rapidly to Matt in Eskimo.

Matt shook his head and tried to explain that he didn't understand, but Ikwa kept talking. Finally Ikwa took Matt's arm, pointed at the black man's skin, and said, "Inuit, Inuit!" Then Matt understood. "Inuit" must be what the Eskimos called themselves. Ikwa thought Matt was another Eskimo because he had brown skin, just as the Eskimos did. Matt looked down at the short fur-covered man, who smelled like seals and whale blubber. He looked into Ikwa's shining black eyes and smiled. From that moment on, the Eskimos called Matt "Miy Paluk," which meant "dear little Matthew," and they loved him as a brother.

In September Matt, Ikwa, Dr. Cook, and the Pearys took the whale boat and went to find more Eskimos. They didn't find a single Eskimo, but they did find some unfriendly walruses.

It began when the boat got mixed up with some walruses (250 walruses, Mrs. Peary said) that were peacefully fishing for clams. One after another the startled walruses poked their heads out of the water, spitting out clam shells and flashing their white tusks. Then an angry bull walrus roared, "Ook, ook, ook!" and headed straight for the boat. The water foamed and boiled as the rest of the herd charged right behind him, speeding along like torpedoes, all roaring their battle cry and tossing their enormous gray wrinkled heads. Matt and the others knew that just one tusk through the bottom of the boat would be the end of them. Ikwa shouted and pounded on the boat to frighten the walruses away, but the walruses weren't frightened. In fact, they were so angry that they tossed the boat up and down furiously. Bracing their feet, Matt and the others fired their guns while Mrs. Peary sat in the bottom of the boat and reloaded the guns as fast as she could. At last the walruses gave up. They dove to the bottom and disappeared, leaving a shaky group of explorers in a still-rocking boat.

Robert Peary

By the end of September, the dull red sun dipped lower each day and finally did not appear at all over the southern horizon. Every day was like a glorious sunset, with a golden, crimson glow on the mountain peaks. Then there was no sunset anymore, just one long night.

By the time the sun was gone, not to return until February, several Eskimo families were living at the camp in stone igloos (snow igloos were only used when the Eskimos traveled, following the animals whose meat and skins they needed).

That winter the men hunted by the full moon—by moonlight so bright that the blue-white ice sparkled. Peary planned for the spring trek. Astrup taught the men to ski. Gibson studied bird and animal life. Verhoeff studied rocks. Dr. Cook *wanted* to study the Eskimos by taking their pictures and measuring their bodies, but the Eskimos refused to let him near them. Finally Matt realized that they were afraid Dr. Cook would go home and make new people from the Eskimo pattern. So Matt got Ikwa to understand, and Dr. Cook got his pictures.

Meanwhile Matt studied with his Eskimo teachers. They taught him easy things, such as never to stand with his feet apart or his elbows sticking out, as this let the cold air close to his body. They taught him hard things, such as how to speak Eskimo. Matt learned, for example, that there is no Eskimo word for "hole." Instead there is a different word for "hole in igloo" or "hole in bear skin" or anything that has a hole.

Matt learned why the Eskimos smelled like walruses and seals and blubber——they *ate* walruses and seals and blubber. They also ate reindeer and polar bears and little auks. They ate the meat while it was still warm and raw and bloody; they ate it when it was frozen solid, by chipping off bite-size chunks; and sometimes they boiled it. They never ate carrots or beans or potatoes or apples or chocolate. In the Arctic the only food came from the bodies of the animals that lived there.

Matt learned how the Eskimos made the skin of a polar bear into clothing. Once the Eskimo man had killed the bear and removed its skin and scraped it as clean as he could, it was up to the Eskimo woman to finish. She had to chew the skin until all the fat was gone and it was completely soft. All day long the woman would fold the skin (with the fur folded inside), chew back and forth along the fold, make a new fold, and continue. It took two days to chew one skin. Then the woman would rest her jaws for one day before beginning on another skin. After the skin had dried, she would cut it up and sew it into a coat or pants. Her needle was made of bone, her thread was made from animal sinew, and her stitches had to be very, very tiny so not a whisper of wind could get through.

An Eskimo woman makes clothing out of an animal skin. Old Eskimo women had very short, flat teeth from chewing skins to soften them.

For Matt's winter outfit the women made stockings of arctic hare fur, tall boots of sealskin, polar bear fur pants, a shirt made of 150 auk skins (with the feathers next to Matt's skin), a reindeer fur jacket, and a white fox fur hood that went around his face. His mittens were made of bearskin with the fur inside.

But the piercing, freezing cold, colder than the inside of a freezer, took Matt's breath away, and the howling arctic wind drove needles of snow and ice into his face. Even his new sealskin boots felt terrible, until he learned to stand still after he put them on in the morning. Then they would freeze instantly to the shape of his feet and wouldn't hurt as much.

Once Matt had his fur clothes, cold or not, he was ready to learn how to drive a sledge pulled by the 80- to 120-pound Eskimo dogs. But first, if a dog got loose, Matt had to catch him. He would drop a piece of frozen meat on the snow and dive on top of the dog as the animal snatched the meat. Then he would "grab the nearest thing grabbable—ear, leg, or bunch of hair," slip the harness over the dog's head, push his front legs through, and tie him to a rock. Finally, Matt said, he would lick his dog bites.

When the dogs were in their traces, they spread out like a fan in front of the sledge. The king dog, who was the strongest and fiercest, led the way in the center. Matt had watched the Eskimos drive the dogs and knew that they didn't use the 30-foot sealskin whip *on* the dogs but *over* the dogs. The trick was to make the whip curl out and crack like a gunshot right over the ear of the dog who needed it. Matt stepped up behind the sledge, shouted, "Huk, huk!" and tried to crack the whip. The dogs sat down. Matt tried again and again and again. After many tries and lots of help from his Eskimo teachers, Matt learned how to snap the whip over the dogs' ears and make them start off at a trot. Then he had to learn how to turn them (they didn't have reins, as horses do), how to make them stop, and how to make them jump over open water with the sledge flying behind.

Dogs in their traces fan out in front of a sledge. If they are starving, the dogs will eat their traces, which are made of sealskin.

There were five Eskimo families at the camp, each family with its own stone igloo. At first it was hard for Matt to go inside the igloos because of their peculiar smell (Eskimos did not take baths, and Matt said that an Eskimo mother cleans her baby just as a mother cat cleans her kittens), but he didn't want to be rude, so he got used to it. Opposite the entrance hole was the bed platform, built of stone and covered with furs. At the end of the bed platform was a small stone lamp, filled with whale blubber for fuel, with moss for the wick. This little lamp was the light and heat and cook stove for the igloo. The Eskimo woman melted snow in a small pan over the lamp and used the water for cooking meat and for drinking. (Eskimos did not build fires for heating or cooking.)

Matt learned how to build a snow igloo when he hunted with the Eskimos, far from the camp. Two Eskimos could cut 50 to 60 snow blocks (each block 6-by-18-by-24-inches) with their long snow knives and build a whole igloo in just one hour. One man would stand in the center and place the blocks in an 8-foot circle around himself. He would add more blocks, spiraling round and round, with the blocks closing in on the center as they rose higher, until the top snow blocks fit perfectly against each other and the roof was complete. Then they would carry in the furs and cooking lamp, and it was home. A chunk of frozen meat, perhaps part of a walrus, might be in the middle of the igloo, handy for snacks and also a good footstool. Snow igloos even had shelves. The Eskimos would stick their snowshoes into the wall and lay mittens on the snowshoe shelf to dry.

The dogs, who had thick silver gray or white hair with a layer of short fine fur underneath to keep them warm, lived outdoors in the snow. They would curl into balls, cover their noses with their tails, and sleep, warm as muffins (usually), even if it was –50°F.

Dogs curl up outside Peary's igloo.

During the full moons Matt and the Eskimos hunted reindeer and arctic hares. The large pure white hares themselves could not be seen against the white snow, only their black shadows. They were like an army of frozen or leaping ghosts. And in the deep blackness of the arctic night, Matt saw hundreds of shooting stars, so thick and close they seemed to burst like rockets. While he watched the stars, the Eskimos explained that what Matt called the Big Dipper was really seven reindeer eating grass, and the constellation he called the Pleiades was really a team of dogs chasing a polar bear.

The Eskimos had no tables or chairs, no books or paper or writing, no money or bills to pay, no king or chief, no doctors or dentists, no schools or churches, no laws, and no wars. They needed shelter from the cold, strong dogs to pull their sledges, and animals they could hunt for furs and meat. Several families usually lived close together to help each other. If one man killed a walrus, he would share it with everyone. Perhaps in a few days another man would kill a bear or a reindeer; then that man would share it too.

Meanwhile in the wooden house, there was more to eat than raw meat, and there was a new cook. Mrs. Peary wrote in her diary for November 17, 1891, "Matt got supper tonight, and will from now until May 1 prepare all the meals under my supervision." For Christmas, at least, he didn't do all the cooking. Mrs. Peary prepared arctic hare pie with green peas, reindeer with cranberry sauce, corn and tomatoes, plum pudding, and apricot pie. Then, wrote Mrs. Peary, "Matt cleared everything away."

In February the sun returned. For days and days before it actually appeared, the sky was a magnificent dawn of pink, blue, crimson, and deep yellow, with rosy clouds. Then the sun appeared in the south at noon, but just for a moment the first day. Each day it rose a little higher. The crystal

Robert Peary's house on McCormick Bay.

clear water in the bay was deep blue, and the air was thick with the sound of wings and songs as thousands of birds swooped and swarmed over the water and up the cliffs.

But Greenland's ice cap, which Matt intended to cross, was a frozen, lifeless desert of snow and howling wind and glaciers and deep crevasses. Even though Matt always covered the inside of his boots with soft dried moss for insulation, his heel froze when he helped haul boxes of pemmican and biscuits up to the ice cap in the beginning of May. (Freezing is very serious. The blood stops moving in the frozen part, and the skin and muscle can soon die.) Matt, who was the best at driving the dogs and at speaking the Eskimo language, had planned to be one of the first men to cross the ice cap, but Peary sent him back to the base camp. There were three reasons: one was the frozen heel; another was that someone had to protect Mrs. Peary at the camp; and the third was that Peary believed an explorer should have a college education in order to know what to do in an emergency.

During the short summer, while the others were gone, Matt went hunting so everyone would have plenty of fresh meat; he learned more of the Eskimo language; his foot healed; and he protected Mrs. Peary from danger.

In the end only Peary and Astrup actually crossed the ice cap. All the others turned back. The Eskimos, who feared Kokoyah, the evil spirit of the ice cap, refused to go at all. Peary did discover a large bay at the northeast corner of Greenland, which he named Independence Bay, but he did not find out if there was a way to get to the North Pole by land. He would have to try again. He asked Matt to come along again too.

Arctic Explorer:

THE STORY OF MATTHEW HENSON

Meet the Author

Jeri Ferris grew up on a small Nebraska farm, with her own horse at home and a library nearby. She once said she had *"the ideal writer's childhood."*

Ms. Ferris taught for several years. When she realized how hard it was to find biographies of great and brave people, she began writing them herself. *"My goal is to make these determined men and women inescapably alive, to make their deeds inescapably real, and to plant the seeds of similar determination and self-confidence in the children who read about them. My goal is that children, no matter their ethnic and social backgrounds and despite the obstacles, will say to themselves, 'I, too, can make a difference.'"*

Theme Connections

Within the Selection

Record your answers to the questions below in the Response Journal section of your Writer's Notebook. In small groups, report the ideas you wrote. Discuss your ideas with the rest of your group. Then choose a person to report your group's answers to the class.

- What steps did Matthew Henson and the other members of his expedition take in order to survive the Arctic winter?
- What did Matthew Henson learn from the Eskimos that helped him survive the harsh Arctic climate?

Across Selections

What other selections have you read in which the main character must survive harsh conditions like Matthew Henson did?

Beyond the Selection

- Think about how "Arctic Explorer: The Story of Matthew Henson" adds to what you know about survival.
- Add items to the Concept/Question Board about survival.

McBroom and the Big Wind

Sid Fleischman
illustrated by Walter Lorraine

I can't deny it——it does get a mite windy out here on the prairie. Why, just last year a blow came ripping across our farm and carried off a pail of sweet milk. The next day it came back for the cow.

But that wasn't the howlin', scowlin', almighty *big* wind I aim to tell you about. That was just a common little prairie breeze. No account, really. Hardly worth bragging about.

It was the *big* wind that broke my leg. I don't expect you to believe that——yet. I'd best start with some smaller weather and work up to that bonebreaker.

I remember distinctly the first prairie wind that came scampering along after we bought our wonderful one-acre farm. My, that land is rich. Best topsoil in the country. There isn't a thing that won't grow in our rich topsoil, and fast as lightning.

The morning I'm talking about our oldest boys were helping me to shingle the roof. I had bought a keg of nails, but it turned out those nails were a whit short. We buried them in our wonderful topsoil and watered them down. In five or ten minutes those nails grew a full half-inch.

So there we were, up on the roof, hammering down shingles. There wasn't a cloud in the sky at first. The younger boys were shooting marbles all over the farm and the girls were jumping rope.

When I had pounded down the last shingle I said to myself, "Josh McBroom, that's a mighty stout roof. It'll last a hundred years."

Just then I felt a small draft on the back of my neck. A moment later one of the girls——it was Polly, as I recall——shouted up to me. "Pa," she said, "do jackrabbits have wings?"

I laughed. "No, Polly."

"Then how come there's a flock of jackrabbits flying over the house?"

I looked up. Mercy! Rabbits were flapping their ears across the sky in a perfect V formation, northbound. I knew then we were in for a slight blow.

"Run, everybody!" I shouted to the young'uns. I didn't want the wind picking them up by the ears. "Will*jill*hester*chester*peter*polly*tim*tom*mary*larry*and-little*clarinda*—— in the house! Scamper!"

The clothesline was already beginning to whip around like a jump rope. My dear wife, Melissa, who had been baking a heap of biscuits, threw open the door. In we dashed and not a moment too soon. The wind was snapping at our heels like a pack of wolves. It aimed to barge right in and make itself at home! A prairie wind has no manners at all.

We slammed the door in its teeth. Now, the wind didn't take that politely. It rammed and battered at the door while all of us pushed and shoved to hold the door shut. My, it was a battle! How the house creaked and trembled!

"Push, my lambs!" I yelled. "Shove!"

At times the door planks bent like barrel staves. But we held that roaring wind out. When it saw there was no getting past us, the zephyr sneaked around the house to the back door. However, our oldest boy, Will, was too smart for it. He piled Mama's heap of fresh biscuits against the back door. My dear wife, Melissa, is a wonderful cook, but her biscuits *are* terribly heavy. They made a splendid door stop.

But what worried me most was our wondrous rich topsoil. That thieving wind was apt to make off with it, leaving us with a trifling hole in the ground.

"Shove, my lambs!" I said. "Push!"

The battle raged on for an hour. Finally the wind gave up butting its fool head against the door. With a great angry sigh it turned and whisked itself away, scattering fence pickets as it went.

We all took a deep breath and I opened the door a crack. Hardly a leaf now stirred on the ground. A bird began to twitter. I rushed outside to our poor one-acre farm.

Mercy! What I saw left me popeyed. "Melissa!" I shouted with glee. "Will*jill*hester*chester*peter*polly*-tim*tom*mary*larry*andlittle*clarinda*! Come here, my lambs! Look!"

We all gazed in wonder. Our topsoil was still there—every bit. Bless those youngsters! The boys had left their marbles all over the field, and the marbles had grown as large as boulders. There they sat, huge agates and sparkling glassies, holding down our precious topsoil.

But that rambunctious wind didn't leave empty-handed. It ripped off our new shingle roof. Pulled out the nails, too. We found out later the wind had shingled every gopher hole in the next county.

Now that was a strong draft. But it wasn't a *big* wind. Nothing like the kind that broke my leg. Still, that prairie gust was an education to me.

"Young'uns," I said, after we'd rolled those giant marbles down the hill. "The next uninvited breeze that comes along, we'll be ready for it. There are two sides to every flapjack. It appears to me the wind can be downright useful on our farm if we let it know who's boss."

The next gusty day that came along, we put it to work for us. I made a wind plow. I rigged a bedsheet and tackle to our old farm plow. Soon as a breeze sprung up I'd go tacking to and fro over the farm, plowing as I went. Our son Chester once plowed the entire farm in under three minutes.

On Thanksgiving morning Mama told the girls to pluck a large turkey for dinner. They didn't much like that chore, but a prairie gust arrived just in time. The girls stuck the turkey out the window. The wind plucked that turkey clean, pinfeathers and all.

Oh, we got downright glad to see a blow come along. The young'uns were always wanting to go out and play in the wind, but Mama was afraid they'd be carried off. So I made them wind shoes—made 'em out of heavy iron skillets. Out in the breeze those shoes felt light as feathers. The girls would jump rope with the clothesline. The wind spun the rope, of course.

Many a time I saw the youngsters put on their wind shoes and go clumping outside with a big tin funnel and all the empty bottles and jugs they could round up. They'd cork the containers jam full of prairie wind.

Then, come summer, when there wasn't a breath of air, they'd uncork a bottle or two of fresh winter wind and enjoy the cool breeze.

Of course, we had to windproof the farm every fall. We'd plant the field in buttercups. My, they were slippery——all that butter, I guess. The wind would slip and slide over the farm without being able to get a purchase on the topsoil. By then the boys and I had reshingled the roof. We used screws instead of nails.

Mercy! Then came the *big* wind!

It started out gently enough. There were a few jackrabbits and some crows flying backward through the air. Nothing out of the ordinary.

Of course the girls went outside to jump the clothesline and the boys got busy laying up bottles of wind for summer. Mama had just baked a batch of fresh biscuits. My, they did smell good! I ate a dozen or so hot out of the oven. And that turned out to be a terrible mistake.

Outside, the wind was picking up ground speed and scattering fence posts as it went.

"Will*jill*hester*chester*peter*polly*tim*tom*mary*larry*and-little*clarinda*!" I shouted. "Inside, my lambs! That wind is getting ornery!"

The young'uns came trooping in and pulled off their wind shoes. And not a moment too soon. The clothesline began to whip around so fast it seemed to disappear. Then we saw a hen house come flying through the air, with the hens still in it.

The sky was turning dark and mean. The wind came out of the far north, howling and shrieking and shaking the house. In the cupboard, cups chattered in their saucers.

Soon we noticed big balls of fur rolling along the prairie like tumbleweeds. Turned out they were timber wolves from up north. And then an old hollow log came spinning across the farm and split against my chopping stump. Out rolled a black bear, and was he in a temper! He had been trying to hibernate and didn't take kindly to being awakened. He gave out a roar and looked around for somebody to chase. He saw us at the windows and decided we would do.

The mere sight of him scared the young'uns and they huddled together, holding hands, near the fireplace.

I got down my shotgun and opened a window. That was a *mistake!* Two things happened at once. The bear was coming on and in my haste I forgot to calculate the direction of the wind. It came shrieking along the side of the house and when I poked the gunbarrel out the window, well, the wind bent it like an angle iron. That buckshot flew due south. I found out later it brought down a brace of ducks over Mexico.

But worse than that, when I threw open the window such a draft came in that our young'uns *were sucked up through the chimney!* Holding hands, they were carried away like a string of sausages.

Mama near fainted away. "My dear Melissa," I exclaimed. "Don't you worry! I'll get our young'uns back!"

I fetched a rope and rushed outside. I could see the young'uns up in the sky and blowing south.

I could also see the bear and he could see me. He gave a growl with a mouthful of teeth like rusty nails. He rose up on his hind legs and came toward me with his eyes glowing red as fire.

I didn't fancy tangling with that monster. I dodged around behind the clothesline. I kept one eye on the bear and the other on the young'uns. They were now flying over the county seat and looked hardly bigger than mayflies.

The bear charged toward me. The wind was spinning the clothesline so fast he couldn't see it. And he charged smack into it. My, didn't he begin to jump! He jumped red-hot pepper, only faster. He had got himself trapped inside the rope and couldn't jump out.

Of course, I didn't lose a moment. I began flapping my arms like a bird. That was such an enormous *big* wind I figured I could fly after the young'uns. The wind tugged and pulled at me, but it couldn't lift me an inch off the ground.

Tarnation! I had eaten too many biscuits. They were heavy as lead and weighed me down.

The young'uns were almost out of sight. I rushed to the barn for the wind plow. Once out in the breeze, the bedsheet filled with wind. Off I shot like a cannonball, plowing a deep furrow as I went.

Didn't I streak along, though! I was making better time than the young'uns. I kept my hands on the plow handles and steered around barns and farmhouses. I saw haystacks explode in the wind. If that wind got any stronger it wouldn't surprise me to see the sun blown off course. It would set in the south at high noon.

I plowed right along and gained rapidly on the young'uns. They were still holding hands and just clearing the tree tops. Before long I was within hailing distance.

"Be brave, my lambs!" I shouted. "Hold tight!"

I spurted after them until their shadows lay across my path. But the bedsheet was so swelled out with wind that I couldn't stop the plow. Before I could let go of the handles and jump off I had sailed far *ahead* of the young'uns.

I heaved the rope into the air. "Will*jill*hester*chester*peter*polly*tim*tom*mary *larry*and*little*clarinda!" I shouted as they came flying overhead. "Hang on!"

Hester missed the rope, and Jill missed the rope, and so did Peter. But Will caught it. I had to dig my heels in the earth to hold them. And then I started back. The young'uns were too light for the wind. They hung in the air. I had to drag them home on the rope like balloons on a string.

Of course it took most of the day to shoulder my way back through the wind. It was a mighty struggle, I tell you! It was near suppertime when we saw our farmhouse ahead, and that black bear was still jumping rope!

I dragged the young'uns into the house. The rascals! They had had a jolly time flying through the air, and wanted to do it again! Mama put them to bed with their wind shoes on.

The wind blew all night, and the next morning that bear was still jumping rope. His tongue was hanging out and he had lost so much weight he was skin and bones.

Finally, about midmorning, the wind got tired of blowing one way, so it blew the other. We got to feeling sorry for that bear and cut him loose. He was so tuckered out he didn't even growl. He just pointed himself toward the tall timber to find another hollow log to crawl into. But he had lost the fine art of walking. We watched him jump, jump, jump north until he was out of sight.

That was the howlin', scowlin' all mighty *big* wind that broke my leg. It had not only pulled up fence posts, but the *holes* as well. It dropped one of those holes right outside the barn door and I stepped in it.

That's the bottom truth. Everyone on the prairie knows Josh McBroom would rather break his leg than tell a fib.

McBroom and the Big Wind

Meet the Author

Sid Fleischman worked as a reporter after he graduated from college. He also wrote novels, suspense stories, and screenplays. Years later, he wrote his first children's book—it was for his own children.

Mr. Fleischman's interest in tall tales grew out of a keen interest in folklore. His McBroom books are filled with exaggeration and humor, characteristics common to tall tales.

Mr. Fleischman writes at a big table cluttered with library books, pens, pencils, letters, notes, and projects. He has been a full-time freelance writer since 1952.

Meet the Illustrator

Walter Lorraine was born in Worcester, Massachusetts, on February 3, 1929. He studied art at the Rhode Island School of Design. Later he was a book designer for a large publishing company and worked with children's book illustrators. Eventually, he started illustrating books himself. Mr. Lorraine says, *"Good illustrators have something to say. Whatever their techniques or styles, they always make a particular individual statement. Whether to convey fact or fiction, they are essentially storytellers who use pictures instead of words."*

Theme Connections

Within the Selection

Writer's Notebook

Record your answers to the questions below in the Response Journal section of your Writer's Notebook. In small groups, report the ideas you wrote. Discuss your ideas with the rest of your group. Then choose a person to report your group's answers to the class.

- How did Josh McBroom and his family survive the first prairie wind they encountered on their farm?
- The big wind brought a black bear to Josh McBroom's house. How did Josh protect himself against the bear?
- How did Josh McBroom's children survive after they were sucked up the chimney?

Across Selections

Josh McBroom and his family struggled to survive the big wind. What other characters have you read about that survived a harsh environment the way Josh McBroom and his family did?

Beyond the Selection

- Select a region of the country and a problem that might exist there because of the region's climate or environment. Write a short tall tale about that region, and share the tale with the members of your group.
- Think about how "McBroom and the Big Wind" adds to what you know about survival.
- Add items to the Concept/Question Board about survival.

Focus Questions How important is hope to survival?
Why do some people panic in difficult situations
while others stay calm and think?

The Grasshopper

David McCord

illustrated by Nelle Davis

Down
a
deep
well
a
grasshopper
fell.

By kicking about
He thought to get out.
    He might have known better,
    For that got him wetter.

To kick round and round
Is the way to get drowned,
    And drowning is what
    I should tell you he got.

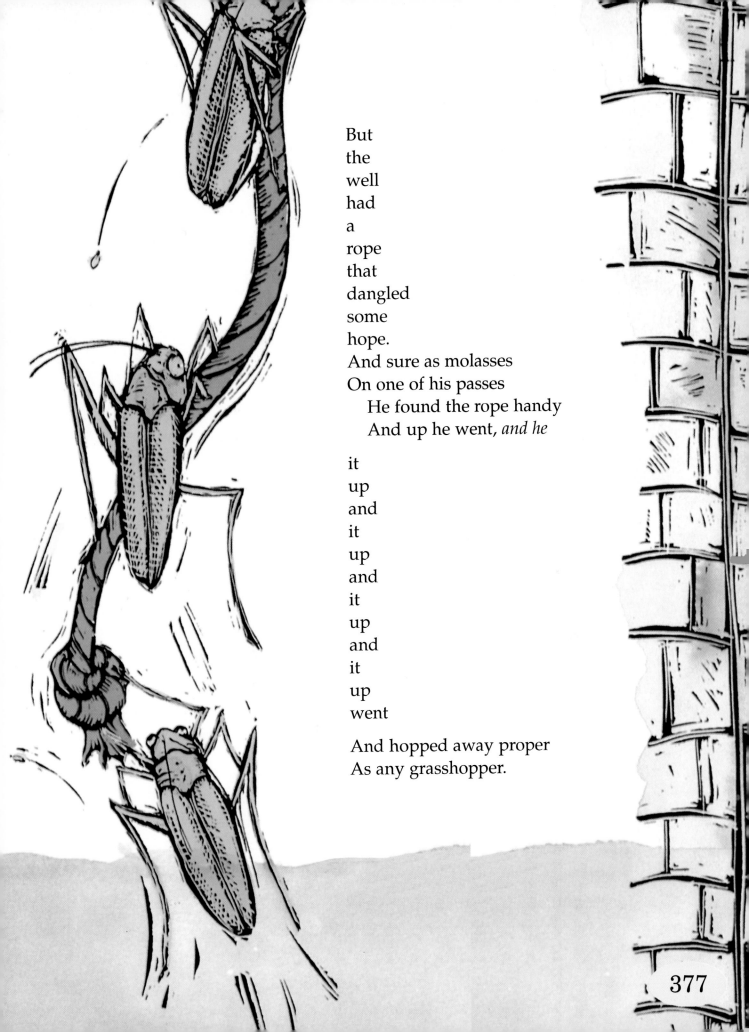

But
the
well
had
a
rope
that
dangled
some
hope.
And sure as molasses
On one of his passes
    He found the rope handy
    And up he went, *and he*

it
up
and
it
up
and
it
up
and
it
up
went

And hopped away proper
As any grasshopper.

Focus Questions What part does luck play in surviving a disaster? Why do disasters have to happen?

The Big Wave

from *The Big Wave*
by Pearl S. Buck
illustrated by Yoriko Ito

Jiya and his family live in a small Japanese fishing village. When a distant volcano erupts, it causes a tidal wave. As the giant wave approaches the village, Jiya's father forces him to climb to safety on a nearby mountain. He climbs to the terraced farm of his friend Kino's family. The rest of Jiya's family stays behind. From the mountaintop, Jiya watches as the wave hits.

Upon the beach where the village stood not a house remained, no wreckage of wood or fallen stone wall, no little street of shops, no docks, not a single boat. The beach was as clean of houses as if no human beings had ever lived there. All that had been was now no more.

Jiya gave a wild cry and Kino felt him slip to the ground. He was unconscious. What he had seen was too much for him. What he knew, he could not bear. His family and his home were gone.

Kino began to cry and Kino's father did not stop him. He stooped and gathered Jiya into his arms and carried him into the house, and Kino's mother ran out of the kitchen and put down a mattress and Kino's father laid Jiya upon it.

"It is better that he is unconscious," he said gently. "Let him remain so until his own will wakes him. I will sit by him."

"I will rub his hands and feet," Kino's mother said sadly.

Kino could say nothing. He was still crying and his father let him cry for a while. Then he said to his wife:

"Heat a little rice soup for Kino and put some ginger in it. He feels cold."

Now Kino did not know until his father spoke that he did feel cold. He was shivering and he could not stop crying. Setsu came in. She had not seen the big wave, for her mother had closed the windows and drawn the curtains against the sea. But now she saw Jiya lying white-pale and still.

"Is Jiya dead?" she asked.

"No, Jiya is living," her father replied.

"Why doesn't he open his eyes?" she asked again.

"Soon he will open his eyes," the father replied.

"If Jiya is not dead, why does Kino cry?" Setsu asked.

"You are asking too many questions," her father told her. "Go back to the kitchen and help your mother."

So Setsu went back again, sucking her forefinger, and staring at Jiya and Kino as she went, and soon the mother came in with the hot rice soup and Kino drank it. He felt warm now and he could stop crying. But he was still frightened and sad.

"What will we say to Jiya when he wakes?" he asked his father.

"We will not talk," his father replied. "We will give him warm food and let him rest. We will help him to feel he still has a home."

"Here?" Kino asked.

"Yes," his father replied. "I have always wanted another son, and Jiya will be that son. As soon as he knows that this is his home, then we must help him to understand what has happened."

So they waited for Jiya to wake.

"I don't think Jiya can ever be happy again," Kino said sorrowfully.

"Yes, he will be happy someday," his father said, "for life is always stronger than death. Jiya will feel when he wakes that he can never be happy again. He will cry and cry and we must let him cry. But he cannot always cry. After a few days he will stop crying all the time. He will cry only part of the time. He will sit sad and quiet. We must allow him to be sad and we must not make him speak. But we will do our work and live as always we do. Then one day he will be hungry and he will eat something that our mother cooks, something special, and he will begin to feel better. He will not cry any more in the daytime but only at night. We must let him cry at night. But all the time his body will be renewing itself. His blood flowing in his veins, his growing bones, his mind beginning to think again, will make him live."

"He cannot forget his father and mother and his brother!" Kino exclaimed.

"He cannot and he should not forget them," Kino's father said. "Just as he lived with them alive, he will live with them dead. Someday he will accept their death as part of his life. He will weep no more. He will carry them in his memory and his thoughts. His flesh and blood are part of them. So long as he is alive, they, too, will live in him. The big wave came, but it went away. The sun shines again, birds sing, and earth flowers. Look out over the sea now!"

Kino looked out the open door, and he saw the ocean sparkling and smooth. The sky was blue again, a few clouds on the horizon were the only sign of what had passed—except for the empty beach.

"How cruel it seems for the sky to be so clear and the ocean so calm!" Kino said.

But his father shook his head. "No, it is wonderful that after the storm the ocean grows calm, and the sky is blue once more. It was not the ocean or the sky that made the evil storm."

お父さん
じゃは大丈夫

"Who made it?" Kino asked. He let tears roll down his cheeks, because there was so much he could not understand. But only his father saw them and his father understood.

"Ah, no one knows who makes evil storms," his father replied. "We only know that they come. When they come we must live through them as bravely as we can, and after they are gone, we must feel again how wonderful is life. Every day of life is more valuable now than it was before the storm."

"But Jiya's family——his father and mother and brother, and all the other good fisherfolk, who are lost——" Kino whispered. He could not forget the dead.

"Now we must think of Jiya," his father reminded him. "He will open his eyes at any minute and we must be there, you to be his brother, and I to be his father. Call your mother, too, and little Setsu."

Now they heard something. Jiya's eyes were still closed, but he was sobbing in his sleep. Kino ran to fetch his mother and Setsu and they gathered about his bed, kneeling on the floor so as to be near Jiya when he opened his eyes.

In a few minutes, while they all watched, Jiya's eyelids fluttered on his pale cheeks, and then he opened his eyes. He did not know where he was. He looked from one face to the other, as though they were strangers. Then he looked up into the beams of the ceiling and around the white walls of the room. He looked at the blue-flowered quilt that covered him.

None of them said anything. They continued to kneel about him, waiting. But Setsu could not keep quiet. She clapped her hands and laughed. "Oh, Jiya has come back!" she cried. "Jiya, did you have a good dream?"

The sound of her voice made him fully awake. "My father—my mother—" he whispered.

Kino's mother took his hand. "I will be your mother now, dear Jiya," she said.

"I will be your father," Kino's father said.

"I am your brother now, Jiya," Kino faltered.

"Oh, Jiya will live with us," Setsu said joyfully.

Then Jiya understood. He got up from the bed and walked to the door that stood open to the sky and the sea. He looked down the hillside to the beach where the fishing village had stood. There was only beach, and all that remained of the twenty and more houses were a few foundation posts and some big stones. The gentle

あ、じやがおきたわ、いゆめみてたの。

383

little waves of the ocean were playfully carrying the light timber that had made the houses, and throwing it on the sands and snatching it away again.

The family had followed Jiya and now they stood about him. Kino did not know what to say, for his heart ached for his friend-brother. Kino's mother was wiping her eyes, and even little Setsu looked sad. She took Jiya's hand and stroked it.

"Jiya, I will give you my pet duck," she said.

But Jiya could not speak. He kept on looking at the ocean.

"Jiya, your rice broth is growing cold," Kino's father said.

"We ought all to eat something," Kino's mother said. "I have a fine chicken for dinner."

"I'm hungry!" Setsu cried.

"Come, my son," Kino's father said to Jiya.

They persuaded him gently, gathering around him, and they entered the house again. In the pleasant cosy room they all sat down about the table.

Jiya sat with the others. He was awake, he could hear the voices of Kino's family, and he knew that Kino sat beside him. But inside he still felt asleep. He was very tired, so tired that he did not want to speak. He knew that he would never see his father and mother any more, or his brother, or the neighbors and friends of the village. He tried not to think about them or to imagine their quiet bodies, floating under the swelling waves.

"Eat, Jiya," Kino whispered. "The chicken is good."

Jiya's bowl was before him, untouched. He was not hungry. But when Kino begged him he took up his porcelain spoon and drank a little of the soup. It was hot and good, and he smelled its fragrance in his nostrils. He drank more and then he took up his chopsticks and ate some of the meat and rice. His mind was still unable to think, but his body was young and strong and glad of the food.

When they had all finished, Kino said, "Shall we go up the hillside, Jiya?"

But Jiya shook his head. "I want to go to sleep again," he said.

Kino's father understood. "Sleep is good for you," he said. And he led Jiya to his bed, and when Jiya had laid himself down he covered him with the quilt and shut the sliding panels.

"Jiya is not ready yet to live," he told Kino. "We must wait."

The body began to heal first, and Kino's father, watching Jiya tenderly, knew that the body would heal the mind and the soul. "Life is stronger than death," he told Kino again and again.

さあじや食べ
鶏肉おいしい

But each day Jiya was still tired. He did not want to think or to remember—he only wanted to sleep. He woke to eat and then to sleep. And when Kino's mother saw this she led him to the bedroom, and Jiya sank each time into the soft mattress spread on the floor in the quiet, clean room. He fell asleep almost at once and Kino's mother covered him and went away.

All through these days Kino did not feel like playing. He worked hard beside his father in the fields. They did not talk much, and neither of them wanted to look at the sea. It was enough to look at the earth, dark and rich beneath their feet.

One evening, Kino climbed the hill behind the farm and looked toward the volcano. The heavy cloud of smoke had long ago gone away, and the sky was always clear now. He felt happier to know that the volcano was no longer angry, and he went down again to the house. On the threshold his father was smoking his usual evening pipe. In the house his mother was giving Setsu her evening bath.

"Is Jiya asleep already?" Kino asked his father.

"Yes, and it is a good thing for him," his father replied. "Sleep will strengthen him, and when he wakes he will be able to think and remember."

"But should he remember such sorrow?" Kino asked.

"Yes," his father replied. "Only when he dares to remember his parents will he be happy again."

They sat together, father and son, and Kino asked still another question. "Father, are we not very unfortunate people to live in Japan?"

"Why do you think so?" his father asked in reply.

"Because the volcano is behind our house and the ocean is in front, and when they work together for evil, to make the earthquake and the big wave, then we are helpless. Always many of us are lost."

"To live in the midst of danger is to know how good life is," his father replied.

"But if we are lost in the danger?" Kino asked anxiously.

"To live in the presence of death makes us brave and strong," Kino's father replied. "That is why our people never fear death. We see it too often and we do not fear it. To die a little later or a little sooner does not matter. But to live bravely, to love life, to see how beautiful the trees are and the mountains, yes, and even the sea, to enjoy work because it produces food for life——in these things we Japanese are a fortunate people. We love life because we live in danger. We do not fear death because we understand that life and death are necessary to each other."

火山

The Big Wave

Meet the Author

Pearl S. Buck was three months old when her parents took her to China, where she grew up. She wrote her first story at age nine. It was published in an English-language newspaper there. Afterward the newspaper printed many of her stories and even paid her for them. She decided then that one day she would be a real writer.

Growing up in China with American parents, Buck saw how people from different backgrounds separated themselves from each other. Because she had both Chinese and American friends, she often felt as though she lived in two worlds. And she realized early that the worlds were not the same. She made it her life's work to try and bring the cultures together and to speak out against every kind of bigotry.

Meet the Illustrator

Yoriko Ito grew up in Japan. When she was a little girl, she knew she wanted to paint. It wasn't until after she came to San Francisco at age 21 that she knew she wanted to study art. However, she says she became a children's book illustrator by accident. She showed her portfolio to some authors at a librarians' conference, and an author introduced her to a publisher. *"I was really lucky,"* says Ms. Ito.

Now Ms. Ito works at the Dreamworks film company. She painted backgrounds for movie animation for *The Prince of Egypt* and *El Dorado.* Ms. Ito advises young artists, *"You have to do your best always. If you believe in something, don't doubt your ability. . . . Remember, you can't please everybody. Trust yourself."*

Theme Connections

Within the Selection

Record your answers to the questions below in the Response Journal section of your Writer's Notebook. In small groups, report the ideas you wrote. Discuss your ideas with the rest of your group. Then choose a person to report your group's answers to the class.

- How did Jiya survive the tidal wave?
- Jiya survived the tidal wave but lost his family. According to Kino's father, what steps did Jiya need to take in order to survive his loss?

Across Selections

Jiya has to deal with the loss of his family. What other characters have you read about that had to survive the loss of a loved one?

Beyond the Selection

- Think about how "The Big Wave" adds to what you know about survival.
- Add items to the Concept/Question Board about survival.

Focus Questions What helps you survive those times when you feel unhappy? How long can a person survive with no one else to talk to?

Solitude

A. A. Milne

illustrated by Ernest H. Shepard

I have a house where I go
   When there's too many people,
I have a house where I go
   Where no one can be;
I have a house where I go,
Where nobody ever says "No";
Where no one says anything——so
   There is no one but me.

Focus Questions Why do some people risk their own safety to help others survive? What can we learn from people who have survived terrible events?

Anne Frank: *The Diary of a Young Girl*

Anne Frank
translated from the Dutch
by B. M. Mooyaart-Doubleday
illustrated by Susan Keeter

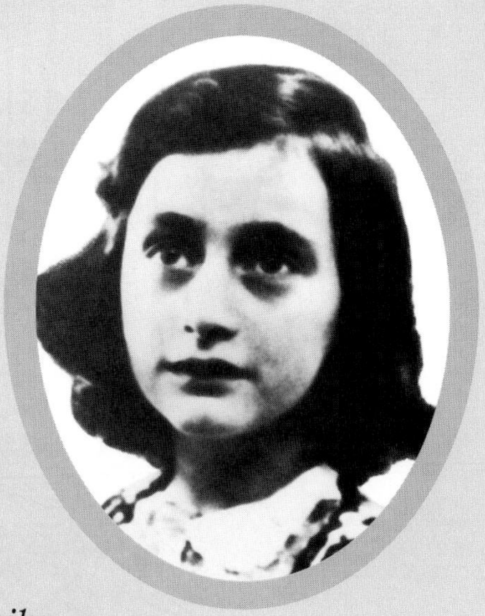

During World War II, many Jewish families in Germany and elsewhere in Europe hid to avoid being sent to concentration camps. Anne Frank and her family moved to Holland to escape the Nazis. When the Nazis came to Holland, the Franks hid for two years in a secret annex in Mr. Frank's office building. During this time, Anne kept a diary of her daily thoughts, feelings, and activities. Her father found these diaries after her death in a concentration camp in 1945 and had them published. These are a few of her first diary entries.

I hope I shall be able to confide in you completely, as I have never been able to do in anyone before, and I hope that you will be a great support and comfort to me.
Anne Frank, 12 June 1942.

Wednesday, 8 July, 1942

Dear Kitty,

Years seem to have passed between Sunday and now. So much has happened, it is just as if the whole world had turned upside down. But I am still alive, Kitty, and that is the main thing, Daddy says.

Yes, I'm still alive, indeed, but don't ask where or how. You wouldn't understand a word, so I will begin by telling you what happened on Sunday afternoon.

At three o'clock (Harry had just gone, but was coming back later) someone rang the front doorbell. I was lying lazily reading a book on the veranda in the sunshine, so I didn't hear it. A bit later, Margot appeared at the kitchen door looking very excited. "The S.S. have sent a call-up notice for Daddy," she whispered. "Mummy has gone to see Mr. Van Daan already." (Van Daan is a friend who works with Daddy in the business.) It was a great shock to me, a call-up; everyone knows what that means. I picture concentration camps and lonely cells——should we allow him to be doomed to this? "Of course he won't go," declared Margot, while we waited together. "Mummy has gone to the Van Daans to discuss whether we should move into our hiding place tomorrow. The Van Daans are going with us, so we shall be seven in all." Silence. We couldn't talk any more, thinking about Daddy, who, little knowing what was going on, was visiting some old people in the Joodse Invalide; waiting for Mummy, the heat and suspense, all made us very overawed and silent.

Suddenly the bell rang again. "That is Harry," I said. "Don't open the door." Margot held me back, but it was not necessary as we heard Mummy and Mr. Van Daan downstairs, talking to Harry, then they came in and closed the door behind them. Each time the bell went, Margot or I had to creep softly down to see if it was Daddy, not opening the door to anyone else.

Margot and I were sent out of the room. Van Daan wanted to talk to Mummy alone. When we were alone together in our bedroom, Margot told me that the call-up was not for Daddy, but for her. I was more frightened than ever and began to cry. Margot is sixteen; would they really take girls of that age away alone? But thank goodness she won't go, Mummy said so herself; that must be what Daddy meant when he talked about us going into hiding.

Into hiding——where would we go, in a town or the country, in a house or a cottage, when, how, where . . . ?

These were questions I was not allowed to ask, but I couldn't get them out of my mind. Margot and I began to pack some of our most vital belongings into a school satchel. The first thing I put in was this diary, then hair curlers, handkerchiefs, schoolbooks, a comb, old letters; I put in the craziest things with the idea that we were going into hiding. But I'm not sorry, memories mean more to me than dresses.

At five o'clock Daddy finally arrived, and we phoned Mr. Koophuis to ask if he could come around in the evening. Van Daan went and fetched Miep. Miep has been in the business with Daddy since 1933 and has become a close friend, likewise her brand-new husband, Henk. Miep came

and took some shoes, dresses, coats, underwear, and stockings away in her bag, promising to return in the evening. Then silence fell on the house; not one of us felt like eating anything, it was still hot and everything was very strange. We let our large upstairs room to a certain Mr. Goudsmit, a divorced man in his thirties, who appeared to have nothing to do on this particular evening; we simply could not get rid of him without being rude; he hung about until ten o'clock. At eleven o'clock Miep and Henk Van Santen arrived. Once again, shoes, stockings, books, and underclothes disappeared into Miep's bag and Henk's deep pockets, and at eleven-thirty they too disappeared. I was dog-tired and although I knew that it would be my last night in my own bed, I fell asleep immediately and didn't wake up until Mummy called me at five-thirty the next morning. Luckily it was not so hot as Sunday; warm rain fell steadily all day. We put on heaps of clothes as if we were going to the North Pole, the sole reason being to take clothes with us. No Jew in our situation would have dreamed of going out with a suitcase full of clothing. I had on two vests, three pairs of pants, a dress, on top of that a skirt, jacket, summer coat, two pairs of stockings, lace-up shoes, woolly cap, scarf, and still more; I was nearly stifled before we started, but no one inquired about that.

Margot filled her satchel with schoolbooks, fetched her bicycle, and rode off behind Miep into the unknown, as far as I was concerned. You see I still didn't know where our secret hiding place was to be. At seven-thirty the door closed behind us. Moortje, my little cat, was the only creature to whom I said farewell. She would have a good home with the neighbors. This was all written in a letter addressed to Mr. Goudsmit.

There was one pound of meat in the kitchen for the cat, breakfast things lying on the table, stripped beds, all giving the impression that we had left helter-skelter. But we didn't care about impressions, we only wanted to get away, only escape and arrive safely, nothing else. Continued tomorrow.

Yours, Anne

Thursday, 9 July, 1942

Dear Kitty,

So we walked in the pouring rain, Daddy, Mummy, and I, each with a school satchel and shopping bag filled to the brim with all kinds of things thrown together anyhow.

We got sympathetic looks from people on their way to work. You could see by their faces how sorry they were they couldn't offer us a lift; the gaudy yellow star spoke for itself.

Only when we were on the road did Mummy and Daddy begin to tell me bits and pieces about the plan. For months as many of our goods and chattels and necessities of life as possible had been sent away and they were sufficiently ready for us to have gone into hiding of our own accord on July 16. The plan had had to be speeded up ten days because of the call-up, so our quarters would not be so well organized, but we had to make the best of it. The hiding place itself would be in the building where Daddy has his office. It will be hard for outsiders to understand, but I shall explain that later on. Daddy didn't have many people working for him: Mr. Kraler, Koophuis, Miep, and Elli Vossen, a twenty-three-year-old typist who all knew of our arrival. Mr. Vossen, Elli's father, and two boys worked in the warehouse; they had not been told.

I will describe the building: there is a large warehouse on the ground floor which is used as a store. The front door to the house is next to the warehouse door, and inside the front door is a second doorway which leads to a staircase. There is another door at the top of the stairs, with a frosted glass window in it, which has "Office" written in black letters across it. That is the large main office, very big, very light, and very full. Elli, Miep, and Mr. Koophuis work there in the daytime. A small dark room containing the safe, a wardrobe, and a large cupboard leads to a small somewhat dark second office. Mr. Kraler and Mr. Van Daan used to sit here, now it is only Mr. Kraler. One can reach Kraler's office from the passage, but only via a glass door which can be opened from the inside, but not easily from the outside.

From Kraler's office a long passage goes past the coal store, up four steps and leads to the showroom of the whole building: the private office. Dark, dignified furniture, linoleum and carpets on the floor, radio, smart lamp, everything first-class. Next door there is a roomy kitchen with a hot-water faucet and a gas stove. Next door the W.C. [water closet]. That is the first floor.

A wooden staircase leads from the downstairs passage to the next floor. There is a small landing at the top. There is a door at each end of the landing, the left one leading to a storeroom at the front of the house and to the attics. One of those really steep Dutch staircases runs from the side to the other door opening on to the street.

The right-hand door leads to our "Secret Annexe." No one would ever guess that there would be so many rooms hidden behind that plain gray door. There's a little step in front of the door and then you are inside.

There is a steep staircase immediately opposite the entrance. On the left a tiny passage brings you into a room which was to become the Frank family's bed-sitting-room, next door a smaller room, study and bedroom for the two young ladies of the family. On the right a little room without windows containing the washbasin and a small W.C. compartment, with another door leading to Margot's and my room. If you go up the next flight of stairs and open the door, you are simply amazed that there could be such a big light room in such an old house by the canal. There is a gas stove in this room (thanks to the fact that it was used as a laboratory) and a sink. This is now the kitchen for the Van Daan couple, besides being general living room, dining room, and scullery.

A tiny little corridor room will become Peter Van Daan's apartment. Then, just as on the lower landing, there is a large attic. So there you are, I've introduced you to the whole of our beautiful "Secret Annexe."

Yours, Anne

Friday, 10 July, 1942

Dear Kitty,

I expect I have thoroughly bored you with my long-winded descriptions of our dwelling. But still I think you should know where we've landed.

But to continue my story——you see, I've not finished yet——when we arrived at the Prinsengracht, Miep took us quickly upstairs and into the "Secret Annexe." She closed the door behind us and we were alone. Margot was already waiting for us, having come much faster on her bicycle. Our living room and all the other rooms were chock-full of rubbish, indescribably so. All the cardboard boxes which had been sent to the office in the previous months lay piled on the floor and the beds. The little room was filled to the ceiling with bedclothes. We had to start clearing up immediately, if we wished to sleep in decent beds that night. Mummy and Margot were not in a fit state to take part; they were tired and lay down on their beds, they were miserable, and lots more besides. But the two "clearers-up" of the family——Daddy and myself——wanted to start at once.

The whole day long we unpacked boxes, filled cupboards, hammered and tidied, until we were dead beat. We sank into clean beds that night. We hadn't had a bit of anything warm the whole day, but we didn't care; Mummy and Margot were too tired and keyed up to eat, and Daddy and I were too busy.

On Tuesday morning we went on where we left off the day before. Elli and Miep collected our rations for us, Daddy improved the poor blackout, we scrubbed the kitchen floor, and were on the go the whole day long again. I hardly had time to think about the great change in my life until Wednesday. Then I had a chance, for the first time since our arrival, to tell you all about it, and at the same time to realize myself what had actually happened to me and what was still going to happen.

Yours, Anne

Anne Frank:
The Diary of a Young Girl

Meet the Author

Anne Frank was four when her family fled to Amsterdam, Holland, to escape the Nazis. The Nazis eventually came to Holland, so the Franks went into hiding. They moved into the attic of her father's warehouse, a place they called the "Secret Annexe." For two years, they did not leave the attic. Anne wrote in her diary about everything that happened there.

Anne's parents had given her the small, clothbound book for her thirteenth birthday. She wrote inside, *"I want to write, but more than that, I want to bring out all kinds of things that lie buried deep in my heart . . . . I want this diary itself to be my friend, and I shall call my friend Kitty."*

In 1944 the Franks were discovered and taken to concentration camps. Of the eight people in the Secret Annex, only Anne's father survived. When he returned to Amsterdam, Miep and Elli gave him the diary they had found in the Annex.

Meet the Illustrator

Susan Keeter has art degrees from Syracuse University. Ms. Keeter's mother and stepfather ran an art school in their home so Ms. Keeter had access to art materials and instruction throughout her childhood.

This story particularly affected Ms. Keeter because her mother was born the same year as Anne Frank. She says, *"I look at my mother, her friends, her work, the beauty she creates and wonder what Anne Frank would have accomplished—how she would have changed the world—if she had been allowed to live a full life."*

Theme Connections

Within the Selection

Record your answers to the questions below in the Response Journal section of your Writer's Notebook. In small groups, report the ideas you wrote. Discuss your ideas with the rest of your group. Then choose a person to report your group's answers to the class.

- What did Anne Frank and her family do in an attempt to escape being sent to a concentration camp?
- How did Anne Frank survive while hiding from the Nazis?

Across Selections

How was Anne Frank's predicament similar to the predicament of the Crafts in "Two Tickets to Freedom"? How are they different?

Beyond the Selection

- What would you miss most if you had to go into hiding, as Anne Frank did, in order to survive?
- Think about how "Anne Frank: The Diary of a Young Girl" adds to what you know about survival.
- Add items to the Concept/Question Board about survival.

Minamoto no Yorinobu Swimming across a bay to attack the rebellious Tadatsune. 1879. **Tsukioka Yoshitoshi.** Woodblock print. Vincent van Gogh Museum, Rijsmuseum, Amsterdam.

Choctaw Removal. 1966. **Valjean McCarthy-Hessing.** Watercolor on paper. The Philbrook Museum of Art, Tulsa, Oklahoma.

Buchenwald Concentration Camp Survivors. 1945. **Margaret Bourke-White.** Photograph.

The Old Plantation. c.1790–1800. **Artist unknown.** Watercolor on laid paper. Abby Aldrich Rockefeller Folk Art Center.

Focus Questions Can people make a difficult situation easier to survive? How do survivors pass on their stories to others?

Music & Slavery

Wiley Blevins

illustrated by Ashley Bryan

Mother was let off some days at noon to get ready for spinning that evening. She had to portion out the cotton they was gonna spin and see that each got a fair share. When mother was going round counting the cards each had spun she would sing this song:

Keep your eye on the sun.
See how she run.
Don't let her catch you with your work undone.
I'm a trouble, I'm a trouble.
Trouble don't last always.

That made the women all speed up so they could finish before dark catch 'em, 'cause it be mighty hard handlin' that cotton thread by firelight.

Bob Ellis
slave in Virginia

The life of many slaves in the United States was often full of fear and misery. Long hours were often spent picking cotton in the hot summer sun. At night, the slaves ate what little food their owners had given them and frequently slept on dirt floors. The slaves lived in run-down, overcrowded cabins and owned only the few clothes and possessions their masters had given them. They lived in fear of being beaten if they did not work hard enough or disobeyed their owners. They were not paid, and they were not allowed to leave their homes without special permission.

These terrible living conditions and lack of freedoms made many slaves want to escape. For most, however, there was no real hope of escape. Each day was a struggle to survive. One way the slaves dealt with these hardships was through music. It was a way to express both their sadness and their hope.

The slaves brought with them from Africa a strong tradition of music. Song and dance were an important part of their daily lives. They sang as they worked. They sang to celebrate. They sang when they were sad. They continued this tradition in the new world.

Slaves also brought instruments with them. The drum was the most important instrument used by them in Africa. However, many slave owners believed drums were being used to send secret messages. Therefore, drums were forbidden on most plantations. Instead, slaves kept the strong rhythms of their songs by clapping their hands, stomping their feet, swaying their bodies, and using other instruments such as the banjo. The banjo, developed by the slaves, became a commonly used instrument and is still in use today.

Many of the songs the slaves sang were developed as they worked in the fields. Singing helped take their minds off the difficulties of their work. These songs often changed over time. Many songs required a leader who would sing one line of the song while the others sang the response. These "call and response" chants were unique to slave music. Some songs that survived have become well-known spirituals, or religious songs. These songs, including "Swing Low Sweet Chariot" and "Go Down Moses," are based on stories in the Bible in which people were kept as slaves. Slaves were punished, often severely beaten, if they spoke against slavery. Through the spirituals, they could sing about the brutality of slavery without fear of being punished. Many of these songs are still sung today and are a tribute to the rich musical heritage of the slaves.

MANY THOUSAND GONE

illustrated by Ashley Bryan

No more auc-tion block for me, No more, No more,

No more auc-tion block for me, Ma - ny thou-sand gone.

No more peck of corn for me,
No more,
No more,
No more peck of corn for me,
Many thousand gone.

No more hundred lash for me,
No more,
No more,
No more hundred lash for me,
Many thousand gone.

Walk Together Children

illustrated by Ashley Bryan

O, Walk to-geth-er child-ren, Don't you get wea-ry,
Sing to-geth-er child-ren, Don't you get wea-ry,

Walk to-geth-er child-ren, Don't you get wea-ry,
Sing to-geth-er child-ren, Don't you get wea-ry,

Walk to-geth-er child-ren, Don't you get wea-ry, There's a
Sing to-geth-er child-ren, Don't you get wea-ry, There's a

great camp meet-ing in the Prom-ised Land.

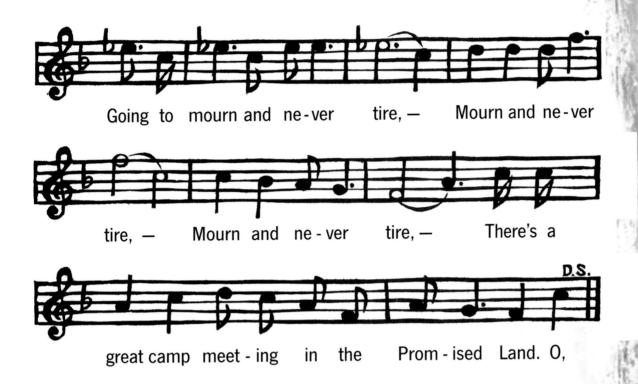

Going to mourn and ne-ver tire, — Mourn and ne-ver

tire, — Mourn and ne-ver tire, — There's a

D.S.

great camp meet-ing in the Prom-ised Land. O,

Music & Slavery

Meet the Author

Wiley Blevins grew up in West Virginia. During his childhood, he heard stories about his grandfather's life on a Virginia plantation. The stories were often about the music and celebrations of the slaves. Mr. Blevins always wondered, *"How could slaves spend so much time singing and celebrating?"*

Mr. Blevins began to study slavery and music further. He says, *"It became clear to me how the music of slaves was a way for them to cope with their brutal living conditions. It was one of their survival mechanisms."*

Meet the Illustrator

Ashley Bryan started writing and illustrating his own books in kindergarten. He bound them and gave them away as gifts for his friends and family. By the time he was in fourth grade, he had already created hundreds of books.

Mr. Bryan now lives in Isleford, Maine, on an island off the coast. He carries a sketchbook to draw people he meets and interesting places he sees as he travels. When he's not traveling, he paints at home during the day and works on his books at night.

Theme Connections

Within the Selection

Record your answers to the questions below in the Response Journal section of your Writer's Notebook. In small groups, report the ideas you wrote. Discuss your ideas with the rest of your group. Then choose a person to report your group's answers to the class.

- Each day was a struggle to survive for the slaves. What conditions made their lives unbearable?
- What did the slaves do to help them survive?

Across Selections

While Anne Frank was in hiding, she wrote in a diary. How is Anne Frank's writing similar to the slaves' use of music?

Beyond the Selection

- The slaves used music to make their lives more bearable. Write lyrics for a song that would make you happy. Share your song with the members of your group.
- Think about how "Music and Slavery" adds to what you know about survival.
- Add items to the Concept/Question Board about survival.

How do you let other people know what you want? Do you have a baby sister or brother? How does the baby tell others what he or she wants? Can you tell what your pet dog or cat or bird wants? How? It's all communication, and it takes as many forms as there are people and animals that need to communicate.

Focus Questions How is animal communication similar to human communication? Do you think people will ever learn to understand what animals are saying?

MESSAGES BY THE MILE

by Margery Facklam

Fin whales swim fast and travel alone, but they stay in touch with other fin whales hundreds of miles away. You might think the world's second-largest animal (only the blue whale is larger) would have the loudest voice, but we can't hear even a trace of the fin whale's long-distance song. Its sound is *infrasonic,* meaning it is *below* the level humans can hear. The rumblings of earthquakes, volcanoes, and severe thunderstorms are also infrasonic as they are building. We may feel them before they erupt, but we don't hear them. Divers swimming near big whales say they can feel the sound tingle right through their bodies. In the days before the churning engines of big ships filled the oceans with noise, the songs of fin whales may have carried for two or three thousand miles.

How whales make their sounds is still a mystery. They have no vocal cords. As one scientist put it, whales have a lot of complicated "plumbing" in their heads, and we don't know how it all works. Whales often sing near canyons on the ocean bottoms. Sounds echo from these deep hollows and trenches. Musicians say the songs sound as if they've been amplified in a recording studio.

Dr. Roger Payne and Dr. Katherine Payne, a husband-and-wife team, studied whale songs for twenty years. They began by recording the sounds made by the humpback whales feeding in the cold waters of the Arctic and Antarctic oceans in the spring. They could hear long, low rumbles, shrill whistles, grunts, eerie groans, and high squeaks like a door opening on a rusty hinge (much like the sounds of the dolphins). Some noises were used when whales met. Perhaps they were asking, "Who are you?" or warning others to stay away; perhaps the sounds were simply a form of greeting. All the "conversations" were short.

It wasn't until the humpback whales had migrated to breeding grounds in warm seas—around Hawaii, California, Bermuda, or Africa—that the Paynes heard the male humpback's beautiful, long melody. The humpback sings this song only when he is alone. His tune is the most complicated of all animal songs, with many notes in different patterns. Most humpback songs last an hour or two, interrupted only when the whale comes up for air. But one scientist taped a song that went on for more than twenty-two hours. The whale was still singing when the scientist got tired and packed up his equipment to go home.

The humpback's songs change each season. At the beginning of the spring migration, the males in one part of the ocean pick up the old melody and begin to make changes in it. They improvise. The song may drop in pitch, or one part may be speeded up while another slows down. As soon as one whale sings a new song, the other whales learn it. We depend on rhymes and repeating choruses to help us remember long songs and poems. Whales do, too. They repeat rhythms and patterns of notes.

Whales from the Pacific Ocean sing a different song from those in the Atlantic. In twenty years of study, the North Atlantic humpbacks have never gone back to an old version of a song after they have changed it. Does an old song go out of style? Is it a message they no longer need? Are they now telling a "story" of things that happened during the most recent migration? Nobody knows.

Some years after the whale studies, Dr. Katherine Payne was watching a group of elephants at the Washington Park Zoo, in Portland, Oregon. The elephants were separated by thick concrete walls, but they called back and forth with their usual trumpetings, snorts, barks, and rumbles. For centuries, people who lived near elephants have heard such rumblings. Some claimed it was only the elephants' stomachs digesting food. But at the zoo that day, Dr. Payne felt a strange throbbing in the air every ten or fifteen seconds.

Later, back in her office at Cornell University, she kept thinking about that feeling. It reminded her of when she was a young girl, singing in the church choir. She had felt the same throbbing from the lowest notes of the big pipe organ. It also felt like the vibrations from the whales' infrasonic songs. Could the elephants be sending infrasonic messages?

Infrasonic calls would explain how herds stay in touch, even though they are separated by thick forests. Infrasonic communication might also help explain some of the elephants' behavior. For example, a group of grandmother and mother elephants traveling with babies, aunts, and baby-sitters sometimes stops suddenly. For a minute or two, they stand still as statues, with their ears fanned out. Then, just as suddenly, they change direction and march away. How do two or three groups of elephants manage to arrive at a waterhole at the same time? They run from different directions and greet each other as old friends. How does a male elephant traveling alone find a female for a mate? If we found that elephants sent infrasonic messages, that would answer a lot of our questions.

Dr. Payne and her team went back to the zoo with recording
equipment that could pick up the sounds we can't hear. When
the tapes were played back at higher speed, the sounds were
clear. There's a spot on an elephant's forehead that trembles
when the animal makes the deep rumbling or purring sounds
that we hear. But whenever the taping equipment registered the
low-level "silent" sounds, the elephant's forehead also fluttered.
Dr. Payne knew she was right. The elephant's secret language
wasn't secret anymore. Like fin whales, elephants communicated
with infrasound.

MESSAGES BY THE MILE

Meet the Author

Margery Facklam says she loves to be a writer because she is never bored. There are always new ideas to develop or research for her to do. Her interest in science began as a child. Growing up, Mrs. Facklam spent every Saturday at the Buffalo Museum of Science. When she was in high school, she worked in the reptile house at the Buffalo Zoo. Later, Mrs. Facklam became a high school science teacher.

Theme Connections

Within the Selection

Record your answers to the questions below in the Response Journal section of your Writer's Notebook. In small groups, report the ideas you wrote. Discuss your ideas with the rest of your group. Then choose a person to report your group's answers to the class.

- How is fin whale communication similar to elephant communication?

- How do infrasonic calls explain how herds of elephants stay in touch?

Beyond the Selection

- Think about how "Messages by the Mile" adds to what you know about communication.

- Add items to the Concept/Question Board about communication.

Focus Questions **Why do poems communicate emotions so well?**
Do animals have their own forms of poetry?

Whalesong

by Judith Nicholls

I am
ocean voyager,
sky-leaper,
maker of waves;
I harm no man.

I know
only the slow tune
of turning tide,
the heave and sigh
of full seas meeting land
at dusk and dawn,
the sad whale song.
I harm no man.

"We'll Be Right Back after These Messages"

by Shelagh Wallace
illustrated by Tony Caldwell

You're watching your favorite show, it's just getting to a really good part and then . . . a commercial. What do you do? Go to the kitchen? Press the mute button? Watch the commercial?

If you're an average TV viewer, you'll find yourself in this situation many, many times—during a year, you see (or perhaps choose not to see) at least 20,000 commercials. Commercials pay for most of the programs you watch: networks charge advertisers to air the advertisers' ads, then use the money they receive to cover the costs of producing the shows. But TV advertising isn't limited to just commercials. There are other kinds of ads on TV as well.

Sometimes you watch an ad on TV without even knowing that's what it is. A well-known soft drink prominently displayed during a prime-time TV show, a Saturday morning cartoon with popular characters that are also toys you can buy, "infomercials," and even music videos are, in fact, advertisements. They're all intended to persuade you to buy something, whether it's a can of cola, an action toy, an amazing new mop, or a compact disc.

How effective are these kinds of ads at convincing you to buy their products? When an American music video channel started showing videos in 1981, music sales boomed. Record companies found that actually being able to see bands perform their songs made people more likely to buy the group's records and concert tickets. The constantly changing camera shots, unusual camera angles and, of course, memorable music are exactly the same things advertisers use in "regular" commercials to get your attention and make sure you remember their ad.

Advertisers use other techniques, as well, to get your attention and hold it for the entire length of a commercial. Here are just some of those techniques:

- Repeating the ad over and over again. Studies show that, if you have a choice, many people are more likely to buy an advertised brand instead of an unadvertised brand, even an unadvertised brand that's cheaper. One reason you're familiar with the advertised brand name is that you've heard the ad for it over and over again.
- Using camera effects and special effects. Close-ups can make products look larger than they are. Computer-generated special effects can make toys appear to do something, such as move by themselves, that they won't actually do when you get them home.

FREE! New! Amazing! Improved!

- Emphasizing "premiums," the toys or prizes that come with certain products. The "special gift inside" may be the only reason you buy the cereal.
- Showing or saying words such as "free," "new," "amazing," and "improved" to get everyone's attention. (Did someone say "free"?)
- Hiring famous people to tell you to buy a certain product. Advertisers conduct surveys to find out which celebrities you trust and like the most, then use those people to promote their products.

There are limits, however, to the extent advertisers can use these techniques to convince you to buy their products. Your government—the Canadian Radio-Television and Telecommunications Commission (CRTC) in Canada and the Federal Communications Commission (FCC) in the U.S.—has hundreds of rules to guarantee that the television industry serves you and the "public interest." As a Canadian or American citizen, you literally own the airwaves that the TV networks use for broadcasting. The networks are allowed to "borrow" the airwaves provided that what they broadcast meets the needs of the public.

The networks, governments, and advertisers agree that children are a special part of the TV audience. Kids under five years of age don't understand that commercials are there to sell them something. (To them, ads are just shorter programs.) And it isn't until kids are about eight years of age that they understand that commercials aren't always literally true. Because of this, the advertising industries in both Canada and the U.S. must obey special rules that restrict what can be advertised to kids under twelve and how it can be advertised to them.

According to the rules, advertisers can't take advantage of you by having a baseball player tell you how great a particular brand of bat is, for example. He can endorse a sports drink, but not a bat or a baseball. What's the difference? Bats and baseballs are too closely identified with what the player does for a living. Seeing him advertise either a bat or a baseball could leave you with the impression that you'll play like him if you buy one, too. Computer-generated effects in commercials are okay, as long as there's at least one part of the ad that shows the product as it actually is. If a toy plane can't fly on its own, the ad has to show someone's hand holding the plane.

"We'll Be Right Back after These Messages"

Meet the Author

Shelagh Wallace was born and raised in Burlington, Ontario. After working for several years in book publishing, Ms. Wallace began writing books herself. She credits her grandfather with encouraging her to write. *"Everyone in my family [is a great reader], but it was my grandfather who wrote stories and encouraged all his grandchildren to write stories as well."* When asked to give advice to aspiring writers, Ms. Wallace replies, *"Read. Read a lot. Read a wide variety of books by many different authors."*

Meet the Illustrator

Tony Caldwell creates his wonderful art from Breckinridge, Colorado, where he is a ski instructor, mountain biker, and rider of horses. A graduate of Maryland Institute College of Art in Baltimore, Tony enjoys assignments which are festive and challenging in color or black and white.

Theme Connections

Within the Selection

Writer's Notebook

Record your answers to the questions below in the Response Journal section of your Writer's Notebook. In small groups, report the ideas you wrote. Discuss your ideas with the rest of your group. Then choose a person to report your group's answers to the class.

- Why are television shows interrupted by commercials?

- How can a television viewer see an advertisement without even knowing it?

- What do advertisers do to communicate their messages and convince you to buy their products?

Across Selections

Television allows people to communicate across vast distances. What other selection have you read that discusses communication across vast distances?

Beyond the Selection

- Is television an effective form of communication? Why? Why not?

- Think about how "We'll Be Right Back After These Messages" adds to what you know about communication.

- Add items to the Concept/Question Board about communication.

Breaking into Print

Before and After the Invention of the Printing Press

Stephen Krensky

illustrated by Bonnie Christensen

In a long room with seven tables and seven windows, a French monk sat hunched over a parchment page. He dipped a goose quill in some ink and began to write. The quill made a scratching sound, like a cat clawing at a closed door.

The monk worked six hours almost every day for many months. He hoped to finish before the first snow fell.

The monk was making a book.

The monastery was a small part of a great empire, an empire with far more soldiers than books. Its emperor, Charlemagne, both read and spoke Latin, but he could write little more than his name.

His scribes, however, created a new script that made writing easier to understand.

Parchment was made from a specially prepared animal skin, usually from sheep or goats. The best parchment, called vellum, was made from calfskin. Monks worked only in natural light. The risk of fire from candles posed too great a danger to their precious manuscripts.

Under Charlemagne's rule (800–814 A.D.) Latin was firmly established as the language of the court and education. Charlemagne's scribes also pioneered leaving spaces between words and starting phrases with capital letters.

In the Middle Ages, people believed in superstitions and magic to explain things such as thunderstorms and diseases. Rome had a population of about 500,000 in 300 A.D. After the fall of its empire, no European city had more than 20,000 people for hundreds of years.

Across the countryside, reading and writing counted for little. Few roads were free of robbers or wolves. In the villages, warring peasants lived and died without ever seeing a book.

In time, the villages knew longer periods of peace. The peasants began to eat better and made goods to trade on market day. Successful merchants learned to read and write so that they could keep records of their business. Sometimes their children were taught as well.

More books were now needed, more than the monks could manage alone. In the new book-making guilds, many hands worked together.

Many such books were made with a new material called paper. It was much cheaper than parchment and especially useful for wood or metal block printing.

Block printing was first developed in Asia in the eighth century. No press was used for the printing process. After the blocks were etched and inked, paper was rubbed on them to make a print.

In faraway China, printers had been using paper for centuries. And around 1050, the Chinese printer Pi Sheng had invented movable type using baked clay tablets. Yet few Chinese printers were excited about the invention. Their alphabet has thousands of characters. Only in a dream could printers create so much type. And even if they managed this feat, organizing the type would turn the dream into a nightmare.

The Koreans made further progress. They were actually printing books with movable type around 1400. But their written language is as complicated as Chinese, which discouraged them from making too much of the process.

In the German town of Mainz, one young man knew nothing of Chinese or Korean printing methods. But he was interested in the idea and process of printing. His name was Johannes Gensfleisch, but he followed the old custom of taking his mother's name: Gutenberg.

As a young goldsmith and gem cutter, Gutenberg had learned how to cut steel punches and cast metal in molds. He knew which metals were hard and which were soft, which melted easily and which could take great heat without melting. Over the next few years, Gutenberg tinkered with the printing process.

Gutenberg cast 290 different letters, numbers, punctuation marks, and other symbols in preparation to printing his first book.

Although he had a simpler alphabet than the Chinese or Koreans, he still faced many obstacles. There was no room for sloppy or careless design. Printed letters had to fit as closely together as handwritten ones. Printed words had to fall in a straight line. Printed lines had to leave even spaces above and below.

Gutenberg also had to find the proper metal to cast letters and the right ink to use. If the metal was too hard, it would break too easily. If the metal was too soft, it would lose its shape too quickly. As for the ink, it could not be too thick or too thin or likely to fade over time.

Gutenberg was very practical. He did not believe in reinventing things that already worked fine. So he adapted a winepress for printing. He made it taller, so that the work could be done at waist height, and he created a rolling tray for sliding the paper in and out.

Gutenberg spent almost twenty years building and tinkering. He invented adjustable molds to make letters in different widths. He found the right alloy for casting his letters. He built the upper and lower type cases for storing capital and small letters. He even created the long, grooved composing stick for quickly assembling lines of print.

Gutenberg's great project was a two-column Bible.

It reflected everything he knew of the art of printing.

Gutenberg began working on the Bible project in 1452. It took more than three years to complete. The Gutenberg Bible, published in 1456, was printed in a run of 200 copies. Though it was started with two presses, six presses were eventually used together. As many as 50 copies were printed on vellum, requiring up to 5,000 animal skins.

Soon, other printers were building on Gutenberg's work. They added more than one ink to a page. They added illustrations to the text.

They began printing more than religious works and public notices. They began printing philosophy and poetry and stories of the imagination.

In almost no time at all, printing grew beyond the reach of one man or firm. New printers were setting up shop as fast as they could learn the craft. A generation earlier, printers had produced a single book in a few months. Now they were printing thousands of books a year.

New schools sprang up to teach people how to read. And since books were no longer rare or costly, students as well as teachers could own them.

Lower costs played a great part in the success of printing. By 1463, ten printed Bibles sold for the price of one manuscript copy. By the year 1500, there were more than 1,000 printers in Europe, and they had printed millions of books.

This freed the students from memorizing so much and gave them more time to think.

There were geography books for Christopher Columbus and science books for Nicolaus Copernicus. And there were art and science and engineering and many other books for Leonardo da Vinci, who studied almost everything.

Reading and writing were no longer just for studious monks or highborn lords and ladies. Books were no longer chained up in private libraries or boldly sold for a king's ransom.

The printing press took learning and knowledge from just a privileged few and shared them with everyone else. And that change, more than any other act, set the stage for the modern world to come.

Despite the success of printed books, some wealthy people looked down on them as plain and coarse. Although many schools were for rich students, some poor students were educated for free.

Breaking into Print

Before and After the Invention of the Printing Press

Meet the Author

Stephen Krensky was always interested in fiction and illustrating, but he never thought of becoming a writer. He didn't write down his stories. He made them up in his head at night, using characters from stories he had read.

In college, Mr. Krensky became interested in writing and illustrating stories for children. Since then he has written more than 40 books on subjects including dinosaurs, summer camp, ancient military leader Alexander the Great, Native American children, and teachers.

"People often ask me how I can write something that twelve-year-olds or nine-year-olds or six-year-olds will want to read. I'm not sure, but I do know that the part of me that was once twelve and nine and six is not neatly boxed and tucked away in some dusty corner of my mind."

Meet the Illustrator

Bonnie Christensen studied at the Center for Book Arts and Parsons School of Design.

Her first book was an alphabet book she was going to print by hand on a press more than 170 years old. But an editor saw samples of her work and bought the book for her publishing company to print.

"I love books," Ms. Christensen says, *"both for children and adults, antique and new, short and long, with or without illustrations, and so I've come to love the book arts, which include printing, papermaking, book-binding and wood engraving."*

442

Theme Connections

Within the Selection

Record your answers to the questions below in the Response Journal section of your Writer's Notebook. In small groups, report the ideas you wrote. Discuss your ideas with the rest of your group. Then choose a person to report your group's answers to the class.

- Why was Gutenberg's printing press more successful at communicating and creating books than the Chinese or Korean printing press?

- How did the printing press take communication, learning, and knowledge from just a privileged few and share it with everyone?

Across Selections

The invention of the printing press allowed a much larger audience to read the same information. How does this compare with the power of television?

Beyond the Selection

- Make a list of all the types of different books you read and how they make your life better.

- Think about how "Breaking into Print: Before and After the Invention of the Printing Press" adds to what you know about communication.

- Add items to the Concept/Question Board about communication.

Symbols. 1984. **Ida Kohlmeyer.** Oil, graphite, and pastel on canvas.
$69\frac{1}{2} \times 69$ in. The National Museum of Women in the Arts,
Washington, D.C., gift of Wallace and Wilhelmina Holladay.

Young Girl Writing a Love Letter.
Johan G. Meyer Von Bremen.
Josef Mensing Gallery, Hamm-Rhynern,
Germany. Photo: SuperStock.

The News Room.
**Jane Wooster
Scott.** Collection
of Vernon Scott IV.
Photo: SuperStock.

445

Koko's Kitten

from *Koko's Kitten*
by Dr. Francine Patterson
photographs by Ronald H. Cohn

Koko's full name is Hanabi-Ko, which is Japanese for Fireworks Child. She was born on the Fourth of July. Every year, I have a party for Koko with cake, sparkling apple cider, and lots of presents.

Koko knows what birthdays are. When asked what she does on her birthday, Koko answered, "Eat, drink, (get) old."

Three days before Koko's party, I said, "I'm going shopping today. What do you want for your birthday?"

"Cereal there. Good there drink," Koko signed.

"But what presents do you want?" I asked.

"Cat," answered Koko.

Later, she repeated, "Cat, cat, cat."

I wasn't surprised that Koko asked for a cat. I have been reading to Koko for many years and two of her favorite stories have been "Puss in Boots" and "The Three Little Kittens."

Koko gets very involved in the stories I read her. When reading the story of the three little kittens who lose their mittens, Koko sees that their mother is angry and that the kittens are crying.

"Mad," Koko signs.

Koko loves picture books. Gorilla books are her favorites. Cat books are next. She likes to go off on her own with a book to study the pictures and sign to herself.

On her birthday, I gave Koko the usual assortment of presents—apple juice, some special fruits and nuts, and a baby doll. I didn't want to give Koko a stuffed toy because I knew she'd eventually destroy it.

The only durable toy cat I could find was in a mail order catalogue and I ordered it right away. It was made of cement and covered with vinyl and black velvet. I chose it because it looked real and it was sturdy—gorilla-proof. The toy cat didn't arrive in time for Koko's birthday, so I decided to save it for Christmas.

In December, I made a list for Koko. I drew about twenty pictures—fruits, vegetables, nuts, dolls, combs, and blankets. Every year, Koko gets a stocking and lots of presents. She loves Christmas.

"What do you want for Christmas?" I asked as I showed Koko the pictures.

Koko carefully studied the booklet. Then she pointed to a doll, nuts—and a cat.

Koko signs "cat"

I bought Koko some nuts and a new doll. I wrapped the toy cat and put it with the rest of her presents.

On Christmas morning, Koko ate her cereal and opened her stocking. It was filled with nuts. Koko threw the nuts aside and went to her next present.

Koko unwrapped a doll.

"That stink," Koko signed.

Then came the velvet cat.

"That red," she signed.

Koko often uses the word red to express anger. Koko was very upset. She started running back and forth, banging on her walls. She was doing display charges past me. They were angry, angry charges.

It is natural for gorillas to display when frightened or in great danger. They run sideways, pound their chests, then go down on all fours, and run back and forth.

But this was Christmas, usually a happy day for Koko, and she was with people she loved.

Later in the day, Barbara, a friend who had known Koko since she was a baby gorilla, arrived.

"That looks like a black cat," Barbara said to Koko. "Would you show it to me?"

Koko signs "mad"

Koko did not answer. She pulled a blanket over her head.

"Could I see it?" Barbara asked.

Koko pulled a rag over the toy cat, then tossed it in the air. "Cat that," Koko signed.

"Please let me see it," said Barbara.

Koko gave her a toy dinosaur instead.

I finally understood Koko's strange behavior. She was unhappy with her Christmas present. I had made a mistake. Koko did not want a cement and velvet toy cat. Koko wanted a real cat. Koko wanted a pet.

Things don't always happen quickly where we live. Every day is full of its own activities. So it was almost six months later when Karen, one of my assistants, arrived with three kittens. The kittens had been abandoned by their mother and raised by a dog, a Cairn terrier.

Karen showed the kittens to Koko.

"Love that," Koko signed.

As we showed Koko the kittens, she gave each one her blow test. When Koko meets a new animal or person, she blows in their face. I think she is trying to get a better scent. When she blows at a person, she expects them to blow back. Maybe she expected the kittens to blow back, too.

The first kitten was smoky gray and white. Koko's blow test took him by surprise. The second kitten was a tailless gray tabby. He was also startled by the blow test. The third kitten, a brown tabby, did not react at all.

After the blow test, Koko seemed to have made some judgments about the kittens.

"Which one do you want?" we asked.

"That," signed Koko, pointing to the tailless tabby.

Koko chooses the tabby

I am not sure why Koko picked the gray tabby as her favorite. I never asked her. Perhaps it was because he didn't have a tail—a gorilla has no tail.

That night, all three kittens went home with Karen. Two days later, the kittens came back for another visit. Koko was happy to see them.

"Visit love tiger cat," Koko signed.

First she picked up the smoky gray and white one. Then Koko took the tailless tabby and carried him on her thigh. After a while, she pushed him up onto the back of her neck.

"Baby," Koko signed.

She cradled the tabby in her legs and examined its paws. Koko squeezed, and the tabby's claws came out.

"Cat do scratch," Koko signed. "Koko love."

"What will you name the kitty?" I asked.

"All Ball," Koko signed.

"Yes," I said. "Like a ball, he has no tail."

Ball stayed overnight as a visiting kitten. By the end of the week, Ball was a permanent member of our household.

Koko had her kitten at last.

For the first few weeks, Ball lived in my house. Every evening at six o'clock, I would take Ball to Koko's trailer for an evening visit. I carried the kitten in my pocket as I prepared Koko for bed. Koko soon grew accustomed to this routine.

"What happens at night?" I asked.

"All Ball," signed Koko.

"Right," I said. "Ball visits you at night."

When he was older, Ball snuck into Koko's trailer by himself. It worried me in the beginning. I did not know how Koko would treat the kitten unsupervised. As it turned out, Koko was always gentle. Ball was never afraid of her.

Kittens should not be separated from their mothers until they are at least six weeks old. Poor Ball was abandoned by his mother at birth, which might have accounted for some of his faults.

Ball was an unusual cat. He was very aggressive. He would go up to people and bite them for no reason. He would bite Koko, too.

"Cat bite. Obnoxious," Koko signed, but she never struck back.

Koko did not like to be scratched or bitten, but she loved Ball in spite of his naughty behavior.

"Tell me a story about Ball," I said.

"Koko love Ball," she signed.

Koko treated Ball as if he were her baby.

The very first time she picked him up, she tried to tuck him in her thigh. That's where mother gorillas put their infants. Older babies are carried on their mothers' backs. Koko tried this with Ball, too.

Koko was a good gorilla mother. She combed and petted Ball to keep him clean. She also examined his eyes, ears, and mouth to make sure he was healthy. It was Koko who discovered Ball's ear mites.

Ball was often a topic of conversation during Koko's lessons.

"Love visit," Koko signed when Ball and I arrived for a morning lesson.

"Ball," I said.

"Trouble," signed Koko. "Love."

Koko seemed to enjoy conversations about her kitten. This dialogue took place between Koko and a research assistant named Janet.

Koko signs "love"

"I'll give you some grapes if you tell me about Ball, the cat," Janet said.

"Soft," Koko signed.

"What kind of animal is he?" Janet asked.

"Cat, cat, cat," Koko answered.

"Do you love Ball?"

"Soft, good cat cat," Koko signed.

In addition to sign language, art is another way I test Koko's perceptions. Ball lay with a green toy on an orange towel. I gave Koko a canvas and some paints and asked her to draw Ball. Koko had ten colors to choose from. First she picked black for Ball's body. Next she picked orange for the towel and green for the toy.

"What about Ball's eyes?" I asked.

Koko picked tan.

Koko loves to play games. Her favorites are "chase," "blow-it," and "tickle."

Koko likes to be tickled, and she thinks that others will like it, too.

"Tickle," Koko signed to Ball when they were lying on the floor together.

Ball was not a good tickler, nor did he like to be tickled. So Koko and I pretended. I tickled Koko while carrying the kitten in my hand. Koko thought this was very funny.

"Chase, blow-it. Enjoy," Koko signed to Ball.

In blow-it, Koko blows as hard as she can into the face of her playmate. It's not hard to understand why this game was not one of Ball's favorites.

Chase is similar to tag. Players run back and forth and chase each other. This is a popular game among gorillas in the wild. But Ball never quite caught on to chase.

"Ball" sitting on Koko's back

Koko did not realize that kittens don't necessarily enjoy gorilla games. Koko did understand that kittens like warmth, affection, and attention. And Koko supplied plenty.

On a foggy December morning, one of the assistants told me that Ball had been hit by a car. He had died instantly.

I was shocked and unprepared. I didn't realize how attached I had grown to Ball, and I had no idea how the news would affect Koko. The kitten meant so much to her. He was Koko's baby.

I went to Koko at once. I told her that Ball had been hit by a car; she would not see him again.

Koko did not respond. I thought she didn't understand, so I left the trailer.

Ten minutes later, I heard Koko cry. It was her distress call—a loud, long series of high-pitched hoots.

I cried, too.

Three days later, Koko and I had a conversation about Ball.

"Do you want to talk about your kitty?" I asked.

"Cry," Koko signed.

"Can you tell me more about it?" I asked.

"Blind," she signed.

"We don't see him anymore, do we? What happened to your kitty?" I asked.

"Sleep cat," Koko signed.

A few weeks later, Koko saw a picture of a gray tabby who looked very much like Ball. She pointed to the picture and signed, "Cry, sad, frown."

It was an unhappy time.

News of All Ball's death traveled quickly. We received thousands of letters. People of all ages wrote to us and expressed their sympathy. Some sent cards, others sent photographs, and many children created pictures. They all had one message: that Koko should have a new kitten.

As we approached Christmas, I wanted to get Koko a new kitten. I had no idea how difficult that would turn out to be.

On December 20, Barbara asked Koko, "What would you like for Christmas?"

"Cat cat tiger cat," was Koko's reply.

We heard of a Manx who was soon expecting a litter. We waited weeks until we discovered that the cat was just getting fat. Christmas came and went.

In January I showed Koko a picture of three kittens. One had a long tail, one had a short tail, and one was tailless.

"When you get another kitty, what kind would you like?" I asked.

"That," Koko signed as she pointed to the tailless cat.

"We'll get you a kitty like that," I said. "Is that okay?"

"Good. Nice," Koko answered.

"How do you feel about kitties?" I asked.

"Cat gorilla have visit," she signed. "Koko love."

Koko was ready for a new kitten if only I could find one.

More time went by. I called the Humane Society. They had no kittens at all—let alone a rare, tailless Manx. I called many other places and was disappointed again and again. I was told that not many kittens were born during that time of year.

The worst part of this period was my feeling that I was letting Koko down. I'd watch as someone would ask Koko, "Where's your cat?" And she would look around almost as if she were doing a double take, as if she were looking for Ball.

Then our luck changed. We received a letter from a breeder of Manx cats who wanted to help. He didn't have any kittens then, but he called other Manx breeders nearby until he located a litter of Manx kittens in Southern California. They were just about ready to leave their mother.

We set the date for March 17. The day before, I told Koko she was getting a new kitty—a red kitty. Red is Koko's favorite color. She was very excited.

Then, another delay.

The breeder called. "I'm sorry," he said. "The kitten is not coming today."

Koko was upset. I was disappointed.

"Trouble," she signed.

"We are having trouble getting you a new kitty. We have been trying very hard," I explained.

Finally, on March 24, a red, tiger-striped Manx was brought to our home. Seeing the kitten, Koko purred with pleasure. It was a wonderful moment. She placed him on her chest and petted him.

"Let me hold the kitty," I said.

But Koko would not let go. She kissed and cradled her kitten.

"Baby," she signed.

Koko was happy. Her new kitten had come to stay.

"Lipstick" playing with Koko

Koko's Kitten

Meet the Author

Dr. Francine Patterson (known as Penny to her friends) has been teaching Koko since the gorilla was one year old. Since she taught Koko sign language, the gorilla easily communicates with humans.

Dr. Patterson has written articles for numerous periodicals including *National Geographic* and *Science*. She has also contributed to several books. She has written two children's books about Koko: *Koko's Kitten* and *Koko's Story*.

Meet the Photographer

Ronald H. Cohn grew up in Chicago, Illinois, within walking distance of the Museum of Science and Industry. He spent all his weekends there. *"That really did it for me,"* he says. *"I had some curiosities, and they were satisfied there. My visits there gave me a very broad interest in all kinds of science."*

Mr. Cohn has been working with Dr. Patterson and Koko from the beginning of the project. *"Koko is like my daughter,"* he says. *"I see her every day."*

Mr. Cohn has this advice for students: *"If you are interested in something, read about it. Try to fulfill your curiosities and find a way to do what you want to do."*

Theme Connections

Within the Selection

Record your answers to the questions below in the Response Journal section of your Writer's Notebook. In small groups, report the ideas you wrote. Discuss your ideas with the rest of your group. Then choose a person to report your group's answers to the class.

- How does Koko communicate with Dr. Patterson?
- What things can Koko communicate to Dr. Patterson?

Across Selections

What other selections have you read in which animals communicate? How are their forms of communication similar? How are they different?

Beyond the Selection

- Think about how "Koko's Kitten" adds to what you know about communication.
- Add items to the Concept/Question Board about communication.

Louis Braille

The Boy Who Invented Books for the Blind

from ***Louis Braille: The Boy Who Invented Books for the Blind***

by Margaret Davidson

illustrated by Bob Dorsey

It's Just a Show-off Trick!

So the busy months passed. And Louis grew happier and happier with his life at school. Only one thing was wrong——but it was the most important thing of all.

Louis was taking reading lessons. But it wasn't anything like what he had dreamed of for so long. In 1820 there was only one way for the blind to read. It was called *raised-print*. Each letter of the alphabet was raised from the page. It stood up from the paper background so it could be felt with the fingers. This sounded easy. But it wasn't.

460

Some of the letters were simple to feel. But others were almost impossible to tell apart. The *Q*'s felt like *O*'s. The *O*'s felt like *C*'s. The *I*'s turned out to be *T*'s and the *R*'s were really *B*'s.

But Louis was determined. Again and again his fingers traced the raised letters until he could tell them apart—most of the time. Then letter by letter he began to feel out words.

But it was so slow! Louis was one of the brightest boys in the school. But often even he forgot the beginning of a sentence before he got to the end of it. Then he had to go back the whole way and start over again.

It would take months to read a single book this way! "This isn't really reading," Louis cried one day. "It's just a show-off trick!"

"It's the best we can do," a teacher answered. "People have tried to find a better way for years."

Louis knew this was true. He knew that people had tried so many things—raised letters, lowered letters, letters of stone and letters of string, letters of wax and letters of wood. One man had even made an alphabet of pins. Louis tried to imagine how it would feel to read a page of pins. Ouch!

Besides, Louis soon learned that in the entire school library there were just fourteen books. Just fourteen! And there were good reasons for this. The raised-print books were very expensive to make. Each one had to be made by hand. They were also big and hard to store. Each letter had to be at least three inches from top to bottom—or blind fingers could not feel it. So only a few words could fit on a page.

No. Louis knew now that there would never be many books for the blind. Not the raised-print way. Then there must be another, better way! There just had to be! Soon that was all Louis could think——or talk——about. And his friends got good and tired of it.

"Do shut up, Louis," they begged.

"But it's so important!" Louis tried to explain. "Don't you see? Without books we can never really learn! But just think what we could grow up to be if only we could read. Doctors or lawyers or scientists. Or writers even! *Anything* almost."

"All right," one of the boys snapped. "We want to read too. Find us a way, if you're so smart."

"I can't," Louis cried. "I'm blind!"

Then one day in the spring of 1821 Captain Charles Barbier came to the Institute. Captain Barbier had worked out a way for his soldiers to send messages to each other in the dark. He called it nightwriting. The Captain thought it might work for the blind too.

Nightwriting used raised dots. A word was broken down into sounds. Each sound was given a different pattern of raised dots. The dots were pushed——or punched——into heavy sheets of paper with a long pointed tool called a *stylus*. When the paper was turned over, raised dots could be felt on the other side.

Dots! At first the blind boys were very excited. There were so many things right about dots! They were so small——just feel how many fit under a single fingertip. And they were so easy to feel!

But before long the boys knew that many things were wrong with Captain Barbier's nightwriting, too. There were so many things it would not do. There was no way to make capital letters or write numbers. There was no way to make periods or commas or exclamation points. It took up far too much room. But most of all it was so hard to learn and hard to feel.

Nightwriting might work well enough for soldiers to send simple notes like "advance" or "enemy is behind you." But it was no way to read or write many words. It was no way to make many books for the blind.

So nightwriting was a failure. Did that mean dots were a failure too? Louis didn't think so. As the days passed it was all he could think of. He even dreamed of dots at night.

And before long Louis made up his mind. He was going to do it himself. He was going to work out a way for the blind to *really* read and write with dots! Quickly and easily. At least he was going to try with all his heart and mind.

Louis set right to work. He was almost never without his tools now. Wherever he went he took heavy sheets of paper, a board to rest them on, and his stylus—the long, thin tool for punching dots. (The stylus was shaped almost exactly like an *awl*—the tool that had made Louis blind.)

Captain Barbier soon heard that someone was trying to make his nightwriting better. He hurried to the Institute to see who it was.

Louis was excited when he learned he was going to meet Captain Barbier, the man who had invented nightwriting. It was Captain Barbier who had worked with dots in the first place! Would the Captain like his ideas? Louis hoped so!

But things went wrong from the start. Captain Barbier's eyebrows rose with surprise as Louis tapped into the room. He had been expecting a man. Not a twelve-year-old boy! Louis couldn't see the look on Captain Barbier's face. But he could hear the chill in his voice.

"I hear you think you have worked out some improvements on my system," the Captain said.

"Yes . . . yes, sir," Louis answered.

"Well?"

"Sir . . . ?" said Louis, confused.

"Explain, explain!"

Louis tried. But the more he talked, the more he could tell that Captain Barbier wasn't really listening.

But Louis kept trying. "S . . . sir. One thing that must be worked out. We must find a way for words to . . . to be spelled the same way again and again."

"Why?" said the Captain. His voice was cold as ice.

"So . . . so we can have books——many books."

"Why?" the Captain asked again. Captain Barbier was like many other people in Louis's day. He felt sorry for blind people. He would never be cruel to them. But he did not think they were as smart as other people——people who could see. He thought blind people should be satisfied with simple things——like being able to read short notes and signs and directions. He certainly didn't think they needed many books!

"Is that all?" said the Captain.

"Yes . . ." Louis was almost whispering now.

"Very interesting," Captain Barbier snapped. "I will think about it." But Louis knew he would not. Captain Barbier was a proud man——too proud. He was used to giving orders and having them obeyed. He might have been able to accept these ideas from another man. But from a boy? A half-grown child? No, he didn't like it. He didn't like it at all!

Captain Barbier said a few more stiff words. Then with a bang of the door he was gone.

Louis sighed. He knew he would get no help from the Captain. He would have to work alone.

The Alphabet of Dots

Louis tried not to waste a single minute. Even when he was home on vacation, he worked on his dots. Often his mother would pack him a lunch of bread and cheese and fruit, and he would wander out to sit on some sunny hillside. Other times he sat by the side of the road, bent over his paper and board. "There is Louis, making his pinpricks," the neighbors said with a smile as they passed. What was he doing? Was it some kind of a game the blind boy was playing to keep himself busy? Louis didn't try to explain. He just went on punching patterns of dots.

At home in Coupvray Louis had plenty of free time to work on his experiments. At school it was not nearly so easy. There were so many other things to do. Louis had to go to class. He had to spend an hour or two in one of the workshops every day. He had to practice his music and do his homework. He had to eat meals with the rest of the boys—or someone would come looking for him.

But Louis still found time to work on his ideas. He worked in bits and pieces. He worked before breakfast. And between classes. He worked after dinner. And late at night.

That was the best time of all. The boys were all asleep, and everything was quiet. Hour after hour Louis bent over his board, experimenting with different patterns of dots.

Sometimes he got so tired he fell asleep sitting up. Sometimes he became so excited he forgot what time it was and worked until he heard the milk wagons rattling by under his window. Louis would raise his head with surprise then. For he knew it was early morning. He had worked the whole night through again! Then Louis would crawl into bed to nap for an hour or two——before he had to get up yawning for breakfast and his first class.

Louis's friends became more and more worried about him.

"You never sleep!"

"Half the time you forget to eat!"

"And for what?" a third boy snapped. "A wild goose chase! That's what!"

"Maybe you're right," Louis always answered them softly. And he kept on working.

Three years went by——three years of hard work and trying and not quite succeeding.

Sometimes Louis got so tired he could hardly lift his hand. And sometimes he became very, very discouraged.

Again and again Louis had simplified Captain Barbier's patterns of dots. But still they were not simple enough. No, reading with dots was still too hard.

Were the boys right? Was this a wild goose chase? Men had been working on this problem for hundreds of years——smart men, important men, older men. And one after another *they* had failed. Who did he think he was? What right did he have to think he could do better than they? "Sometimes I think I'll kill myself if I don't succeed," Louis said to Gabriel.

Then Louis had a new and very different idea. It seemed so simple——after he'd had it. Captain Barbier's nightwriting had been based on *sounds*. But there were so many sounds in the French language. Sometimes it took almost a hundred dots to write out a simple word. This was far, far too many to feel easily with the fingertips. But what if he used dots in a different way? What if the patterns of dots didn't stand for sounds at all? What if they stood for the letters of the alphabet instead? There were only twenty-six of them, after all!

Louis was filled with excitement. He was sure he was right! Now he worked even harder. And everything began to fall into place.

First Louis took a pencil and marked six dots on a heavy piece of paper. He called this six-dot pattern a *cell*. It looked like this:

He numbered each dot in the cell:

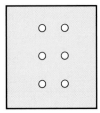

Then he took his stylus and raised dot number one—that would stand for *A*:

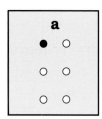

He raised dots number one and two—and that would stand for *B*:

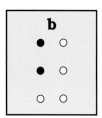

Raised dots number one and four would be *C*:

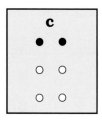

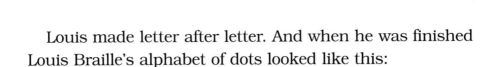

Louis made letter after letter. And when he was finished Louis Braille's alphabet of dots looked like this:

a	b	c	d	e	f	g
h	i	j	k	l	m	n
o	p	q	r	s	t	u
v	w	x	y	z		

Louis ran his fingers over his alphabet. It was so simple! So simple! Fifteen-year-old Louis Braille felt like shouting or crying or laughing out loud. All the letters of the alphabet had been made out of the same six dots——used over and over again in different patterns! He knew it wouldn't look like much of anything to people who could see. But it wasn't supposed to! It was meant to be felt! Quickly. Easily. And it worked!

471

Louis Braille

The Boy Who Invented Books for the Blind

Meet the Author

Margaret Davidson has written several biographies for children. Some of her books have been written under the names Mickie Compere and Mickie Davidson.

Ms. Davidson says about writing books, *"I've been asked [how I came to write books], and the only valid answer I've been able to scare up is that I loved to read when I was a child. It was a whole world to me."*

When she's not writing, Ms. Davidson enjoys art, reading, and visiting museums.

Meet the Illustrator

Bob Dorsey has been a professional illustrator for 17 years, working with a wide range of media and a variety of subjects. Some of his favorite projects include portraits, wildlife, children, and sports. Mr. Dorsey is well known for the many portraits that he has done for the National Baseball Hall of Fame in Cooperstown, New York. His paintings have been exhibited throughout the United States.

Theme Connections

Within the Selection

Writer's Notebook Record your answers to the questions below in the Response Journal section of your Writer's Notebook. In small groups, report the ideas you wrote. Discuss your ideas with the rest of your group. Then choose a person to report your group's answers to the class.

- How did Louis Braille help blind people communicate better?

- How did soldiers send messages to each other in the dark?

Across Selections

How are Louis Braille and Gutenberg in "Breaking into Print: Before and After the Invention of the Printing Press" similar?

Beyond the Selection

- How did the work of Louis Braille make a difference to people? Share your thoughts with the members of your group.

- Think about how "Louis Braille: The Boy Who Invented Books for the Blind" adds to what you know about communication.

- Add items to the Concept/Question Board about communication.

Connections

Diane Siebert

illustrated by Aaron Meshon

Extending high above the ground,
They stretch forever, wrapped around
The voices sent to rendezvous
With other voices passing through.

And as they travel far away,
The wind-blown conversations sway
As rows and rows of resting birds
Perch happily on miles of words.

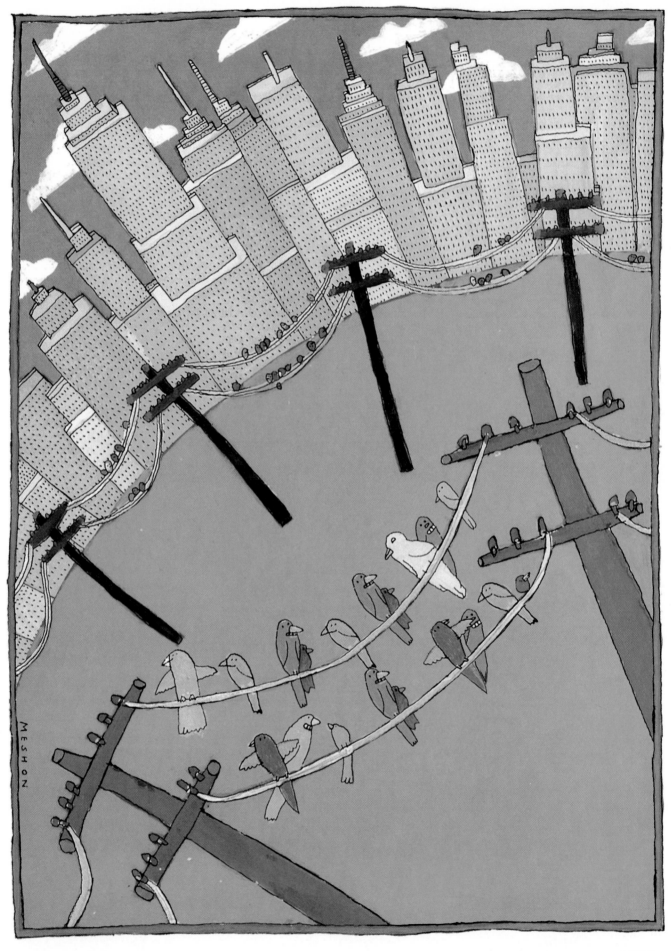

475

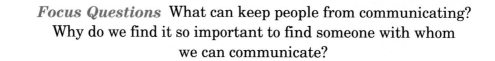

My Two Drawings

from *The Little Prince*
written and drawn by **Antoine de Saint-Exupéry**
translated from the French by Richard Howard

Once when I was six I saw a magnificent picture in a book about the jungle, called *True Stories*. It showed a boa constrictor swallowing a wild beast. Here is a copy of the picture.

In the book it said: "Boa constrictors swallow their prey whole, without chewing. Afterward they are no longer able to move, and they sleep during the six months of their digestion."

In those days I thought a lot about jungle adventures, and eventually managed to make my first drawing, using a colored pencil. My drawing Number One looked like this:

I showed the grown-ups my masterpiece, and I asked them if my drawing scared them.

They answered, "Why be scared of a hat?"

My drawing was not a picture of a hat. It was a picture of a boa constrictor digesting an elephant. Then I drew the inside of the boa constrictor, so the grown-ups could understand. They always need explanations. My drawing Number Two looked like this:

The grown-ups advised me to put away my drawings of boa constrictors, outside or inside, and apply myself instead to geography, history, arithmetic, and grammar. That is why I abandoned, at the age of six, a magnificent career as an artist. I had been discouraged by the failure of my drawing Number One and of my drawing Number Two. Grown-ups never understand anything by themselves, and it is exhausting for children to have to provide explanations over and over again.

So then I had to choose another career, and I learned to pilot airplanes. I have flown almost everywhere in the world. And, as a matter of fact, geography has been a big help to me. I could tell China from Arizona at first glance, which is very useful if you get lost during the night.

So I have had, in the course of my life, lots of encounters with lots of serious people. I have spent lots of time with grown-ups. I have seen them at close range...which hasn't much improved my opinion of them.

Whenever I encountered a grown-up who seemed to me at all enlightened, I would experiment on him with my drawing Number One, which I have always kept. I wanted to see if he really understood anything. But he would always answer, "That's a hat." Then I wouldn't talk about boa constrictors or jungles or stars. I would put myself on his level and talk about bridge and golf and politics and neckties. And my grown-up was glad to know such a reasonable person.

My Two Drawings

Meet the Author/Illustrator

Antoine de Saint-Exupéry loved aviation. He joined the French Army Air Force and later became a commercial pilot. As a writer he combined his thrill for flying with adventure to create exciting adult novels and of course the story of *The Little Prince*. *The Little Prince* happened by accident. One day while Saint-Exupéry was at lunch with his publisher, he began to doodle on his napkin. His publisher saw the drawing of what Saint-Exupéry called "just a little fellow I carry around in my heart" and suggested the author create a children's book. Writing *The Little Prince* was a joyful task for Saint-Exupéry.

Meet the Translator

Richard Howard is an American poet and translator. He has translated over 100 books from French to English, including modern French fiction and poetry from the nineteenth century. Richard Howard uses his poems to bring past artists, writers, and musicians to life. In each poem, he has a historical character speak about their life and times.

Theme Connections

Within the Selection

Record your answers to the questions below in the Response Journal section of your Writer's Notebook. In small groups, report the ideas you wrote. Discuss your ideas with the rest of your group. Then choose a person to report your group's answers to the class.

- Why didn't the grown-ups understand what the pilot was trying to communicate with his first drawing?
- How did the pilot change his drawing to better communicate his message?

Across Selections

In "My Two Drawings" we see that there are two parts to every communication: someone says something, and someone else has to understand that person. Where do you see this in other readings?

Beyond the Selection

- Think of a story you have read, and draw a picture to illustrate one scene from the story. Share your pictures with the other members of your group.
- Think about how "My Two Drawings" adds to what you know about communication.
- Add items to the Concept/Question Board about communication.

A Changing America

First were the Native Americans. Different tribes and societies occupied parts of North America. Then the Europeans came and began to set up colonies. That was more than 150 years before the United States came into being. What was life like during those years? It wasn't all log cabins and teepees and battles over territory. A complex society grew up that led to the America we know today. So it's *your* history—even if your ancestors didn't come over on the *Mayflower*!

Early America

by Trevor Matheney

When the colonists arrived in America, they were beginning a new life in what to them was a "new world." They weren't completely aware of the long and varied history of the place they called the Americas.

Hopewell Culture (300 B.C.–A.D. 500), Ohio: Raven or crow with a pearl eye cut from a sheet of copper

There is evidence that long before Columbus in 1492 or John Cabot in 1497 ever set foot in the Americas, nomadic groups had traveled from Asia and spread out through what is now the United States and South America. These people formed tribes such as the Hopewell and Powhatan and great civilizations such as the Aztec and Inca. In addition, artifacts that have been found suggest visits by the Japanese, Chinese, and Phoenicians.

By the early 1500s many Spanish, English, French, and Portuguese explorers, fishermen, and traders were traveling to the Americas and returning with tales of giant forests, huge stretches of land, and plenty of clear blue waters.

This was particularly interesting to European men. For the most part in Europe at that time, only the oldest son could inherit the land of his father. Thus, for many younger sons the only way to have land of their own was to leave Europe. The idea of settling in the New World of the Americas became very attractive.

Other people wanted to escape some of the problems they faced in Europe. In many places in Europe, people were not allowed religious freedom. Some of these people felt they would be able to worship as they pleased in the New World.

Spain and England were the first countries to build settlements in the Americas. These settlements were called colonies. The first Spanish settlement was established at St. Augustine, Florida, in 1565.

Spanish settlement at St. Augustine, Florida

Sir Walter Raleigh's expedition to
Roanoke Island, 1585

In 1585, the English began a colony on Roanoke Island off the coast of what is now North Carolina. This colony failed. However, another attempt to colonize Roanoke Island was made in 1587. It was here that Virginia Dare, the first English child born in America, was born. In 1590, when supply ships returned from England to the Roanoke Colony, everyone had disappeared. No one knows what happened to these early colonists. Because of this, the Roanoke Colony has become known as the Lost Colony.

The Jamestown Colony, founded in 1607, and the Plymouth Colony, founded in 1620, were the first two English colonies that survived. The Jamestown Colony grew into what was called the Virginia Colony. The Plymouth Colony was located in what is now Massachusetts and is where the Pilgrims first settled.

The colonists had to face the hardships of living in a new, unfamiliar land. Many died of disease or starvation. Most of the early colonists were farmers, growing corn, beans, and other food and raising their own animals. They made their own clothes, built their own homes, and worked long, hard days. Few colonial children went to school. Often parents used the Bible to teach their children to read. A few colleges were eventually started for men only. The first college in the colonies was Harvard, founded in 1636 in Massachusetts.

The Native Americans helped these early colonists survive their first years in the New World. However, some Native American groups were upset at having their lands taken by these new people who often brought with them unfriendly ways and diseases deadly to the Native Americans. As more and more colonists arrived, they began taking land from these groups. Several wars were fought between the colonists and the Native Americans. In 1675, a Native American leader named King Philip led the Wampanoag and Narragansett tribes in a war against the colonists in Massachusetts and Rhode Island. These were the same tribes who had helped the colonists survive their first years in the New World. Now, they were angry. Both tribes were nearly destroyed in this war. Clashes between the colonists and the Native Americans continued throughout the colonial period.

Native Americans helping English: Dutch fur trader

Although the colonies were governed by England, not all colonists were English. Many were from Germany, France, the Netherlands, Sweden, Ireland, and Scotland. Others were brought from Africa as indentured servants and later, slaves. By 1700 there were about 250,000 colonists living in the thirteen English colonies in America.

The colonies were different in many ways. For example, in Massachusetts, many of the colonists came as families looking for land to settle. The Rhode Island and Pennsylvania colonies were settled by religious groups in search of freedom to worship as they pleased. The New York Colony became a very culturally and ethnically diverse colony. People from all countries began to settle there.

Many early colonists were unmarried men under the age of twenty-five. In the Maryland Colony, most colonists were single men who arrived as indentured servants. They would work for a period of time, up to seven years, before being given their freedom. In exchange, they received food and shelter, and often learned a trade. Over half of these Maryland colonists died of starvation and disease within a few years of arriving in the colonies.

As the number of indentured servants decreased, there was a shortage of workers in the colonies. To fill this shortage, the colonists turned to slavery. In some colonies, over one-fourth of the population consisted of African slaves. However, not all colonial Africans were slaves. Some had come to America as indentured servants and when their indenture was served they were free to work as they saw fit.

England was not the only country to own land in America. Spain owned what is now Florida, and France owned much of the land west of the thirteen English colonies. This prevented the English colonists from spreading out. Because of this, the population in the English colonies became more concentrated. Cities and towns grew out of the early settlements.

The colonists began to feel they lived in a country so different from England that English law and the English government no longer served them well. These ideas would lead to the Revolutionary War, in which the thirteen English colonies would become the United States of America.

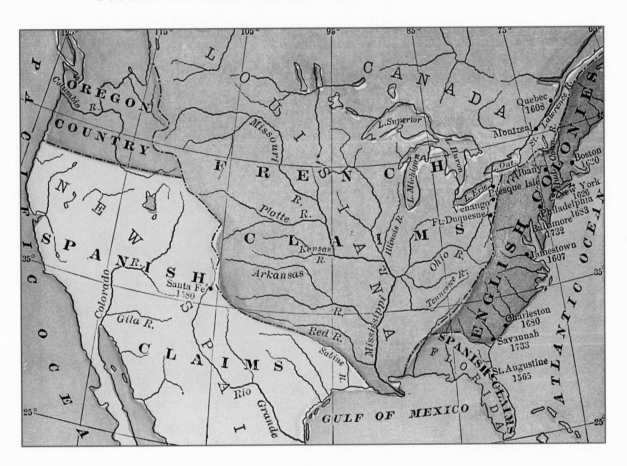

Early America

Meet the Author

Trevor Matheney is a pen name of Wiley Blevins, who wrote "Music and Slavery" from Unit 4. Mr. Blevins grew up in the South and eventually became a teacher. He has taught both in the United States and in Ecuador. Currently Mr. Blevins lives in New York City, where he is a writer and an editor.

Theme Connections

Within the Selection

Writer's Notebook

Record your answers to the questions below in the Response Journal section of your Writer's Notebook. In small groups, report the ideas you wrote. Discuss your ideas with the rest of your group. Then choose a person to report your group's answers to the class.

- What are some of the reasons colonists settled in Colonial America?
- What hardships did the colonists face in Colonial America?
- Why were several wars fought between Native American groups and the colonists in Colonial America?

Across Selections

In this selection, you learned about early America. What information presented in this selection was similar to information presented in "The Colonies"?

Beyond the Selection

- Think about how "Early America" adds to what you know about the theme A Changing America.
- Add items to the Concept/Question Board about the theme A Changing America.

Focus Questions Why would people take such a risky journey to go live in America? Were the childen aboard the Mayflower very different from children now?

The Voyage of the Mayflower

Patricia M. Whalen
illustrated by James Watling

Pelted by rain under a black sky, the ninety-foot *Mayflower* rolled and pitched on mountainous waves. Its masts were bare because during a storm, a sailing ship must lower all its sails and drift with the wind to avoid capsizing or breaking apart.

Below the main deck, the passengers huddled in the dark. They could hear the wind howling and the waves thudding against the vessel's wooden sides and washing over the deck. Seawater dripped down on them through the canvas covering the deck gratings and seeped through the seams in the planking. The passengers were soaked and shivering; several were seasick besides. As frightened adults tried to comfort terrified children, they prayed for safety in the storm and an end to the long, terrible voyage.

Suddenly, above the din of the storm, they heard the noise of splitting timber. One of the beams supporting the deck had cracked! The ship was in danger of sinking. Then someone remembered a great iron screw brought from Holland. Carefully, the ship's carpenter positioned it beneath the beam and braced it. It would hold; the passengers and crew could reach land safely.

Crossing the Atlantic in 1620 was extremely risky. A wooden ship could leak or break apart in a storm. Since the sails could be raised only in fair weather, it was impossible to predict how long a voyage would last. To avoid the stormy autumn months, ships usually made the crossing in spring or summer. They almost never sailed alone.

Aware of these dangers, the Pilgrims had planned to cross the ocean in two ships in the summer of 1620. The English Separatists from Holland (who called themselves Saints) borrowed money from London businessmen and purchased a small ship, the *Speedwell*. For the Separatists' safety, and to help them establish a profitable colony, the businessmen recruited additional volunteers in London. The

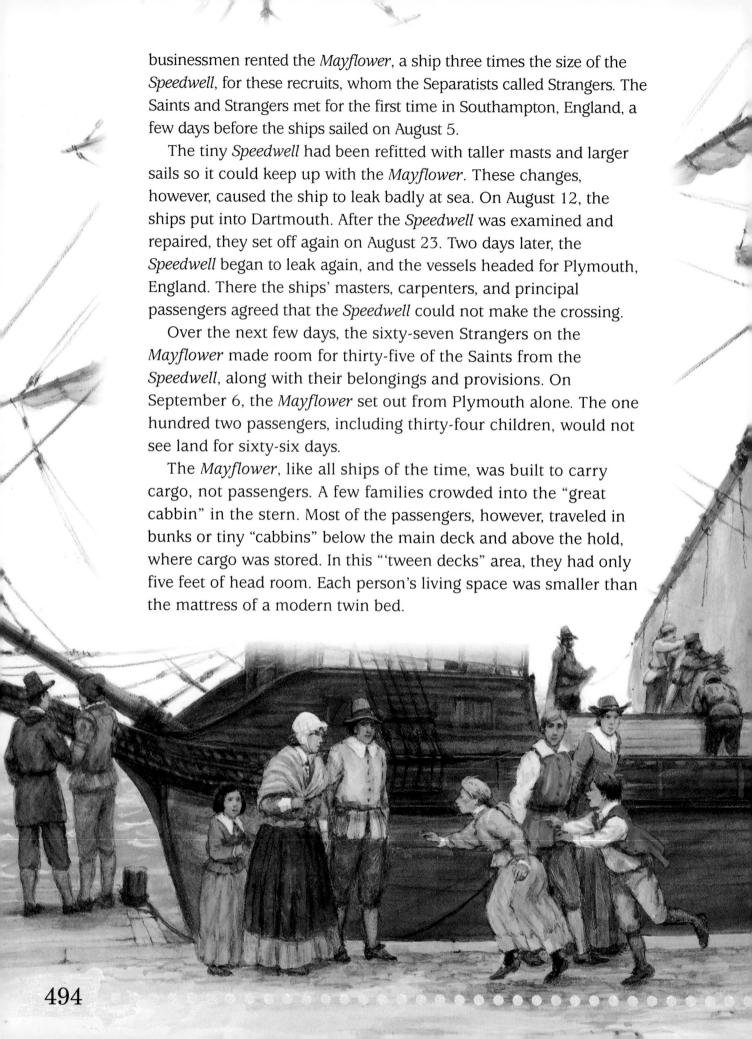

businessmen rented the *Mayflower*, a ship three times the size of the *Speedwell*, for these recruits, whom the Separatists called Strangers. The Saints and Strangers met for the first time in Southampton, England, a few days before the ships sailed on August 5.

The tiny *Speedwell* had been refitted with taller masts and larger sails so it could keep up with the *Mayflower*. These changes, however, caused the ship to leak badly at sea. On August 12, the ships put into Dartmouth. After the *Speedwell* was examined and repaired, they set off again on August 23. Two days later, the *Speedwell* began to leak again, and the vessels headed for Plymouth, England. There the ships' masters, carpenters, and principal passengers agreed that the *Speedwell* could not make the crossing.

Over the next few days, the sixty-seven Strangers on the *Mayflower* made room for thirty-five of the Saints from the *Speedwell*, along with their belongings and provisions. On September 6, the *Mayflower* set out from Plymouth alone. The one hundred two passengers, including thirty-four children, would not see land for sixty-six days.

The *Mayflower*, like all ships of the time, was built to carry cargo, not passengers. A few families crowded into the "great cabbin" in the stern. Most of the passengers, however, traveled in bunks or tiny "cabbins" below the main deck and above the hold, where cargo was stored. In this "'tween decks" area, they had only five feet of head room. Each person's living space was smaller than the mattress of a modern twin bed.

The Pilgrims suffered other discomforts. Many were seasick, particularly at the beginning of the voyage. In storms, they were constantly wet and cold. They could not bathe or wash and dry their clothes and bedding. For toilet purposes, they used buckets.

In fair weather, the adults and children who had recovered from seasickness could leave their dim, foul-smelling quarters for the wind and spray of the main deck. The adults took deep breaths of the cold, tangy air and stretched cramped muscles. The younger children, forbidden to run around, played quiet games. Damaris Hopkins, age three, and Mary and Remember Allerton, ages four and six, "tended the baby" (played with dolls). Six- and nine-year-old brothers Wrestling and Love Brewster played "I Spy" and "Hunt the Slipper" with six- and seven-year-old Jasper and Richard More. Finger games such as cat's cradle and paper, scissors, stone were popular with eight-year-old Humility Cooper, Ellen More, John Cooke, John Billington, and Bartholomew Allerton. Elizabeth Tilley, age fourteen, and Mary Chilton and Constance Hopkins, both fifteen, helped prepare the meals.

For cooking, the passengers built charcoal fires in metal braziers set in sandboxes. There was so little space, however, that only a few people could cook at once. When storms made lighting fires dangerous, everyone ate cold meals.

After morning prayers, they ate a simple breakfast of cheese and ship's biscuit (hard, dry biscuit). If cooking was allowed, they might have porridge. Their midday meal might consist of ship's biscuit and cheese or, in fair weather, cooked "pease pottage," boiled salt fish, pork, or beef and any freshly caught bonito or porpoise. Before retiring, they had a light supper. Everyone, even the children, drank beer with their meals because it was preferred to water.

Not until December 11, more than a month after first sighting land, did the Pilgrims decide where they would build their colony. One day, before an exploring party left the *Mayflower,* the

passengers and crew had another narrow escape. In his family's "cabbin," fourteen-year-old Francis Billington tried making "squibs" (small fireworks) by lighting short pieces of rope. He then fired a couple of muskets and a fowling piece near an open, half-full barrel of gunpowder. No one knows why his mischief did not blow up the ship.

The *Mayflower* remained anchored offshore during the winter while the Pilgrims built their new homes. On April 5, 1621, the ship set sail for England. With the prevailing winds and currents, it made the return trip in only thirty-one days.

The Voyage of the Mayflower

Meet the Illustrator

James Watling was educated at the Barron School of Art and Leeds College of Art. He began teaching in 1954, first in secondary schools, then at McGill University in Montreal after he moved to Canada from England. He retired as an Associate Professor in Art Education in 1995. Some of Mr. Watling's interests include gardening, woodworking, nature, and wildlife. He has been illustrating since the 1960s and continues this today.

Theme Connections

Within the Selection

Record your answers to the questions below in the Response Journal section of your Writer's Notebook. In small groups, report the ideas you wrote. Discuss your ideas with the rest of your group. Then choose a person to report your group's answers to the class.

- Why was it extremely risky for the Pilgrims to cross the Atlantic and come to America?
- What discomforts did the Pilgrims face in their journey to America?

Across Selections

The Pilgrims took a big risk and sailed to America. What other stories have you read in which a character or characters took similar risks?

Beyond the Selection

- The children on the *Mayflower* played quiet games like "I Spy," cat's cradle, and paper, scissors, stone to pass the time. Do you like to play games? Share some games you like to play with the other members of your group.
- Think about how "The Voyage of the Mayflower" adds to what you know about the theme A Changing America.
- Add items to the Concept/Question Board about the theme A Changing America.

Sampler. c.1792. **Patty Coggeshall.** Linen embroidered with silk thread.
$19\frac{1}{2} \times 16\frac{5}{8}$ in. The Metropolitan Museum of Art, New York, NY.

The Mason Children:
David, Joanna, and
Abigail. 1670.
Attributed to the
Freake-Gibbs Painter.
Fine Arts Museum of San
Francisco.

Quilled Buckskin Robe. National Museum of
the American Indian, Smithsonian Institution.

Pocahontas

from *The Virginia Colony*

by Dennis B. Fradin

illustrated by Robert Roth

This painting of Pocahontas, done while she was touring England shortly before her death, shows her in English clothing.

Exactly when and where the Native American girl named Matoaka was born is not known, but it probably was in eastern Virginia around 1595. When the Jamestown colonists arrived in 1607, Matoaka was about twelve years old. Little is known about Matoaka's life away from the colonists, but when she was with them, she lived up to her nickname, Pocahontas, which means "The Playful One."

After Pocahontas saved John Smith's life in early 1608, there was a short time of peace between the colonists and the Native Americans. During this time Pocahontas often came to Jamestown, where she would challenge the young men to compete with her at performing handsprings and running races. The English youths taught her a phrase: "Love you not me?" which Pocahontas would repeat to them. In return, Pocahontas taught Captain Smith and the other colonists some Native American words.

In the spring of 1608, John Smith got into an argument with Pocahontas's people during a bargaining session and took seven of them captive. Powhatan tried to get the prisoners released, but nothing worked until he sent Pocahontas to Jamestown as his agent. Captain Smith and the other leaders of Jamestown let the prisoners go for the sake of Pocahontas.

About a year after this incident, Smith left Virginia, and relations between the Native Americans and the colonists worsened. Those few times when the Native Americans and the colonists met peacefully, Pocahontas and her people asked what had become of Captain Smith. The colonists always said that he was dead.

In 1613 Pocahontas was staying in a Native American village along the Potomac River when she was kidnapped and taken first to Jamestown and then to Henrico. In Henrico she was given fancy English petticoats and dresses to replace her deerskin clothes, taught the English language, and renamed Rebecca. How Pocahontas felt about this we do not know. We do know, however, that Pocahontas met the tobacco planter John Rolfe in the summer of 1613 and that the next spring the two were married in a ceremony that was Jamestown's big social event of the year.

In 1616 Pocahontas and her husband went with their year-old son, Thomas, and several other Native Americans to England. She was introduced to royalty and invited to balls and banquets. In England, Pocahontas also learned a startling piece of news: John Smith was still alive! One day in the fall of 1616 Captain Smith called at the house where she was staying near London.

Pocahontas, who by this time was ill because of England's damp and chilly weather, was both pleased and upset at the sight of Smith. "They did tell us always you were dead," she said. Pocahontas then teased Smith for having forgotten her, reminded him that she had adopted

him long ago, and called him "Father." When Smith said that she should not call him "Father," Pocahontas answered, "I tell you then I will, and I will be forever and ever your countryman."

A few minutes later Captain Smith left, and the two never met again. In March of 1617, just as the Rolfes were about to sail home to Virginia, Pocahontas died of smallpox. The woman who had saved John Smith's life and who had once performed handsprings in Jamestown was only twenty-two years old when she died. Thomas Rolfe, her son, was educated in England. At age twenty he returned to Virginia, where he became a popular citizen and even helped defend the colony against the Native Americans.

Pocahontas

from *The Virginia Colony*

Meet the Author

Dennis Fradin taught elementary school students before he became an author. Now he has written almost 150 books. He is a man who loves his work. He says, *"I have the time of my life as a children's book author. Each day I take about five steps from my bedroom into my office, where I spend my time reading, writing, rewriting, and phoning people for information. Often I travel to do in-person research."*

Mr. Fradin researches his books very carefully and sometimes rewrites them five or six times. He says, *"I also check over all my facts line by line to make sure everything is accurate. So all that keeps me pretty busy. I try not to let a day of the year go by without working."*

Meet the Illustrator

Robert Roth grew up on Long Island, New York, and studied art at the Rhode Island School of Design.

Mr. Roth has been drawing since he could pick up and hold a pencil. Almost everywhere he goes he carries a sketchbook. He likes to draw from real life outside the studio to keep his eye alert and his work fresh.

Theme Connections

Within the Selection

Record your answers to the questions below in the Response Journal section of your Writer's Notebook. In small groups, report the ideas you wrote. Discuss your ideas with the rest of your group. Then choose a person to report your group's answers to the class.

- Why was Matoaka nicknamed Pocahontas, which means "The Playful One"?
- John Smith held seven of Powhatan's people captive. How did Powhatan manage to get them released?

Across Selections

In this selection, we read that Pocahontas' people and the colonists argued. What have you read in other selections that can help you better understand why they were arguing?

Beyond the Selection

- Think about how "Pocahontas" adds to what you know about the theme A Changing America.
- Add items to the Concept/Question Board about the theme A Changing America.

Focus Questions Were all the colonists in favor of the Revolution?
Could the colonies have broken from England without a war?

Martha Helps the Rebel

A Play by Carole Charles
illustrated by Charles Shaw and Dennis Hockerman

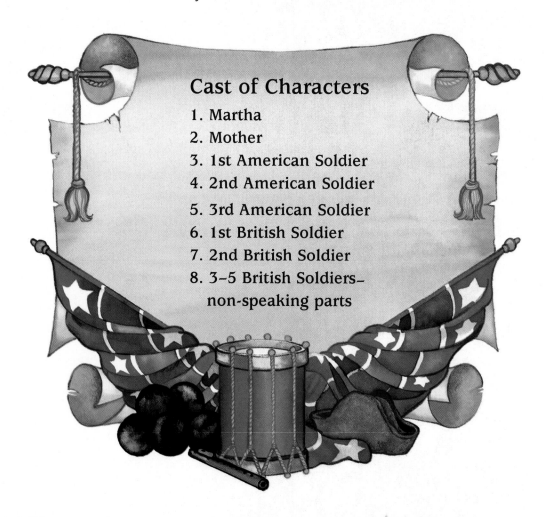

Cast of Characters

1. Martha
2. Mother
3. 1st American Soldier
4. 2nd American Soldier
5. 3rd American Soldier
6. 1st British Soldier
7. 2nd British Soldier
8. 3–5 British Soldiers–
   non-speaking parts

(Setting: South Carolina, 1780. From the back of their farmhouse, a mother and her ten-year-old daughter, Martha, watch three American soldiers walk through the nearby woods.)

Martha: Look at the soldiers, ma!

Mother: I see them, Martha. They must be coming from Charleston.

Martha: Are they American soldiers?

Mother: Yes.

Martha: I wish I were big enough to be a soldier like pa. I'd chase all the British soldiers right back to England! Would you like to be a soldier, ma?

Mother: *(musing)* Sometimes I would. But you and I need to take care of the farm until your pa comes home.

(Three American soldiers walking through the woods. British soldiers in hiding nearby.)

1st Am. Soldier: *(sings)* "Come all you brave soldiers, Both valiant and free, It's for independence, We all now agree."

2nd Am. Soldier: Hey, quiet down! Everyone in South Carolina can hear you.

1st Am. Soldier: Good! Then all the British soldiers in the colony will run at the sound of my voice. *(Sings the song again, just as loudly.)*

3rd Am. Soldier: Come on, quiet down. If any British soldiers have landed this far south, I'd like to hear them before they hear us.

1st Am. Soldier: Ah, there aren't any British around here.

3rd Am. Soldier: Maybe not. That's what we're supposed to find out.

(Woods. 1st Am. soldier whistling the tune from previous scene.)

2nd Am. Soldier: When we get back to Charleston, I'd like to . . .

(Interrupted by a musket shot, Whistling stops abruptly. 2nd Am. soldier yells and falls dead.)

3rd. Am. Soldier: British! Stay down!

(Shots fired from both sides.)

1st Am. Soldier: *(whispering)* Let's run for it. We'll never be able to hold them off here.

3rd Am. Soldier: All right . . . now!

(Musket shot strikes 3rd Am. soldier, who yells and falls.)

1st Am. Soldier: Oh, no! *(Fiercely, to himself)* I have to get out of here!

(Soldier exits, running, crouched. Sound of feet running, crashing through low brush. Muskets fire several more times.)

(Woods. American soldier enters, running through low brush. About eight British soldiers pursue. American soldier exits on other side.)

1st Br. Soldier: Let's get him!

2nd Br. Soldier: *(panting heavily)* I can hardly run with this heavy pack.

3rd Br. Soldier: *(also panting)* Hey, just a minute. Slow down. Listen, he can outrun us easily. We're wearing winter uniforms and carrying packs. All the American has to carry is a musket.

1st Br. Soldier: But we have to stop him before he reaches Charleston. The American army must not know our position or strength.

3rd Br. Soldier: *(still breathing heavily)* I know. So let's outsmart that American soldier. Hide the packs somewhere in the bushes. Then spread out and we'll search the ways to Charleston. He'll have to stop for food and water, perhaps for rest. If we move quickly, we'll find him.

(Martha grooms a riding horse. Mother enters. Mother and Martha see the American soldier running through the woods as if pursued.)

Martha: Ma, look!

Mother: I see. Martha, ride old Jonathan as fast as you can to that soldier. Bring him back by the stream bed so no one will see him. I'll wait in the kitchen.

Martha: What if there are British soldiers right behind him?

Mother: You said you wanted to fight. This is your chance. Hurry, before it's too late.

(Martha and horse exit. Sound of hoofbeats.)

(Kitchen. Mother is lowering a quilting frame from the ceiling. Frame has a nearly completed quilt attached. Soldier and Martha enter from side. Soldier appears haggard, exhausted.)

Mother: Martha, go back outside and ride old Jonathan hard around the pasture, as though you were exercising him. If anyone comes, I don't want a panting horse tied to my front porch.

Martha: Yes, ma. *(Exits.)*

Soldier: Ma'am, I . . .

Mother: *(interrupting)* We can talk later. Right now I want you up on those rafters, right over the spot where the quilting frame will be.

Soldier: Up there? But . . .

Mother: *(interrupting)* Soldier, if you want to live, you'd better get up on those rafters, and fast!

(American soldier balanced on the rafters. Mother raising the quilting frame. British soldiers can be seen through a window, approaching the house from the woods.)

Am. Soldier: Ma'am, you don't know how much I appreciate your help.

Mother: *(speaking as she raises the frame)* It's all right. My husband is a soldier with the Continental Army too. Maybe someone will help him one day.

Am. Soldier: I'm very grateful for . . .

Mother: *(interrupting)* Hush! *(whispering)* Soldiers coming! Don't make a sound!

(Loud knocks on the door.)

Br. Soldier: *(from outside)* Open up! *(More loud knocks.)* Open up, I say!

(Kitchen. American soldier completely hidden from view by quilt and frame. Mother has lifted hot skillet off fireplace in pretense of busyness. Loud knocks continue.)

Mother: Just a minute!

(More loud knocks. British soldiers push open the door and enter the kitchen.)

Br. Soldier: Sorry, ma'am. We're looking for someone.

Mother: *(indignant)* You might have waited until I opened the door!

(Soldiers begin searching the house.)

Mother: What are you doing!

Br. Soldier: Looking for someone, like I said. Arnold, you keep watch outside. Two of you search the barn and grounds. The rest of you search every inch of this house.

Mother: You have no right to search my house!

Br. Soldier: You have nothing to be afraid of, ma'am, *(threateningly)* unless we find an American soldier here.

(Kitchen. Mother seated. British soldiers still searching. Martha comes running in.)

Martha: Ma! What are they doing?

Mother: They're just looking for someone, Martha.

Br. Soldier: Where have you been, little girl?

Martha: *(defiant)* My name is Martha, not "little girl"! I've been out riding my horse.

Br. Soldier: *(quiet but threatening)* You wouldn't have been hiding an American soldier somewhere, would you?

Martha: *(still defiant)* I told you, I was riding my horse.

Mother: Martha, come sit down with me. They'll be leaving soon.

Martha: *(through clenched teeth)* I hope so!

(Kitchen. American soldier climbing down from rafters. Twilight.)

Mother: It's safe now. The British have gone.

Soldier: Thank you. I'm very grateful. *(Thoughtful)* Do you know if there are many British around?

Mother: We haven't seen British soldiers for several months, until today.

Martha: *(excited)* I'll bet there are thousands of British just over the hill, ready to attack Charleston!

Soldier: *(laughing gently)* Well, perhaps. But we rather expect an attack from the sea. That's how they attacked at the beginning of the war.

Martha: Maybe they're trying to trick you! You should go look for yourself. I'll bet there are thousands of British over there, just polishing their muskets and laughing.

Soldier: *(slowly)* That is possible. Perhaps I should take a look as soon as it's dark.

(Early morning, outside the farmhouse. Mother milking a cow. Martha enters, carrying a basket of eggs. Soldier rushes on stage.)

Soldier: You were right, Martha! The British are landing along the coast. It looks as though they are preparing to march on Charleston.

Mother: *(very nervous)* Keep your voice down! The British came back again last night. They're still looking for you, and for any other American soldiers. All the roads are guarded.

Soldier: And I know why! Most of our troops in Charleston are guarding the coast. If the British attack from the south, they will meet almost no resistance.

Martha: You'll have to tell them! You'll have to get through!

Mother: But how? It would be easier for . . . for this cow to pass the British. An American soldier couldn't make it!

Martha: I have an idea!

(Martha, mother, and soldier taking clothes out of a chest. Soldier half dressed as an old farmer.)

Mother: Pa won't mind our giving these clothes to you. They just might help you get past the British.

Martha: You really look like a farmer! *(Laughs with delight.)*

Soldier: Martha, you had a good idea. And making me look so old is the best part of the disguise.

(Dirt road. British soldiers standing guard, blocking road. American soldier disguised as old farmer enters, accompanied by Martha, who leads a milk cow.)

"Farmer": Afternoon, gentlemen.

1st Br. Soldier: Hold on, old man. Where are you taking the cow?

"Farmer": Yonder, to the next town. The little girl has a cousin who wants to buy her milk cow.

1st Br. Soldier: She looks old enough to take an old gentle cow to the next town by herself. Why are you going, mister?

Martha: I'll tell you why. Because I'm afraid to go by myself, that's why. I've never seen so many soldiers around here. I . . . I'm just afraid.

2nd Br. Soldier: Ah, let them go. You're scaring the little girl. The old man is harmless.

"Farmer": *(moving on)* Afternoon, gentlemen.

(American soldier disguised as farmer and Martha walk off with cow. British soldiers still stand guard. British troops approach in formation from south.)

1st Br. Soldier: I wish we knew what happened to that American soldier. If he makes it to Charleston, he'll tell them all about us.

"Farmer", offstage: *(sung in cracked old man's voice)* "Come all you brave soldiers, Both valiant and free, It's for independence, We all now agree."

Martha Helps the Rebel

Meet the Illustrator

Charles Shaw once served in the Army National Guard. He loves to illustrate the Texas frontier, children, and jazz musicians. His work can be found in a number of Texas museums and historical societies. Mr. Shaw is so well-known for his illustrations of Texas frontier life that the University of Texas asked him to create illustrations for a book called *Texas*, written by the famous novelist James Michener. Mr. Shaw has also contributed his illustrations to many other books and magazines.

Meet the Illustrator

Dennis Hockerman has been a designer and illustrator for 23 years. Besides illustrating children's books, he has worked for the greeting card, gift wrap, and toy industries. In his spare time, Mr. Hockerman enjoys working at his printing press creating hand-colored etchings. He works out of his home in Wisconsin, where he lives with his wife, three children, and pets.

Theme Connections

Within the Selection

Record your answers to the questions below in the Response Journal section of your Writer's Notebook. In small groups, report the ideas you wrote. Discuss your ideas with the rest of your group. Then choose a person to report your group's answers to the class.

- Why did the British soldiers want to stop the American soldier?
- How did Martha help the American troops during the Revolutionary War?

Across Selections

What does the American soldier have in common with Anne Frank and her family from "Anne Frank: The Diary of a Young Girl"?

Beyond the Selection

- Think about how "Martha Helps the Rebel" adds to what you know about the theme A Changing America.
- Add items to the Concept/Question Board about the theme A Changing America.

Prophecy in Flame

by Frances Minturn Howard
illustrated by Antonio Castro

Grandfather wrote from Valley Forge,
"My dear, I miss you; times are harder;
The cheeses sent from home received,
A fine addition to our larder."

Grandfather wrote, "The volunteers
Are leaving—going home for haying;
We lose militia day by day;
But still a few of us are staying."

Grandfather wrote, "Last night I gave
My blanket to a soldier who
Was wrapped in rags; Phoebe, my dear,
The nights are cold. I dream of you."

520

Grandfather wrote, "That grand old man
Who bears us up seems not to tire;
I speak of General Washington,
Who last night shared with us his fire."

Grandfather dipped his quill and wrote,
Sanded and sealed his letter; sent it
Off with a splash of sealing wax,
Thinking of her for whom he meant it,

Nor dreamed that soldiers hungering here
Would feed a nation's new desire,
And men unborn would warm themselves
At that same small, fierce-flickering fire.

GOING WEST

from *Children of the Wild West*
by Russell Freedman

It was a typical wagon train of the 1840s. The swaying wagons, plodding animals, and walking people stretched out along the trail for almost a mile.

Near the end of the train, a boy holding a hickory stick moved slowly through the dust. He used the stick to poke and prod the cows that trudged beside him, mooing and complaining.

"Get along!" he shouted. "Hey! Hey! Get along!"

Dust floated in the air. It clogged the boy's nose, parched his throat, and coated his face. His cheeks were smeared where he had brushed away the big mosquitoes that buzzed about everywhere.

Up ahead, his family's wagon bounced down the trail. He could hear the *crack* of his father's whip above the heads of the oxen that pulled the wagon. The animals coughed and snorted. The chains on their yokes rattled with every step they took.

His mother sat in the front seat of the wagon, holding the baby on her lap. His sisters had gone off with some other girls to hunt for wild herbs along the road.

The family was traveling west along the Oregon Trail in what someday would be the state of Wyoming. They followed the sandy banks of the North Platte River past rocky hills dotted with sagebrush and greasewood. This was Indian country, the land of the Oglala Sioux.

Back in Missouri, their wagon had been a brand-new prairie schooner with red wheels, a blue body, and a fresh white canvas top. Now the top was stained and patched, the paint faded and crusted with mud. The wagon creaked and groaned, but it was still sturdy. On this hot July afternoon, the canvas cover had been rolled back and bunched so that any breezes could blow through the wagon.

The wagon was crammed with the family's possessions—with food, clothing, and furniture; with tools, bedding, kitchenware, and tent supplies. Tied to its side were a plow and a hoe. Hanging from a rope was a sealed pail of milk that bounced steadily as the wagon jolted along. By evening, the milk would be churned into butter.

There were forty wagons in the party, and nearly two hundred men, women, and children. A few of the pioneers rode saddle horses, but most of them walked. The only ones riding inside the wagons were little children with their mothers, and people who were sick or injured. Following the wagons were herds of milk cows and beef cattle, along with extra oxen, mules, and horses.

The pioneers had been up since four that morning, when the sentries started the day by firing their rifles. Hurrying about in the darkness, they had kindled fires, put on kettles of water, milked cows, pulled down tents, loaded wagons, and fixed breakfast. By seven, they were ready to roll. The train captain gave the signal to move out. Slowly the lead wagons rolled forward, and the others fell into line.

At noon they stopped for an hour's rest. The teams of oxen and mules were turned loose from the wagons but were not unyoked. Blankets and buffalo robes were spread out beside the trail. The pioneers ate a cold lunch, relaxed a bit, then rolled down the trail again.

As they moved along, they passed the splintered wreck of an abandoned wagon. Every two or three miles, they saw wooden grave markers where pioneers had been laid to rest beside the trail. As the day wore on, children began to climb aboard the wagons, finding nooks and corners where they could curl up and nap.

Late that afternoon, near a grove of willows, the train captain gave the signal to stop for the night. One after another, the wagons pulled off the trail and began to form a large circle, or corral. The wagons were locked together, front to rear, with chains; the front tongue of one wagon reached under the rear wheels of the next. A gateway was left open to admit the livestock. Then the last wagon was rolled into place, sealing the corral.

Safely inside, the pioneers tended their cattle, pitched tents, and started campfires for the evening meal. Families sat together eating beans, dried buffalo meat, and camp-baked bread from tin plates.

By 8 P.M., sentries had taken their posts around the corral. Children ran past playing tag. Some girls sat in a circle, sharing secrets and laughing. A boy lay sprawled on his belly beside a campfire, studying a tattered copy of the *Emigrants Guide to Oregon and California*. Grown-ups stood in small groups, chatting and planning the day ahead.

Gradually the pioneers drifted off to their tents and wagons, where they huddled under blankets and fell asleep. Even in July, the night was chilly at this high altitude. They had traveled perhaps fifteen miles that day, nearly seven hundred miles since leaving Missouri in May. They still had more than twice that distance to go.

527

The first pioneers to travel west by wagon train had set out from Missouri in the spring of 1841. Each year after that, emigrants streamed westward in ever-increasing numbers. By 1869, when the first transcontinental railroad was completed, more than 350,000 pioneers had followed the ruts of the Oregon Trail across the continent.

At the beginning, most of them headed for the Pacific Coast. They went west to claim free land in the Oregon and California territories, to strike it rich by mining gold and silver, to settle in a new country where there was plenty of elbowroom and boundless opportunity.

They called themselves "emigrants" because, as they started their journey, they were actually leaving America. During the early 1840s, the United States ended at the banks of the Missouri River. The region that later would be Kansas and Nebraska had been set aside by the United States government as Indian territory. California was still a northern province of Mexico. The vast wilderness of the Oregon country was claimed jointly by the United States and Great Britain. Gradually these western territories would become part of the United States. But when the first emigrants set out, they were entering a foreign land.

GOING WEST

Meet the Author

Russell Freedman grew up in San Francisco. His parents were good friends with several authors. The authors would often come to the Freedman home to discuss the news of the day. These discussions helped Russell learn to develop his own thoughts. Later, as a reporter, Mr. Freedman came across a story about a sixteen-year-old boy who invented the braille typewriter. This story led to his first book, *Teenagers Who Made History*.

Mr. Freedman travels widely to do the research for his books. When he is not writing, he enjoys attending films, concerts, and plays.

Theme Connections

Within the Selection

Record your answers to the questions below in the Response Journal section of your Writer's Notebook. In small groups, report the ideas you wrote. Discuss your ideas with the rest of your group. Then choose a person to report your group's answers to the class.

- Why did the pioneers have to take all their possessions?

- Who rode in the wagons and who walked alongside the wagons?

Across Selections

- What other selections have we read about people who left their homes to set out for a new land?

Beyond the Selection

- Think about how a car trip across America would be alike and different from the way pioneer children traveled.

- Add items to the Concept/Question Board about the theme A Changing America.

- Think about how "Going West" adds to what you know about the theme A Changing America.

THE CALIFORNIA GOLD RUSH

West With the Forty-Niners

by Elizabeth Van Steenwyk

It could be said that the story of the gold rush really began on the day in 1839 when John Augustus Sutter first arrived in California. He brought little with him from Switzerland except his dream of creating a farming empire in this sleepy possession of Mexico. Mexico had broken away from Spanish rule in 1821 and claimed California for itself. Millions of acres in California that once belonged to Spain were now owned by Mexican officials. Thousands of cattle grazed and grew fat on these huge land grants. They became California's leading, and only, product. The time and place seemed to be perfect for making Sutter's dream come true.

Sutter applied for Mexican citizenship. In 1840 he received a land grant of nearly 50,000 acres (20,235 hectares), in the Sacramento Valley. He built a fort made of adobe near the south bank of the American River. From this fort, he controlled the surrounding land, which he named New Helvetia. (Helvetia is another name for Switzerland.)

Meanwhile, overland emigrants from the United States began to arrive in the valley. They had followed trails established by fur trappers. After 1841, this route through the midsection of the country became known as the California Trail.

Settlers in this period before the gold rush also came by ship. More than 200 Mormons came ashore at Yerba Buena (soon to be called San Francisco). They had sailed around Cape Horn, the southernmost tip of South America, hoping to escape from the religious persecution they had experienced in the East. Many of them found work at Sutter's Fort.

By January 1848, Sutter's Fort was a lively place with a population of nearly 300. More settlers arrived every day, and a sawmill was urgently needed. Sutter appointed a carpenter named James Wilson Marshall to supervise construction of a sawmill about 45 miles (72.4 km) east of the fort. The location was at a bend in the south fork of the American River in the Coloma Valley.

On the afternoon of January 14, Marshall walked along a ditch that channeled water from the river to the sawmill. Earlier, he thought he had seen some shiny pebbles in the ditch and wanted to examine them more closely. He picked up a pebble about the size of a pea, and his heart began to race. It looked too yellow to be silver but didn't seem bright enough to be gold. He pounded it. It bent but didn't break. Could it be?

Marshall hurried back to some workmen, who were resting at the end of a long day. He announced that he had just found gold. At first, they were unimpressed. Only Henry Bigler, a Mormon from Virginia, thought it might be significant. In his diary, he wrote, "This day some kind of mettle [metal] was found in the tail race that looks like goald [gold]."

The next day, the workmen decided to have a better look at the shiny pebbles. Within minutes, they realized James Marshall knew what he was talking about. He really had discovered gold!

As news of James Marshall's gold discovery at the sawmill reached the Mormons at Sutter's mill, they, too, began to look for gold. They discovered enough to abandon their regular work and begin mining in earnest. This second site became known as Mormon Island.

After Marshall told Sutter of his discovery, Sutter tested the pebbles for himself and became convinced they were gold. He established legal claim to the land, buying it directly from the Indians. Then he asked his workers to say nothing of the discovery for six weeks.

But even Sutter himself could not keep quiet. He wrote to his friend, Mariano Vallejo, less than a week later, saying that he had discovered a "mina de oro."

By the second week of March, news of the discovery reached San Francisco. It traveled by word of mouth until the fifteenth, when the news appeared in print for the first time. However, the story appeared on the last page of the San Francisco *Californian* and was only one paragraph long. Even a second story in the other weekly newspaper, the *California Star*, did little to interest the local folks.

The owner of the *Star* was an enterprising man named Sam Brannan. He decided to put out a special edition and send it to the folks in the eastern United States. With this edition, he hoped to persuade people to move to San Francisco and buy the lots he owned. Then he would make a profit for himself.

San Francisco citizens remained skeptical about the gold discovery. But ranchers near Sutter's Fort began to believe it after they saw the results of the Mormon diggings at a flour mill site. They came and staked out claims for themselves.

Sam Brannan arrived next. After he saw that workers at Sutter's Fort were in a frenzy over the discovery, he bought up future store locations. Those who already had been prospecting displayed their pouches of gold dust as they prepared to dig for more. Sam Brannan realized that something important had happened here. He was determined to be a part of it.

On May 12, Brannan returned to San Francisco, displaying a bottle full of gold dust and shouting, "Gold! Gold! Gold from the American River." Excited people gathered around to ask questions and wonder. But they

didn't wonder long. On May 12, there were six hundred men in the city. Three days later, there were two hundred. The others had gone to the gold field. By the end of the month, the city had nearly closed down. Even the newspapers ceased operation—there was no one left to read them. Soon, men from all over California left other jobs and headed for the hills.

Two thousand copies of Sam Brannan's special edition *Star* reached Missouri by the end of July. Many newspapers reprinted stories from it, but most people dismissed the gold discovery idea. It was unimportant, they said, or too good to be true. So, they ignored it.

But the news wouldn't die. Stories continued to trickle back East in letters by private citizens and reports from government officials. Throughout the summer and fall, newspapers featured more stories about the great wealth to be found in the West. What most Americans needed, however, was official support for these tall tales. Finally, on December 5, 1848, President James K. Polk delivered a message to Congress. In it, he said that the news of California's gold discovery had been verified. Those tales weren't fiction; they were fact!

The gold rush was on!

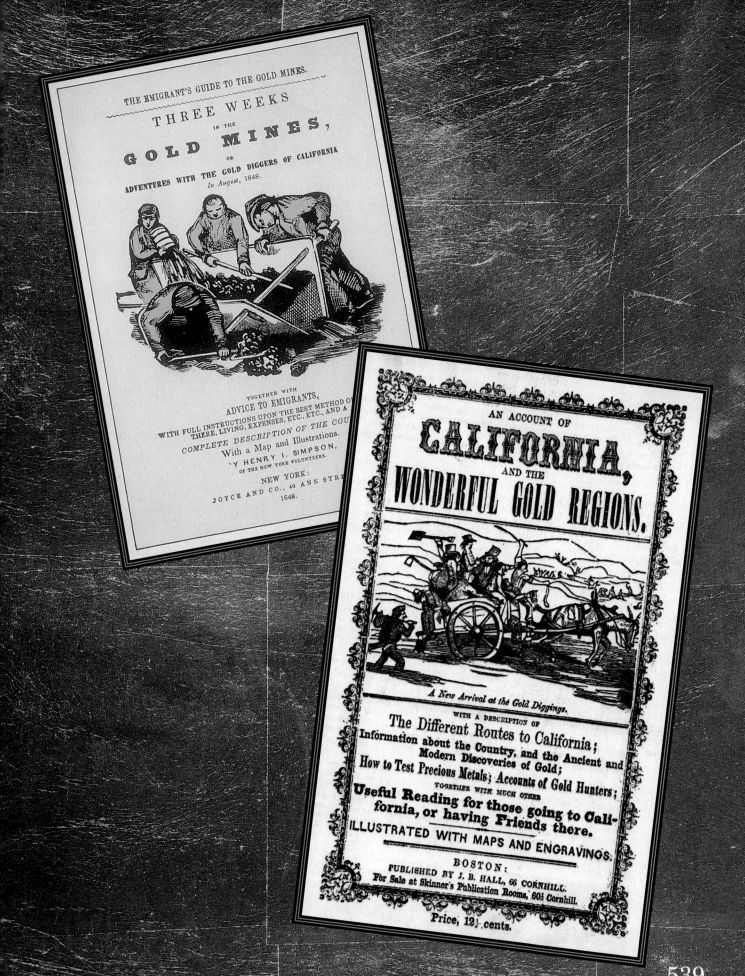

THE CALIFORNIA GOLD RUSH

West With the Forty-Niners

Meet the Author

Elizabeth Van Steenwyk was born in 1928 in Galesburg, Illinois. She has written many books, both fiction and nonfiction, on such topics as figure skating, horses, American presidents, and California history. Her book *The Best Horse* was made into a motion picture. When asked why she writes for children, Elizabeth Van Steenwyk replies, *"I write for young children because there are so many more possibilities than limitations."*

Theme Connections

Within the Selection

Record the answers to the questions below in the Response Journal section of your Writer's Notebook. In small groups, report the ideas you wrote. Discuss your ideas with the rest of the group. Then choose a person to report your group's answers to the class.

- How did the California Gold Rush help America expand into California?

- How did the people in the East learn about the discovery of gold in California?

Across Selections

- What other stories have we read about people moving to new places?

Beyond the Selection

- Think about what "The California Gold Rush" tells you about the theme A Changing America.

- Add items to the Concept/Question Board about the theme A Changing America.

The GOLDEN SPIKE

by Dan Elish

illustrated by Alan Reingold

The one-street town of Promontory, Utah, was buzzing with activity on May 10, 1869. A crowd of one thousand people lined the streets. Reporters from nearly every paper in the country were on hand. A band from Salt Lake City raised its trombones and trumpets, ready to play. Top-level railroad executives milled about, waiting for the ceremony to begin—the ceremony that would mark the completion of the transcontinental railroad.

Work on this great project had begun a full eight years before. The Central Pacific line had started in San Francisco and built east, while the Union Pacific

Railroad had started in Omaha, Nebraska, and built west. Now these two great lines were to finally meet and for the first time in history connect the eastern and western United States.

And now, the crowd—mostly Irish and Chinese laborers who had borne the brunt of the work—pushed close.

"Gentlemen," said Leland Stanford, president of the Central Pacific, "with your assistance we will proceed to lay the last tie, the last rail, and drive the last spike."

With great pomp, Stanford picked up a silver-headed sledge hammer, lifted it over his head, aimed at a gold spike, and swung with all his might...only to miss!

The Irish and Chinese workers howled. Stanford was getting a taste of just how hard it was to build a railroad.

Now Thomas Durant, the vice president of the Union Pacific, took up the sledgehammer, and swung a mighty blow.

He missed as well.

As a worker was hastily summoned to pound in the final spike, a telegrapher sent the signal to the nation: "It's done!"

From New York to San Francisco the country cheered as one.

Back at Promontory, two great locomotives inched forward just close enough so that the two engineers could lean forward and shake hands with each other.

A San Francisco author, Bret Harte, wrote a poem to commemorate the event:

What was it the engines said,
Pilots touching, head to head,
Facing on a single track,
Half a world behind each back?

It was the joining of two worlds: East meets West. Before the railroad, Americans thought of the West as a wilderness populated mostly by Indians. On that day the fabric of American life changed forever. Farmers and ranchers had a new, more efficient way to send their goods to market. Settlers rushed west, and western cities grew up. America finally had the technological means to grow and thrive—and become the America that we know today. For the first time in history, a vast country was made one.

Meet the Author

Dan Elish When Dan Elish graduated from college, he thought he wanted to write music and lyrics. One day after rereading *Charlie and the Chocolate Factory*, he was surprised to see how much of the book's humor could be enjoyed by adults as well as children. *"This book prompted me to try one of my own,"* he said. He thought it would only take him a few months to write a book for children. Instead it took him a year and a half to write his first book, *The Worldwide Dessert Contest*!

Meet the Illustrator

Alan Reingold began his career as an illustrator after graduating from The Rhode Island School of Design. Since then, he has been commissioned to illustrate cover and interior art for domestic and international magazines. His realistic images can also be seen on movie posters, in national ad campaigns, and on book covers. Alan's first *Time* magazine cover hangs in the permanent collection of The National Portrait Gallery in Washington, D.C. Alan teaches illustration at Parsons School of Design.

Theme Connections

Within the Selection

Writer's Notebook

Record your answers to the questions below in the Response Journal section of your Writer's Notebook. In small groups, report the ideas you wrote. Discuss your ideas with the rest of your group. Then choose a person to report your group's answers to the class.

- What job did the Golden Spike complete?

- Why was the Golden Spike event so important to the country?

Across Selections

- The California Gold Rush was 20 years before the transcontinental railroad was completed. How did the California gold rush and the railroad help the west grow?

Beyond the Selection

- Think about how "The Golden Spike" tells you about the theme A Changing America.

- Add items to the Concept/Question Board about the theme A Changing America.

Pronunciation Key

a as in **a**t

ā as in l**a**te

â as in c**a**re

ä as in f**a**ther

e as in s**e**t

ē as in m**e**

i as in **i**t

ī as in k**i**te

o as in **o**x

ō as in r**o**se

ô as in b**ou**ght and r**a**w

oi as in c**oi**n

o͝o as in b**oo**k

o͞o as in t**oo**

or as in f**or**m

ou as in **ou**t

u as in **u**p

ū as in **u**se

ûr as in t**ur**n, g**er**m, l**ear**n, f**ir**m, w**or**k

ə as in **a**bout, chick**e**n, penc**i**l, cann**o**n, circ**u**s

ch as in **ch**air

hw as in **wh**ich

ng as in ri**ng**

sh as in **sh**op

th as in **th**in

t͟h as in **th**ere

zh as in trea**s**ure

The mark (´) is placed after a syllable with a heavy accent, as in **chicken** (chik´ ən).

The mark (´) after a syllable shows a lighter accent, as in **disappear** (dis´ ə pēr´).

548

Glossary

A

abandon (ə ban´ dən) *v.* To give up something; to stop working on something.

abolitionist (ab´ ə lish´ ən ist) *n.* A person who wants to end slavery.

abreast (ə brest´) *adv.* Alongside of; next to.

accomplished (ə kom´ plisht) *adj.* Good at something because of practice.

accustomed (ə kus´ təmd) *adj.* Used to or familiar with something.

adjustable (ə jus´ tə bəl) *adj.* Able to be changed in size or position.

adobe (ə dō´ bē) *n.* A brick made out of clay.

advertise (ad´ vûr tīz´) *v.* To promote a product or service through print, radio, or television.

agate (ag´ it) *n.* A playing marble with swirls or stripes of several colors in it.

agent (ā´ jənt) *n.* Someone who represents or stands in for another person.

aggressive (ə gre´ siv) *adj.* Working hard with a lot of energy and drive to get something.

alarmingly (ə lär´ ming lē) *adv.* Filled with a sense of danger.

allotment (ə lot´ mənt) *n.* A share or part of something.

alloy (a´ loi) *n.* A mixture of metals.

ambitious (am bish´ əs) *adj.* Motivated to succeed.

amplify (am´ plə fī´) *v.* To make louder.

amputation (am´ pyōō tā´ shən) *n.* The act of cutting off a body part such as an arm or a leg.

analyze (a´ nəl īz´) *v.* To study something carefully.

anatomy (ə nat´ ə mē) *n.* The structure of the human body.

ancestor (an´ ses tər) *n.* A forefather; a parent, grandparent, great-grandparent, and so on.

anesthesia (an´ əs thē´ zhə) *n.* A loss of feeling brought about by drugs so that surgery can be performed.

antibiotic (an´ ti bī ot´ ik) *n.* A chemical that kills disease germs.

antibody (an´ ti bo´ dē) *n.* Substance produced by the body that destroys or weakens germs.

antiseptic (an´ tə sep´ tik) *adj.* Free from germs; germ-killing.

appeal (ə pēl´) *v.* To make an earnest request.

appetizing (a´ pə tī´ zing) *adj.* Arousing the desire for food.

applicant (a´ pli kənt) *n.* A person who tries for a certain job or position.

appointment (ə point´ mənt) *n.* A job or office.

arctic (ärk´ tik) *adj.* Having to do with the region of the North Pole.

arrangement (ə rānj´ mənt) *n.* Plan or agreement.

artifact (är´ tə fakt´) *n.* A handmade object from an earlier time or culture.

Pronunciation Key: at; lāte; câre; fäther; set; mē; it; kīte; ox; rōse; ô in bought; coin; bŏŏk; tōō; form; out; up; ūse; tûrn; ə sound in about, chicken, pencil, cannon, circus; chair; hw in which; ring; shop; thin; ŧħere; zh in treasure.

artificial (är´ tə fish´ əl) *adj.* Made by humans rather than produced by nature.

asepsis (ā sep´ sis) *n.* The methods used to make sure there are no germs.

assert (ə sûrt´) *v.* To say firmly.

Word History

Assert is a French word that comes from the Latin word *asserere*. It can be traced back to the terms *ad-*, which means "toward," and *serere*, which means "to join."

asthma (az´ mə) *n.* A disease involving coughing and difficulty with breathing.

astronaut (as´ trə nôt´) *n.* A person who travels in space.

astronomer (ə stro´ nə mər) *n.* A person who studies objects outside Earth's atmosphere.

authoritative (ə thor´ i tā´ tiv) *adj.* Bossy; masterful.

awl (ôl) *n.* A tool with a sharp point used for making small holes in wood, leather, or tin.

B

bacteria (bak tēr´ ē ə) *n. pl., sing.* **bacterium.** Disease germs; one-celled organisms that can be seen only with a microscope.

bank (bangk) *v.* To tilt an aircraft to one side while flying it.

bargaining (bär´ gə ning) *n.* Discussing terms; talking or arguing in order to agree upon something.

barge (bärj) *v.* To rudely push oneself into a place.

befall (bi fôl´) *v.* To happen to.

benefit (be´ nə fit´) *n.* Something given to workers in addition to pay, such as insurance, paid vacations, or sick days.

bioethics (bī´ ō e´ thiks) *n.* The study of ethics in biological research.

blood pressure (blud´ presh´ ər) *n.* The amount of force with which blood presses against the insides of the body's blood vessels.

blubber (blub´ ər) *n.* Whale fat.

bonito (bə nē´ tō) *n.* A fish similar to the tuna, found in the Atlantic Ocean.

boom (bōōm) *v.* To grow suddenly and rapidly.

boundless (bound´ ləs) *adj.* Having no limits.

bow (bou) *n.* The curved front part of a boat.

brace (brās) *n.* A pair; a couple.

brainstorm (brān´ storm) *v.* To come up with many ideas quickly.

brandish (bran´ dish) *v.* To shake; to wave threateningly.

brazier (brā´ zhər) *n.* A metal frame for holding fire.

brush (brush) *n.* A growth of shrubs, small trees, and bushes.

brutality (brōō tal´ i tē) *n.* Cruelty; extremely harsh treatment.

buzz (buz) *v.* A low humming sound.

C

calculate (kal′ kyə lāt′) *v.* To measure; to figure out.

capacity (kə pas′ i tē) *n.* The ability.

capsize (kap′ sīz) *v.* To overturn in the water, as a boat.

captivity (kap ti′ və tē) *n.* Being held and confined.

card (kärd) *n.* An instrument used for combing cotton or wool fibers.

caribou (kar′ ə boo′) *n.* A large deer, related to the reindeer.

cartilage (kär′ tl ij) *n.* Firm yet flexible tissue that is inside the human body.

catgut (kat′ gut) *n.* A strong thread made of dried animals' intestines, used in surgery to make stitches.

cell (sel) *n.* A small unit of organization.

century (sen′ chə rē) *n.* 100 years.

chafing (chā′ fing) *n.* A rubbing.

chartreuse (shär trooz′) *n.* A yellowish-green color.

chattel (chat′ l) *n.* Anything movable that is owned by someone.

chemist (kem′ ist) *n.* A scientist who studies what substances are made of.

chorus (kōr′ əs) *n.* Part of a song that is repeated after each verse.

citizen (si′ tə zən) *n.* A person born in or made a member of a country.

civilization (siv′ ə lə zā′ shən) *n.* A culture, society, or group of human beings who have developed art, education, agriculture, trade, science, government, and so on.

claim (klām) *v.* A section of land declared as one's own.

clog (klôg) *v.* To block or fill up.

colleague (kol′ ēg) *n.* A member of the same profession as another person.

colonist (kol′ ə nist) *n.* A person who is a member of a settlement formed by people who have come to a new land.

colony (kol′ ə nē) *n.* A settlement formed by people who have come to a new land.

Word Derivations

Below are some words derived from the word *colony*.

colonial	colonies	colonize
colonially	colonist	colonized
colonialism	colonization	colonizing

comfortable (kəmpf′ tər bəl) *adj.* Providing physical ease and well-being.

commotion (kə mō′ shən) *n.* Noisy disturbance.

community (kə mū′ ni tē) *n.* All the people living in the same area; the area surrounding the place where you live.

complicated (kôm′ plə kā′ təd) *adj.* Hard to understand.

complication (kom′ pli kā′ shən) *n.* Another disease that makes a person's original disease get worse.

compound (kom′ pound) *n.* A closed-in area containing homes or other buildings.

Pronunciation Key: at; l**ā**te; c**â**re; f**ä**ther; s**e**t; m**ē**; **i**t; k**ī**te; **o**x; r**ō**se; **ô** in b**ou**ght; c**oi**n; b**oo**k; t**oo**; f**or**m; **ou**t; **u**p; **ū**se; t**û**rn; **ə** sound in **a**bout, chick**e**n, penc**i**l, cann**o**n, circ**u**s; **ch**air; **hw** in **wh**ich; ri**ng**; **sh**op; **th**in; **th**ere; **zh** in trea**s**ure.

compromise (kom´ prə mīz´) *n.* A settlement made by both sides giving up a little.

Word History

The French word **compromise** can be traced back to the Latin word *compromittere*. In Latin, *com-* means "with" or "together," while *promittere* means "to promise."

computer-generated (kəm pū´ tər je´ nə rā´ təd) *adj.* Made or drawn on a computer.

concentrated (kon´ sən trā´ tid) *adj.* Packed closely together.

concentration camp (kôn´ sən trā´ shən kamp) *n.* A fenced and guarded camp for keeping prisoners of war, refugees, and political prisoners.

conclusive (kən kloo´ siv) *adj.* Answering a question completely.

condemnation (kon´ dem nā´ shən) *n.* A judgment of guilty.

condominium (kôn´ də mi´ nē əm) *n.* An apartment building owned by the person or persons living in it.

confide (kən fīd´) *v.* To tell secrets to; to discuss private thoughts.

confidence (kon´ fi dəns) *n.* A belief in one's own ability.

confirm (kən fûrm´) *v.* To make sure.

connect (kə nekt´) *v.* To hook up with; to introduce someone to.

conscious (kon´ shəs) *adj.* Aware of; noticing the needs of.

consent (kən sent´) 1. *n.* Agreement; permission. 2. *v.* To agree.

console (kən sōl´) *v.* To comfort.

constellation (kon´ stə lā´ shən) *n.* A group of fixed stars having a name.

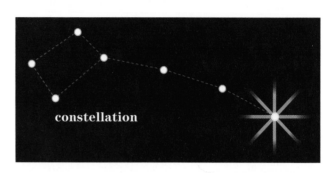

constellation

consternation (kon´ stər nā´ shən) *n.* Dismay; dread; anxiety.

Word History

Consternation came into usage in the English language around 1611. It comes from the Latin terms *consternare*, which means "to throw into confusion," and *-ation*, which means "act" or "process."

consult (kən sult´) *v.* To ask advice.

consumptive (kən sump´ tiv) *adj.* Sick with the disease tuberculosis, a lung infection.

contaminated (kən tam´ ə nā´ təd) *adj.* Unclean; mixed with something dirty.

Continental Army (kon´ tən en´ təl är´ mē) *n.* American Army that fought the British during the Revolutionary War.

continue (kən tin´ ū) *v.* To keep going; to last.

contract (kon´ trakt) *n.* A formal, written agreement.

controversial (kôn´ trə vûr´ shəl) *adj.* Subject to debate or disagreement.

conversation (kôn´ vər sā´ shən) *n.* Oral exhange of observations, opinions, or ideas.

conveyance (kən vā´ əns) *n.* The act of taking something from one place to another.

convince (kən vins´) *v.* To cause one to believe something.

coronary artery (kor´ ə ner ē är´ tə rē) *n.* An artery in the heart that supplies blood to the parts of the heart.

corps (kor) *n.* A group formed for a specific purpose.

county seat (koun´ tē sēt´) *n.* The town in which the government of a county is housed.

cradle (krā´ dl) *v.* To hold gently in one's arms.

crevasse (krə vas´) *n.* A deep crack in a glacier or in the Earth's surface.

crimson (krim´ zən) *adj.* Deep red in color.

crouch (krouch) *v.* To stoop or bend low, usually by bending the legs.

crude (kro͞od) *adj.* Rough; simple.

culturally (kul´ chər ə lē) *adv.* Having to do with the civilization of a given race or nation.

cunning (ku´ ning) *adj.* Tricky.

curandera (ko͞o´ rän de´ rä) *n.* A woman healer who uses folk medicine such as herbs and other plants to cure illness.

customer (kus´ tə mûr) *n.* Person who buys something.

D

daub (dôb) *v.* To cover or coat by smearing something on.

defiant (di fī´ ənt) *adj.* Standing up against authority; resisting.

delectable (di lek´ tə bəl) *adj.* Very tasty.

demanding (di mand´ ing) *adj.* Requiring a lot of time or energy.

demonstrate (de´ mən strāt´) *v.* To show or prove.

deposit (di pôs´ ət) *n.* Money or valuable things in a bank or safe place.

desert (di zûrt´) *v.* To abandon.

design (di zīn´) *n.* A drawing or outline made to serve as a guide or pattern.

desolately (des´ ə lit lē) *adv.* In a hopeless or lonely way.

desperately (des´ pər it lē) *adv.* Hopelessly.

destination (des´ tə nā´ shən) *n.* The place where a journey ends.

determined (di tûr´ mənd) *adj.* Having a strong desire to complete something.

digestion (dī jes´ chən) *n.* The breakdown and absorption of food by the body.

din (din) *n.* A lot of noise; clamor; uproar; racket.

discard (dis kärd´) *v.* To throw away.

discourage (dis kûr´ ij) *v.* To keep from doing something.

disinfect (dis´ in fekt´) *v.* To cleanse of infection; to make free of germs.

Pronunciation Key: **a**t; l**ā**te; c**â**re; f**ä**ther; s**e**t; m**ē**; **i**t; k**ī**te; **o**x; r**ō**se; **ô** in b**ou**ght; c**oi**n; b**oo**k; t**oo**; f**or**m; **ou**t; **u**p; **ū**se; t**û**rn; **ə** sound in **a**bout, chick**e**n, penc**i**l, cann**o**n, circ**u**s; **ch**air; **hw** in **wh**ich; ri**ng**; **sh**op; **th**in; **th**ere; **zh** in trea**s**ure.

dispel (di spel´) *v.* To drive away; to banish.

Word History

The word **dispel** comes from the Latin word *dispellare* and can be broken down into *dis-*, which means "apart," and *pellare*, which means "to drive." The prefix *dis-* can also mean "the opposite of," but not in this case.

display (di splā´) *v.* To show.

distinctly (di´ stin(k)t´ lē) *adv.* Very clearly.

distress (di stres´) *n.* Great pain, sorrow, or anxiety.

diverse (di vûrs´) *adj.* Different; varied.

document (do´ kyə ment´) *v.* To observe and record for future study.

don (don) *v.* To put on.

douse (dous) *v.* To splash.

dressing (dres´ ing) *n.* The cloth or other material used to cover a wound.

dubiously (doo´ bē əs lē) *adv.* Doubtfully; in an unsure way.

durable (door´ ə bəl) *adj.* Able to last a long time; able to hold up to rough handling.

ear mite (ēr mīt) *n.* A small bug that lives in the ears of animals.

effective (i fek´ tiv) *adj.* Able to get results.

emigrant (e´ mi grənt) *n.* Someone who leaves his or her homeland to settle in a new one.

eminent (em´ ə nənt) *adj.* Celebrated; well-known; grand.

empire (em´ pīr) *n.* A group of countries, lands, or peoples under one government or ruler.

enchain (en chān´) *v.* To tie down or hold back.

encounter (in koun´ tər) *n.* Casual or unplanned meeting.

energetic (e´ nûr je´ tik) *adj.* Having energy; spirited.

enlightened (in lī´ tənd) *adj.* Free from ignorance.

entrepreneur (än´ trə prə nûr´) *n.* Someone who starts a business and then manages it.

enviously (en´ vē əs lē) *adv.* With jealousy.

epidemic (ep´ i dem´ ik) *n.* An outbreak of disease that spreads quickly to many people.

equipment (i kwip´ mənt) *n.* Instruments or tools.

erupt (i rupt´) *v.* To break out suddenly and with great force.

escort (i skort´) *v.* To go with and protect.

establish (i stab´ lish) *v.* To start, create, or found.

etch (ech) *v.* To make a pattern or design on a hard surface.

ethnically (eth´ nik lē) *adv.* Having to do with the national origins of a people.

excel (ik sel´) *v.* To do better than others.

executive (ig ze´ kū tiv) *n.* A person who directs or manages.

exhaust (ig zôst´) *v.* To tire out.

expectancy (ik spek´ tən sē) *n.* A state of waiting for something to happen. **life expectancy:** The number of years the average person will live.

expedition (ek´ spi dish´ ən) *n.* A journey made to accomplish something.

express (iks pres´) *n.* A rapid system of delivering goods or mail.

extent (ik stent´) *n.* The amount or limit.

external (ek stûr´ nl) *adj.* Outside; outward.

F

fabric (fab´ rik) *n.* An underlying structure or foundation.

facilities (fə sil´ i tēz) *n. pl.* Things designed to make a task easier or more convenient.

failure (fāl´ yər) *n.* Something that does not turn out well; something that is not a success.

faint (fānt) *adj.* Dim; weak; not clear.

falter (fôl´ tər) *v.* To be tongue-tied; to talk awkwardly.

farmer's market (fär´ mərz mär´ kət) *n.* A place where people come to buy and sell fruits and vegetables for a short period of time.

fascinate (fa´ sən āt´) *v.* To completely and fully interest someone.

fatal (fāt´ l) *adj.* Deadly; causing death.

fee (fē) *n.* Money requested or paid for some service or right.

feebly (fē´ blē) *adv.* Weakly.

feisty (fī´ stē) *adj.* Full of energy.

ferry (fer´ ē) *v.* To carry across a river or a bay. —*n.* A boat that carries passengers, vehicles, or goods across a river or a bay; a ferryboat.

fiber (fī´ bər) *n.* Material or cloth.

Word Derivations

Below are some words derived from the word *fiber*.

fiberboard	fiberglass	fiber optics
fiberfill	fiberize	fibers
fibered	fiber-optic	fiberscope

fibrous (fī´ brəs) *adj.* Containing fibers, or long, narrow strips or cords.

fierce (fērs´) *adj.* Wild or threatening in appearance.

flank (flangk) *n.* The side.

forceps (for´ səps) *n.* Small pliers used in surgery.

fortunate (for´ chə nət) *adj.* Lucky.

fowling piece (fou´ ling pēs´) *n.* A shotgun used for shooting wild birds.

fragrance (frā´ grəns) *n.* A sweet smell that is pleasing.

freight (frāt) *n.* Cargo; goods.

frenzy (fren´ zē) *n.* Wild excitement.

frustrate (frəs´ trāt) *v.* To make someone feel upset, helpless, or powerless in a situation.

fugitive (fū´ jə tiv) *n.* Person who runs away.

fund (fund) 1. *v.* To pay for. 2. *n.* Money collected and saved for a special purpose.

G

game (gām) *n.* Wild animals that are hunted.

game reserve (gām′ ri zûrv′) *n.* An area of land set aside for wild animals to live in without being hunted.

gaudy (gô′ dē) *adj.* Showy or flashy in a crude way.

generation (jen′ ə rā′ shən) *n.* 1. A group of people who are all about the same age. 2. The process of bringing into existence.

gesture (jes′ chər) *n.* A body movement that shows meaning.

gibbon (gi′ bən) *n.* A tailless ape from southeastern Asia.

glacier (glā′ shər) *n.* A large, slow-moving mass of ice.

glassy (glas′ ē) *n.* A glass marble with colored swirls.

gore (gor) *v.* To wound using a horn or tusk.

gorge (gorj) *n.* A steep, narrow opening between mountains; a small canyon.

gossamer (gos′ ə mər) *adj.* Light; thin; flimsy.

greasewood (grēs′ wood′) *n.* A shrub that grows in the western United States.

grindstone (grīnd′ stōn′) *n.* A round, flat stone used to sharpen tools.

grippe (grip) *n.* Influenza; the flu.

guild (gild) *n.* During the Middle Ages, a group of merchants or crafters.

H

haggard (hag′ ərd) *adj.* Having a worn look because of being very tired, afraid, or hungry.

hammer out (ham′ ər out) *v.* To discuss until an agreement is reached.

hardship (härd′ ship) *n.* Trouble; misfortune.

harness dressing (här′ nəs dres′ ing) *n.* A mixture used to polish leather.

harvest (här′ vist) 1. *n.* The act or process of gathering a crop. 2. *v.* To gather a crop.

haughty (hô′ tē) *adj.* Full of pride.

Word History

Haughty comes from the French word *haut*, which is derived from the Latin word *altus*. *Altus* means "high." **Haughty** came into the English language during the 15th century.

headland (hed′ lənd) *n.* A high piece of land that sticks out into a large body of water.

heap (hēp) *n.* A pile; a mound.

hearthstone (härth′ stōn) *n.* The stone floor of a fireplace.

heave (hēv) *n.* An upward movement.

hemorrhage (hem′ ər ij) *n.* Heavy bleeding.

herb medicine (ûrb´ me´ də sən) *n.* Plant with healing properties used to treat diseases or injuries.

heritage (hâr´ ə tij) *n.* Something handed down to a person from his or her ancestors.

hibernate (hī´ bər nāt´) *v.* To pass the winter in a long sleep.

highborn (hī´ born) *adj.* Born to the noble class.

highwayman (hī´ wā´ mən) *n.* A robber who steals from travelers on a road.

horizon (hə rī´ zən) *n.* The distant line where the ocean and the sky seem to meet.

hose (hōz) *n.* Stockings.

house (houz) *v.* To provide shelter for.

hullabaloo (hə lə bə lōō´) *n.* An uproar.

hurtle (hûrtl) *v.* To move rapidly and with great force.

hygiene (hī´ jēn) *n.* Keeping oneself clean in order to stay healthy.

I

ice cap (īs´ kap) *n.* A thick layer of ice covering an area.

idly (īd´ lē) *adv.* Lazily.

imagine (i ma´ jən) *v.* To form a mental image of.

immaculate (i mak´ yə lit) *adj.* Extremely clean; spotless.

immune (i mūn´) *adj.* Free from; not able to get a certain disease.

impair (im pâr´) *v.* To weaken; to injure.

impracticable (im prak´ ti kə bəl) *adj.* Not possible with the methods or equipment available.

impression (im presh´ ən) *n.* An idea; a picture in the mind.

improvement (im proov´ mənt) *n.* Way of making something better.

improvise (im´ prə vīz´) *v.* To make changes in a song as it is being sung.

incision (in sizh´ ən) *n.* A cut made into the body during surgery.

indentured servant (in den´ chərd sûr vənt) *n.* A person who came to America under a contract to work for someone else for a period of time.

independence (in´ də pen´ dən(t)s) *n.* Freedom.

indescribably (in´ di skrī´ bə blē) *adv.* Unusually; extraordinarily.

indignantly (in dig´ nənt lē) *adv.* With anger; with an insulted feeling.

induct (in dukt´) *v.* To admit as a member.

in earnest (in ûr´ nəst) *adv.* Seriously.

ineffectively (in´ i fek´ tiv lē) *adv.* Uselessly; in vain.

infect (in fekt´) *v.* To introduce disease germs.

infirm (in fûrm´) *adj.* Weak; sickly.

infirmary (in fûr´ mə rē) *n.* A place where sick people are treated.

infomercial (in´ fō´ mər´ shəl) *n.* Extra-long television commercials.

infrasonic (in´ frə sô´ nik) *adj.* Having a sound of such low frequency that people cannot hear it.

inherit (in her´ it) *v.* To receive another's property after his or her death.

insulation (in´ sə lā´ shən) *n.* A material that keeps heat from being lost.

intern (in´ tûrn) *n.* A doctor who is being trained at a hospital.

internal (in tûr´ nl) *adj.* Inside; inner.

Pronunciation Key: at; l**ā**te; c**â**re; f**ä**ther; s**e**t; m**ē**; **i**t; k**ī**te; **o**x; r**ō**se; **ô** in b**ou**ght; **c**oin; b**oo**k; t**oo**; f**or**m; **ou**t; **u**p; **ū**se; t**û**rn; **ə** sound in **a**bout, chick**e**n, penc**i**l, cann**o**n, circ**u**s; **ch**air; **hw** in **wh**ich; ri**ng**; **sh**op; **th**in; **th**ere; **zh** in trea**s**ure.

interracial (in´ tər rā´ shəl) *adj.* Including people of different races.

interrupt (in´ tə rupt´) *v.* To stop for a time; to break off.

intimidate (in tim´ i dāt´) *v.* To threaten; to frighten.

inundate (in´ ən dāt´) *v.* To swamp; to flood; to overwhelm.

investment (in vest´ mənt) *n.* The use of money to gain profit; The money spent to start or improve a business or savings program.

irrigate (ir´ i gāt) *v.* To wash with water or another liquid.

J

jolt (jōlt) *v.* To move in a sudden, rough way.

K

kidnap (kid´ nap) *v.* To seize and carry off a person.

kindle (kin´ dəl) *v.* To begin burning or cause to burn.

kindling (kind´ ling) *n.* Small pieces of wood or scraps used for starting a fire.

L

labor (lā´ bər) *n.* The beginning of the process of birth.

laborer (lā´ bər´ ər) *n.* One who works for pay.

land grant (land´ grant´) *n.* A gift of land from the government to a person.

lanyard (lan´ yərd) *n.* A woven friendship bracelet.

lapse (laps) *v.* To fall; to sink.

Word History

The word **lapse** came into English language usage around 1526. It comes from the Latin word *labi,* which means "to slip."

league (lēg) *n.* A distance of roughly three miles.

limited (li´ mə təd) *adj.* Having boundaries or limits.

listlessly (list´ ləs lē) *adv.* Without energy or interest.

livestock (līv´ stôk´) *n.* Farm animals, such as cattle, horses, or sheep.

lull (lul) 1. *v.* To put to sleep by soothing. 2. *n.* A short period of calm or quiet.

luxurious (lug´ zhoor´ ē əs) *adj.* Giving much comfort and joy.

M

maintenance (mānt´ nəns) *n.* The work of keeping something in good condition.

mandolin (man´ də lin´) *n.* A stringed musical instrument.

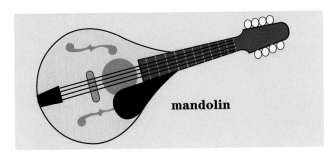

mandolin

maneuver (mə noo´ vər) *v.* To change the position of something; to move in a planned way.

manipulate (mə nip´ yə lāt´) *v.* To handle or control.

manufacturing (man´ yə fak´ chə ring) *adj.* Making and selling products.

manuscript (man´ ū skript) *n.* A handwritten document.

market (mär´ kit) *n.* A demand for something that is for sale.

Word Derivations

Below are some words derived from the word *market*.

market order	market share	marketer
market price	marketability	marketing
market research	marketable	marketplace
market researcher	marketed	unmarketable

marketing (mär´ ki ting) *n.* All the activities that lead to selling a product, including advertising, packaging, and selling.

mast (mast) *n.* A pole supporting a ship's sails.

masterpiece (mas´ tər pēs´) *n.* A great work of art.

meditation (me´ də tā´ shən) *n.* A practice of quiet thinking.

melody (me´ lə dē) *n.* Series of musical tones; part of a song.

menacing (men´ is ing) *adj.* Dangerous; threatening.

merchandise (mûr´ chən dīz´) *n.* Things for sale; goods.

mesa (mā´ sə) *n.* High, flat land, like a plateau but smaller.

meticulously (mə tik´ yə ləs lē) *adv.* In an extremely careful and precise way.

microbe (mī´ krōb) *n.* An organism that is too small to be seen without a microscope.

middlings (mid´ lingz) *n.* A wheat by-product used in animal feed.

migrate (mī´ grāt´) *v.* To move from one place to another.

mild mannered (mī(ə)ld´ ma´ nûrd) *adj.* Gentle in nature.

milk wagon (milk´ wa´ gən) *n.* A horse-drawn wagon used to deliver milk very early in the morning.

mill (mil) *v.* To move around in a confused way.

misery (mi´ zə rē) *n.* Suffering.

mite (mīt) *adj.* A little bit.

mock (mok) *adj.* Fake.

Word Derivations

Below are some words derived from the word *mock*.

mock turtle soup	mockery	mockingbird
mocked	mock-heroic	mockingly
mocker	mocking	mock-up

Pronunciation Key: **at**; **lāte**; **câre**; **fä**ther; **set**; **mē**; **it**; **kīte**; **ox**; **rōse**; **ô** in b**ou**ght; c**oi**n; b**ŏŏk**; t**ŏŏ**; f**or**m; **out**; **up**; **ūse**; t**ûr**n; **ə** sound in **a**bout, chick**e**n, penc**i**l, cann**o**n, circ**u**s; **ch**air; **hw** in **wh**ich; ri**ng**; **sh**op; **th**in; **t/h**ere; **zh** in trea**s**ure.

monastery (mo′ nə stâr′ ē) *n.* A house for monks.

monies (mun′ ēz) *n. pl.* Funds; a plural of *money.*

monk (mungk) *n.* A man who belongs to a religious order.

mural (myŏŏr′ əl) *n.* A large painting, often on a wall.

musket (mus′ kit) *n.* An old-fashioned kind of gun, used before the modern rifle.

muslin (muz′ lin) *n.* A kind of cotton cloth.

muster (mus′ tər) *v.* To gather.

mystified (mis′ tə fīd′) *adj.* Bewildered; confused.

N

native (nā′ tiv) *adj.* Belonging to by birth.

nauseate (nô′ zē āt′) *v.* To make sick to the stomach.

net (net) *v.* To earn or get as a profit.

nomadic (nō mad′ ik) *adj.* Wandering from place to place.

O

obligation (ô′ blə gā′ shən) *n.* Responsibility; something a person is supposed to do.

obnoxious (əb nok′ shəs) *adj.* Annoying or offensive.

Word History

The word **obnoxious** comes from the Latin word *obnoxius* and can be broken down into the following parts: *ob-*, which means "in the way of" or "exposed to," and *noxa*, which means "harm." "Exposed to something harmful" is actually an archaic, or out-of-date, definition of **obnoxious.**

odds (odz) *n.* The chances that something will or will not happen.

omen (ō′ mən) *n.* A sign of a future event.

ominous (om′ ə nəs) *adj.* Unfavorable; threatening misfortune.

ongoing (on′ gō′ ing) *adj.* Continuing, steady.

organic (or gan′ ik) *adj.* Grown without chemicals; natural.

ornery (or′ nə rē) *adj.* Disagreeable.

overawed (ō′ vər ôd′) *adj.* Extremely respectful or fearful.

overlapping (ō′ vər la′ ping) *n.* Way of lying on top of something and partly extending over it.

P

P.S. Public School.

pachyderm (pak′ i dûrm′) *n.* Any large, thick-skinned, hoofed animal, such as the elephant.

page (pāj) *v.* To call for someone over a loudspeaker.

parch (pärch) *v.* To make hot and thirsty.

parchment (pärch´ mənt) *n.* Specially prepared animal skin, usually from sheep or goats, made into a tough translucent paper for writing.

passage (pas´ ij) *n.* A narrow corridor; a hallway.

pattern (pa´ tûrn) *n.* An arrangement of markings.

peculiar (pi kūl´ yər) *adj.* Strange; unusual.

pemmican (pem´ i kən) *n.* A mixture of powdered dried meat, dried berries, and fat.

perception (pər sep´ shən) *n.* The ability to experience things through one's senses.

persecution (pûr´ si kū´ shən) *n.* The mistreatment or harassment of a person or group of people.

persuade (pər swād´) *v.* To talk into believing.

pesky (pes´ kē) *adj.* Annoying.

physician (fə zi´ shən) *n.* Doctor.

physicist (fi´ zə sist) *n.* A person who studies matter and energy and how the two work together.

pilgrim (pil´ grim) *n.* 1. A person who travels to a holy place. 2. **Pilgrim:** A member of a religious group that came to America to find freedom of religion.

pitch (pich) *n.* A dark, sticky substance used to make things waterproof. —*v.* To lurch or fall suddenly.

plague (plāg) *n.* Any widespread disease; a disease that is spread in an epidemic.

plodding (plod´ ing) *adj.* Moving in a slow, heavy way.

plunge (plunj) *v.* To fall suddenly.

pneumonia (noŏ mōn´ yə) *n.* A disease of the lungs.

poacher (pō´ chər) *n.* A person who catches animals in a place where hunting is against the law.

pomp (pomp) *n.* A magnificent display or ceremony.

poppet (pop´ it) *n. British dialect.* A nickname showing affection, meaning "child."

popular (pop´ yə lər) *adj.* Well-liked by many.

porcelain (por´ sə lin) *n.* A fine, delicate china.

port (port) *n.* A place or town where ships come to load or unload.

portion (por´ shən) *v.* To share among; to distribute.

potential (pə ten´ shəl) *adj.* Possible.

poultice (pōl´ tis) *n.* A wad of something soft and moist, placed over a wound to heal it.

practitioner (prak ti´ shə nər) *n.* One who performs a professional service.

prairie schooner (prer´ ē skoō´ nər) *n.* A type of covered wagon used by pioneers.

precision (pri sizh´ ən) *n.* Exactness; accuracy with details.

pretense (prē´ tens) *n.* A false show or appearance for the purpose of deceiving others.

prevailing (pri vā´ ling) *adj.* The most frequent; occurring most often.

privileged (priv´ lijd) *adj.* Enjoying luxuries and special treatment.

procession (prə se´ shən) *n.* A line of people moving forward in an orderly and ceremonial manner.

product (prô´ dukt´) *n.* Anything that is made or created.

profitable (prô´ fə tə bəl) *adj.* Able to make money.

profusely (prə fūs´ lē) *adv.* In abundance; in large amounts.

prominently (prô´ mə nənt lē) *adv.* Noticeably.

promote (prə mōt´) *v.* To advance in rank, position, or grade.

prospect (prô´ spekt) 1. *n.* A future possible event; something that could happen. 2. *v.* To search or explore for gold or other mining products.

prostration (pros trā´ shən) *n.* Exhaustion; extreme tiredness.

provide (prə vīd´) *v.* To supply what is needed.

provisions (prə vizh´ ənz) *n.* Things that are supplied for a special task, especially food and the necessary tools.

pulse (puls) *n.* The regular beating of the heart.

pursue (pər soo´) *v.* To chase.

Q

qualified (kwä´ lə fīd´) *adj.* Having the skills or education needed for a certain job or position; capable.

quarters (kwor´ tərz) *n.* Living accommodations; a place to live.

queer (kwēr) *adv.* Strange.

quill (kwil) *n.* A hollow wing or tail feather used for writing.

R

racket (rak´ ət) *n.* Noise indicating confusion.

rafter (raf´ tər) *n.* Any of the long, heavy pieces of wood or metal that support a roof.

raised print (razd´ print´) *n.* A type of print for blind people in which letters of the alphabet are raised from the page so that they can be felt.

rambunctious (ram bungk´ shəs) *adj.* Active and noisy in a violent way.

ransom (ran´ səm) *n.* A large amount of money paid to free something or someone from captivity.

ration (rash´ ən) *n.* A fixed allowance of something; a limited share.

reasonable (rēz´ nə bəl) *adj.* Possessing sound judgment.

reception (ri sep´ shən) *n.* A party held to welcome someone.

reconsider (rē´ kən si´ dər) *v.* To think about again.

recruit (ri kroot´) 1. *v.* To gain fresh people for a task. 2. *n.* A new member of a group or organization.

reflect (ri flekt´) *v.* To represent; to show.

Word Derivations

Below are some words derived from the word *reflect*.

reflected	reflection	reflector
reflecting	reflective	reflects

refugee camp (re´ fyoo jē kamp) *n.* A place where people who are forced to leave their homes live temporarily.

register (re´ jə stər) *v.* To show or record, as on a scale or meter.

related (ri lā´ təd) *adj.* Having some connection.

relations (ri lā´ shənz) *n.* The connections between people; people's associations with each other; the dealings people have with each other.

relay (rē´ lā´) 1. *n.* The passing along of something (like a message). (rē´ lā´) 2. *v.* To send along; to pass from one person to another.

relieved (ri lēvd´) *adv.* Comforted.

rendezvous (ron´ di vōō´) *v.* To meet or get together at a certain place.

renew (ri nōō´) *v.* To repair; to restore.

resentment (ri zent´ mənt) *n.* A feeling of being insulted.

reservation (rez´ ər vā´ shən) *n.* The land set aside for Native Americans to live on.

restaurateur (res´ tə rə tûr´) *n.* Someone who owns or runs a restaurant.

restore (ri stor´) *v.* To bring something back to its original condition.

resume (ri zōōm´) *v.* To start up again; to continue.

Word History

The word **resume** came into English usage in the 15th century. It comes from the Latin word *resumere.* *Resumere* can be broken down into the word parts *re-*, which means "again," and *sumere*, which means "to take up."

retire (ri tīr´) *v.* To go away to a private place.

rugged (ru´ gəd) *adj.* Sturdy and strong.

S

S.S. or **Schutzstaffel** (shōōts´ stä´ fəl) *German.* A special Nazi police force.

sac (sak) *n.* An inner body structure that is like a bag.

sandspit (sand´ spit) *n.* A bar of raised sand that juts out from an island.

satchel (sach´ əl) *n.* A small bag; a school bag.

Word History

Satchel comes from an older English word, *sachel.* *Sachel* is derived from the Latin word *saccus*, which means "bag." This word came into the English language during the 14th century.

scalpel (skal´ pəl) *n.* A small, straight, light knife used by surgeons.

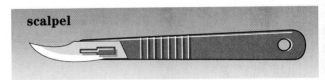
scalpel

scholarship (sko´ lər ship´) *n.* Money given to a student, often to help pay for college.

scribe (skrīb) *n.* A person who copies manuscripts by hand.

scullery (skul´ ə rē) *n.* A small room off the kitchen where dishes are washed, vegetables are prepared, and other chores are done.

scythe (sīth) *n.* A tool with a blade and a long handle used for cutting or mowing grass or crops.

seep (sēp) *v.* To flow a little at a time.

sentries (sen´ trēz) *n.* People stationed to keep watch; a guard.

serpent (sûr´ pənt) *n.* A snake.

563

**Pronunciation Key: at; lāte; câre; fäther;
set; mē; it; kīte; ox; rōse; ô in bought;
coin; book; too; form; out; up; ūse; tûrn;
ə sound in about, chicken, pencil, cannon,
circus; chair; hw in which; ring; shop;
thin; there; zh in treasure.**

serum (sēr´ əm) *n.* The liquid part of blood.

service (sûr´ vəs) *adj.* Providing useful work rather than products.

settlement (set´ l mənt) *n.* A colony; a new community in a new land.

shan't (shant) Contraction of **shall not:** Will not.

sheepfold (shēp´ fōld´) *n.* A pen or shelter for sheep.

ship (ship) *v.* To send by boat, train, truck, airplane, or other mode of transportation.

shock (shok) 1. *n.* A thick, bushy mass. 2. A dangerous condition in which a person's blood circulation becomes extremely slow.

siege (sēj) *n.* A group of illnesses, one after the other.

sign (sīn) *v.* For the hearing impaired, to make hand motions that mean something.

significant (sig ni´ fi kənt) *adj.* Important.

silkworm gut (silk´ wûrm gut´) *n.* Silk thread used in surgery.

simulate (sim´yə lāt) *v.* To make something seem like something else; to imitate.

sinew (sin´ū) *n.* A tough substance that joins muscle to bone; a tendon.

site (sīt) *n.* The ground occupied by a building.

situation (si´ chə wā´ shən) *n.* A position or state of affairs.

skeptic (skep´ tik) *n.* One who is doubtful.

skirt (skûrt) *v.* To move around the edge of.

sledge (slej) *n.* A sled or sleigh.

slop (slop) *n.* Food waste, usually garbage, fed to animals.

snare (snâr) *n.* A trap.

sole (sōl) *adj.* Single; one and only.

solution (sə loo´ shən) *n.* A liquid that has something dissolved in it.

sorrowfully (sär´ ō f(ə) lē) *adv.* Full of grief or sadness.

sound (sound) *adj.* Secure; safe; sensible.

specialize (spe´ shə līz´) *v.* To concentrate on one activity or subject.

specific (spi si´ fik) *adj.* Exact; particular.

spout (spout) *v.* To come out through a narrow opening with great force.

spout

startling (stärt´ ling) *adj.* Surprising; astonishing.

stave (stāv) *n.* One of the thin, curved wood strips used to make a barrel.

steadily (sted´ ə lē) *adv.* In a regular or methodical way.

sterilize (ster´ ə līz´) *v.* To make free from germs.

sternum (stûr´ nəm) *n.* The breastbone; the flat, narrow, bony area to which the ribs are attached.

stethoscope (steth´ ə skōp´) *n.* An instrument for listening to sounds within the body.

Word History

Stethoscope comes from the French word *stéthoscope*. *Stéthoscope* is derived from the Greek word *stethos*, which means "chest," and *-scope*, which means "instrument." The word came to mean an instrument for listening to the chest.

stifled (stī´ fəld) *adj.* Suffocated or smothered.

stock (stok) *n.* All of the animals on a farm; livestock.

strain (strān) *v.* To overwork; to work to the utmost.

Word Derivations

Below are some words derived from the word *strain*.

restrain	restrains	straining
restrained	strained	strains
restraining	strainer	unrestrained

studious (stoo´ dē əs) *adj.* Dedicated to study and learning.

sturdy (stûr´ dē) *adj.* Strong.

stylus (stī´ ləs) *n.* A pointed writing instrument.

suburb (su´ bərb) *n.* A community at the edge of, but outside of, a large city.

summon (sum´ ən) *v.* To send for; to call someone to come.

superstition (soo´ pər stish´ ən) *n.* A belief in magic; a belief that is not based on reason.

supervise (soo´ pûr vīz´) *v.* To watch over or direct.

suture (soo´ chər) *v.* To stitch together; to sew up.

swallow (swä´ lō´) *n.* A type of bird.

sympathy (sim´ pə thē) *n.* A feeling of understanding for another's sadness or hurt.

symptom (simp´ təm) *n.* A sign that indicates what kind of illness someone has.

T

taut (tôt) *adj.* Stretched tight; tense.

technique (tek nēk´) *n.* Way of handling something.

thatched (thacht) *adj.* Covered with straw.

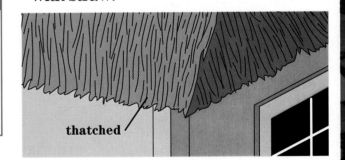

thatched

thrash (thrash) *v.* To thresh; to beat the grain from stalks; to beat.

threshold (thresh´ ōld) *n.* The bottom part of a doorway; the sill.

thrive (thrīv) *v.* To progress, grow, or prosper well.

throes (thrōz) *n.* Any violent spasm or struggle.

tidal (tīd´ l) *adj.* Having to do with the rise and fall of the sea.

tide (tīd) *n.* A current or flowing water.

Word Derivations

Below are some words derived from the word *tide.*

ebb tide	tidal wave	tidemark
high tide	tide table	tides
low tide	tideland	tidewater
tidal	tideless	tideway

timid (ti´ məd) *adj.* Shy; feeling or showing a lack of courage.

tinker (ting´ kər) *v.* To experiment with something.

toll (tōl) *n.* Damage; destruction.

toll-gate (tōl´ gāt) *n.* A gate where people must pay in order to use a road.

tongue (tung) *n.* A piece of board that fits into the groove of another board.

tottery (tot´ ə rē) *adj.* Unsteady; shaky.

trace (trās) *n.* One of the two straps or chains that connect an animal to a load being pulled.

tradition (trə dish´ ən) *n.* A custom that has been handed down or preserved through many generations.

traffic (tra´ fik) *n.* The people being serviced by a business.

transcontinental (trans´ kon tə nen´ təl) *adj.* Stretching across a continent.

transfusion (trans fū´ zhən) *n.* A transfer of blood into a person.

Word History

Transfusion came into English usage in the 16th century. It can be traced back to the Latin word *transfundere. Trans-* means "across" or "beyond," and *fundere* means "to pour." The suffix *-ion,* a Latin term, means "act" or "process." In this case, the word came to mean the act or process of pouring blood beyond one person to another.

treacherous (tre´ chə rəs) *adj.* Not safe because of hidden dangers.

trek (trek) *n.* A difficult journey or trip.

tribute (trib´ ūt) *n.* Praise given in recognition of worth or value.

trickle (trik´ əl) *v.* To flow.

trifling (trī´ fling) *adj.* Not important.

trot (trot) 1. *n.* A slow run. 2. *v.* To run slowly.

troublesome (trə´ bəl səm) *adj.* Causing problems or difficulties.

trough (trôf) *n.* A container holding the drinking water or food for animals.

U

uncharted (un chär´ tid) *adj.* Not shown on a map; not explored; not known.

unconscious (ən kon´ shəs) *adj.* Without physical or mental awareness; senseless.

unfortunate (ən forch´ nət) *adj.* Unlucky.

unsupervised (ən soo' pər vīzd) 1. *adj.* Without being watched over by someone. (from **supervise** 2. *v.* To watch over, oversee.)

usher (ush' ər) *v.* To escort or take someone someplace.

V

vaccine (vak sēn') *n.* A preparation, usually liquid, given to prevent a disease.

valiant (val' yənt) *adj.* Courageous or brave.

vanish (va' nish) *v.* To disappear suddenly.

vendor (ven' dər) *n.* A person or company that sells a product.

venture (ven' chər) *n.* An uncertain undertaking; a new situation with a doubtful outcome.

veranda (və ran' də) *n.* A covered balcony; a porch.

verge (vûrj) *n.* The place where something begins; the brink.

verify (vâr' ə fī) *v.* To declare something real, authentic, or true.

via (vī' ə) *adv.* By way of; passing through.

vibration (vī brā' shən) *n.* Slight, rapid movements of an object.

vinyl (vī' nl) *n.* A plastic-like fabric made by humans.

vital (vīt' l) *adj.* Necessary for life.

Word History

The French word **vital** can be traced back to the Latin word *vita*, which means "life." The word came into the English language during the 14th century.

vouch (vouch) *v.* To bear witness; to confirm.

W

W.C. Water closet: A bathroom.

warden (wor' dn) *n.* An officer in charge; a supervisor.

weed-infested (wēd' in fes' td) *adj.* Filled with unwanted or undesirable plants.

wick (wik) *n.* A braided or twisted string of a soft substance that soaks up the fuel in a candle or lamp and holds the flame.

wreckage (rek' ij) *n.* The remains of something that has been wrecked or destroyed.

Y

yearn (yûrn) *v.* To long for.

yoke (yōk) *n.* A wooden frame used to join together two work animals.

Z

zephyr (zef' ər) *n.* The west wind.

567

Acknowledgments

"Prophecy in Flame" from ALL KEYS ARE GLASS by Frances Minturn Howard, Boston, Massachusetts, copyright © 1950. Used by permission of the estate.

"Going West" from CHILDREN OF THE WILD WEST by Russell Freedman. Copyright © 1983 by Russell Freedman. Reprinted by permission of Clarion Books/Houghton Mifflin Company. All rights reserved.

From THE CALIFORNIA GOLD RUSH, text copyright © 1991 by Elizabeth Van Steenwyk. Reprinted with permission of Franklin Watts, a division of Grolier Publishing. All rights reserved.

"The Golden Spike" from THE TRANSCONTINENTAL RAILROAD, text copyright © 1993 by Dan Elish. Reprinted with permission of the author. All rights reserved.

Photo Credits

7, NASA; 8 (t), Wells Fargo Bank, (c) ©Neil Johnson, (bl) ©1994 Jim McHugh/Outline Press Syndicate, Inc.; 11 (t), ©Brian Payne/Black Star, (b) Courtesy Archives & Special Collections on Women in Medicine, Allegheny University of the Health Sciences; 12, ©Library of Congress/PHOTRI; 14, ©Tui De Roy/Minden Pictures; 15, ©Ron Cohn/The Gorilla Foundation; 16, ©North Wind Picture Archive; 17 (t), ©Western History/Genealogy Department, Denver Public Library, (b) ©Bettmann/Corbis; 18-19, NASA; 30, 46, file photo; 64, ©Paul Abdoo; 82-85, NASA; 86, ©Stanford News Services; 87, ©Jim Ruymen/UPI/Corbis-Bettmann; 88 (l), ©Walt Frerck/UPI/Corbis-Bettmann, (r) NASA; 89-93, NASA; 94 (t), NASA, (b) ©AP/Wide World Photos; 95, ©AP/Wide World Photos; 96, Gail Sakurai; 97, NASA; 98, The Art Institute of Chicago, Gift of Mrs. Richard E. Danielson and Mrs. Chauncey McCormick. Photograph ©2000, The Art Institute of Chicago, All Rights Reserved; 99 (t), The Metropolitan Museum of Art, Rogers Fund, 1936. (JP 2581) Photograph ©1991 The Metropolitan Museum of Art, (b) Estate of Margaret Bourke-White Estate, courtesy Life Magazine ©Time Inc.; 112, Doris Ettlinger; 126, file photo; 126-130, ©Aaron Haupt; 127 (l), ©David Young-Wolff/PhotoEdit, (b) ©Aaron Haupt; 128 (t), ©Aaron Haupt, (b) ©Myrleen Ferguson/PhotoEdit; 131, Aaron Haupt; 132-134, Wells Fargo Bank; 136, ©Bettmann/Corbis; 139, Wells Fargo Bank; 140, ©Bettmann/Corbis; 141, ©Bettmann/Corbis; 143, Wells Fargo Bank; 146-153, ©Neil Johnson; 154 (t), Charlotte A. Watson Fund, 1942, Albright-Knox Art Gallery, Buffalo, New York, (b) Scala/Art Resource, NY; 155 (t), The Brooklyn Museum, Brooklyn, New York. John B. and Ella C. Woodward Memorial Funds, (b) SuperStock; 157, ©1994 Alan Levenson; 159, 160, ©1994 Jim McHugh/Outline Press Syndicate, Inc.; 163, ©1997 David McNew; 164-166, 169, ©1994 Jim McHugh/Outline Press Syndicate, Inc.; 170 (t), Marlene Targ Brill; 186, Diane Paterson; 200, file photo; 204 (t), ©Archive Photos; 217, 219, Bettmann/Corbis; 221, ©AP Wide World Photo; 222 (t), file photo, (b) Jim Roldan; 238, file photo; 254 (t), Carol Saller, (b) Gerald Talifero; 256 (t), ©Erich Lessing/Art Resource, NY, (b) Nicolo Orsi Battaglini/Art Resource, NY; 257 (t, b), Scala/Art Resource, NY; 258 ©Brian Payne/Black Star; 286 (t), Paula G. Paul, (b) Robert Collier-Morales; 288, Courtesy Archives & Special Collections on Women in Medicine, Allegheny University of the Health Sciences; 306 (t), Marion Marsh Brown, (b) Diane Magnuson; 318 (t), Maia Wojciechowska, (b) Ramon Gonzalez Vicente; 332, Scott O'Dell; 335, ©Robert E. Peary/National Geographic Image Collection; 339, ©Library of Congress/PHOTRI; 340, ©Dartmouth College Library; 343, 344, ©Corbis; 347, Courtesy of The Peary-MacMillan Arctic Museum, Bowdoin College; 350-351, 353, ©Dartmouth College Library; 355, 357, ©Bettmann/Corbis; 359, Library of Congress/PHOTRI; 374, file photo; 388 (t), ©Archive Photos, (b) Yoriko Ito; 392, ©UPI/Corbis-Bettmann; 402 (t),©UPI/Corbis-Bettmann, (b) Susan Keeter; 404 (t), Robert Schaap Collection, Vincent van Gogh Museum, Rijsmuseum, Amsterdam, (b) Museum purchase, The Philbrook Museum of Art, Tulsa, Oklahoma; 405 (t), Margaret Bourke-White, Life Magazine ©Time Inc., (b) Abby Aldrich Rockefeller Folk Art Center. Photo:©Colonial Williamsburg Foundation; 412, file photo; 417, ©Tui De Roy/Minden Pictures; 418, ©Charles Nicklin/Al Giddings Images, Inc.; 419, ©Michael Durham/Oregon Zoo; 420-421, ©Hal Beral/Corbis; 425, ©Daniel J. Cox/Natural Selection; 432 (t), courtesy Shelagh Wallace; 442, ©Richard Sobol; 444, The National Museum of Women in the Arts, Washington, D.C. Gift of Wallace and Wilhelmina Holladay; 445 (t, b), SuperStock; 447-459, ©Ron Cohn/The Gorilla Foundation; 472, Bob Dorsey; 480, ©Agence France Presse/Archive Photos; 484, ©Werner Forman Archive/Field Museum of Natural History, Chicago/Art Resource, NY; 485, ©St. Agustine Foundation at Flagler College; 486, ©Stock Montage, Inc.; 487, 489, ©North Wind Picture Archive; 490, ©Werner Forman Archive/Field Museum of Natural History,Chicago/Art Resource, NY; 498, James Watling; 500, The Metropolitan Museum of Art, Rogers Fund, 1913. Photograph ©The Metropolitan Museum of Art; 501 (t), Fine Arts Museum of San Francisco, Gift of Mr. and Mrs. John D. Rockefeller 3rd, 1979.7.3, (b) Quilled Buckskin Robe, National Museum of the American Indian, Smithsonian Institution; 502, ©National Portrait Gallery, Washington DC. Photo: Art Resource, NY; 506, Dennis B. Fradin; 518, Charles Shaw; 529, ©Corbis; 533, ©North Wind Picture Archive; 534, 537, Stock Montage, Inc.; 538 (l), Stock Montage, Inc., (r) ©Bettmann/Corbis; 539, ©Bettmann/Corbis.

Unit Opener Acknowledgments

Unit 1 photo by NASA; Unit 2 illustrated by Robert Byrd; Unit 3 illustrated by Rusty Fletcher; Unit 4 illustrated by Mary Beth Schwark and Bob Kuester; Unit 5 illustrated by Ruth Flanigan; Unit 6 illustrated by Jan Adkins.